Irma Kurtz

Irma Kurtz was born in New Jersey and grew up in New York. ... graduating in English Literature from Barnard College, ... bia University, in 1956, she moved to Europe, first to ... d then to London where, in 1970, she joined the brand ... *smopolitan* as its first agony aunt.

... r her years in London, Irma Kurtz has contributed to ... ly every national paper and is a frequent broadcaster on radio ... nd TV. Recently she moved to Bloomsbury after twenty years ... n Soho, and describes herself as a 'last-time buyer'. She also keeps a small hiding place in an unfashionable region of northern France. The mother of a son, Irma Kurtz became a grandmother in March 2005.

Praise for *About Time*:

'Ir... ...urtz is not going gently into that good night of the T... ...ge ... she tells not only her own story but has also d... ...the likes of super-granny Jane Fearnley-Whittingstall, ...thy publican Norman Balon ... to say what, besides ... ...fulness and bloody-mindedness, keeps them going. ... ...sior!' *The Times*

...e warned, Kurtz refusing to take getting old quietly is just the beginning' *Sunday Times*

About Time

Growing Old Disgracefully

IRMA KURTZ

JOHN MURRAY

First published in Great Britain in 2009 by John Murray (Publishers)
An Hachette UK Company

First published in paperback in 2010

1

A CIP catalogue record for this title is available from the British Library

ISBN 978-0-7195-6986-9

Typeset in Bembo by Palimpsest Book Production Limited,
Grangemouth, Stirlingshire

Printed and bound by Clays Ltd, St Ives plc

John Murray policy is to use papers that are natural,
renewable and recyclable products and made from wood grown in
sustainable forests. The logging and manufacturing processes are expected
to conform to the environmental regulations of the country of origin.

John Murray (Publishers)
338 Euston Road
London NW1 3BH

www.johnmurray.co.uk

For Jasper, beloved newcomer,
From Granny Soho

Contents

I

My Old Folks

THE YOUNG WANT it all. And why not? The trouble is they want it now; they want it all right now, today, immediately, right this minute and to hell with tomorrow. First-time house-buyers would eagerly sell years of their old age to the highest bidder if they could for money in hand immediately and consider it a bargain, too. Ask a twenty-year-old in the pub which he craves more at this moment: to live to be one hundred or his next smoke and, if he gets lucky, a white night later with the girl across the bar? Or that woman past her mid-thirties, burbling about how glad she is that she has chosen a career instead of children? Ask her whether she can ever imagine a time not very far ahead when she has neither and can no longer choose?

Yes, the young want it all, only not tomorrow: they have no ambition for longevity. They do not aim for great age or think it has anything to do with them, and they never have. Girls born as I was, in the first third or so of the twentieth century to parents who grew up in the nineteenth century, would have traded any amount of mere time for the one, the only one: the man we had been told and taught would come along to rescue and complete us.

Hollywood movies back then were in black and white, like so many influential ideas from America. The blonde always got the guy in the last reel. Brunettes too young to bleach resented the colour bias, and if it did not worry my own little brown and plaited head unduly, that was because I realised early on he whose destiny was also mine could not be an ordinary man who saw as men ordinarily see. Besides, if the onscreen brunette is curvy with a hint of dominatrix in her style, her unfortunate *chevelure* need not put paid to romantic expectations the way, say, grey hair would. Who woos a decrepit princess? Who applauds a creaky knight in tarnished armour? Gnomes and witches and ogres are not only old, but evil too, and they sleep alone. To be old and no longer fanciable? Ugh!

'I'd rather die,' says a girl and turns again to her mirror.

My generation was commonly the second and not uncommonly the first to be born in the United States. Grandparents were rare among young Americans; they belonged to the old countries – the countries of the old – where a few still clung on to life but many more were dying. American kids of my landlocked era could not visit Grandpa for Christmas in Sicily, or nip over to pay respects to Grandma's grave in Cork or Minsk or Treblinka. Our family trees were sawn off at the root. My father, born on the cusp of the twentieth century in a Manhattan tenement flat, was the first of seven brothers and two sisters who never met their grandparents nor any of their countless European relatives, all turned into smoke over Polish hills long before air travel became everyday transport, except for the rich or for bombs.

By the time I was born in September 1935, Western civilisation's battle against nature was in its early days and technology had barely begun its domination of earth's bounty. I was nearly a teenager before we acquired our first television set, black and white of course, with an outsize magnifying glass placed in front of the screen so the whole family could watch at the same time. Sons back then were raised to win the bread, daughters to anticipate a vocation, not a job. After a little girl passed through the phase of wanting to be a ballet dancer, then a nurse, before settling on her predestined career of marriage and motherhood, she probably wanted to be a teacher. Grade-school teachers, who in those days were all single women, were seen by us children as a genre apart, like angels or royals or clowns, exempt from ordinary time. Teachers could be ancient, yes, most of them were and thus venerable, too; but not just plain old. Old has never been a respectful adjective for a human being. I was one of a handful of my classmates who did not want to dance or nurse, and only briefly to teach when I grew up; I was also one of very few in my class who had a generation of the aged close at hand.

'Child, you do not know what good is,' my great-grandmother complained when I pushed away my green vegetables.

Perhaps I did not. But when 'Gay Gammaw' stroked my cheek with her crumpled hand, I knew what old was.

My paternal grandparents lived next door to us in Jersey City; a flat roof between our apartments served as garden and throughway as well as a line of defence against their traditional kosher ways and comical Yiddish resignation which my mother found antipathetic and passé. Mother was a second-generation American on her maternal side, born in the heartland of Indiana to a local girl and a scholarly German Jew, Morris Auerbach. He died of tuberculosis in a sanatorium in Denver, Colorado, when Mother was just six. Mother's mother, my Grandma Annie, was also an only child. She spoke not a word of any tongue save English with a gen-you-whine Midwestern twang. She was suspected by my paternal grandparents of eating bacon, which indeed she did, as did their son, my father, though they never saw him doing it for we scurried to hide forbidden foods whenever the rap of Grandpa Joe's cane was heard on our stairs. In fact, they suspected my blue-eyed Grandma Annie of being a Christian, which she was not, merely a generation further away from the terrors and the *shtetls*. Dutifully and reluctantly, they invited her to their family celebrations of Hanukkah and

3

Passover; in the same spirt she attended. Her own mother, my 'Gay Gammaw', born in an outlying area of what was then Transylvania, had escaped the pre-Nazi pogroms, God alone knows how.

None of my old people spoke of the past. They had risked everything and lost most of it to make their descendants Americans; finally they silenced their very memories in case the tales should stigmatise and endanger us. Nor did they teach us their languages – Yiddish, Russian, German, Czech, Polish and Hungarian – addressing us only in accented and fragmented English. How enriched my life would have been if only my immigrant old people had not been so self-sacrificing. Short-term memory is overrated; machines can be set to manage most of it. However, the memory of an aged man or woman, even while it is failing as a faculty, can deepen into what is virtually a new emotion, expressing itself in abstractions and in inventions, too, in tales containing history and truths that at their best ascend to art. The neglect and scorn of antique memories by a jejune society amounts to the passive theft of each life's final treasure: its unique body of reminiscence.

Every day, my own deepening memory returns to me another leathery and oaken detail: for example, of the waiting room for my father's dental surgery. It is separated by a small lobby from our living apartment. Stacks of *Life* and *Look* magazines are piled on the carved sideboard for the distraction of nervous patients awaiting treatment. A bubbling fish-tank holds a colony of circling guppies, lazy and anonymous. I know they eat their offspring though I have never been able to catch them at it. Two big sash windows look out on a three-storey, red-brick tenement across the street, a tramline, and a pharmacy with a barber's pole in front of it, twisting red and white; the stripe of blue that I see was not actually there, only painted in later by my expatriate memory.

In that solemn room where children are not allowed to play, one cloudy afternoon my father lifts me in his arms to look down into a long wooden box and upon the closed face and folded hands of one who was and is no longer my darling Gay Gammaw. For decades I took it for granted that I must have been too young to have imprinted the picture I can still see with my mind's eye of the powdery white mask beneath me, so quiet, so elsewhere. In adulthood I assumed that the pale image in my secret album had to be one of memory's graphic interpolations, an editorial full stop tacked onto my first lost relationship. And then a few years ago I came across my Baby Book in a drawer of Mother's desk, containing this passage in her trim backward-sloping hand:

'Dad'n held you. You looked down upon Gay Gammaw as she lay in her coffin. Dad'n took you away hurriedly because the look on your little face hurt us all very much. You wanted to cry, to ask questions. I hope you have lost for ever the pained enquiry in your heart that day. But never forget her. She was good and she loved you dearly and from the first moment you saw her you too loved your "Gay Gammaw".'

Gay Gammaw missed the opportunity to love my brother, too, when he arrived at last into her line of women a year after her death. Her own daughter, my Grandma Annie, however, leaped at the chance to prefer him; she moved east permanently after his birth, joined us at our country house on the lake during the long holidays, and in winter she lived in a rented flat near our own in town. Grandma Annie detested my father, referred to him as 'that man' in conversations with my mother, and chose not to sit at table when he was with us on summer weekends but to take her meals standing in the kitchen. Between Grandma Annie and me there simmered an overheated indifference that occasionally bubbled up into real hatred.

'You'll never be the woman your mother is,' she used to

taunt me long before I realised that I was bound to become any sort of woman at all.

One pleasure of increasing age is to reread books beloved in youth, sometimes to love them again, and just as often to reread and love at last books that bored or bothered long ago. Only yesterday I was reading a Carson McCullers short story published in the year of my birth and out of the shadowy prose sprang a forgotten American word: 'chifferobe'. Originally it must have been a frenchified chiffonier, preferable to a vulgar 'chest of drawers' among terribly nice middle-Americans even as they mutated it with 'wardrobe'. 'Chifferobe' was one of Grandma Annie's words. Seeing 'chifferobe' again in all its ill-educated gentility, I remembered how Grandma Annie never cared a 'hill of beans' for religion; how when she went to visit her second cousin in Tampa, she stayed in a 'hoe-tul', with the emphasis on the first syllable. I also remembered once overhearing her ask my mother: 'Myra, what do Lisbons do in bed?' Oh yes, and she was glad, too, she would never be buried in a Christian cemetery because 'There are too many of those fancy Muslims in them.' And then I had to remember more.

I am twelve years old; Grandma Annie is in her sixties, about a decade younger than I am now. My parents have gone out. My little brother is asleep next door, still in the bottom of the double-decker bed that we used to share until I was old enough for a room of my own. I leave off reading now in my room and slip out to forage for a shortbread cookie. Grandma Annie is alone in the dimly lit hall. She wears the ruffled navy-blue dress with white polka dots. Her greying hair is in its customary chignon. A few hairpins have tumbled to the floor. And Grandma Annie is thumping her forehead against the wall and she is crying: 'What's wrong with me? What's wrong with me? What's wrong with me?'

I creep away, scared by what I ought not to have seen and cramming it into a dark corner of the chifferobe that is memory.

Sometimes when I was little I would look up from my scribbling, as I can almost do now, and see Grandma Annie chewing the side of her tongue and staring at me narrowly, silently. Whenever she washed my hair, the shampoo stung my eyes and she tore at the tangles as she brushed it afterwards. Would her wretched distaff-line never be broken by a stalwart youth to make his women proud and support them in their old age? She wanted me gone or at least replaced. Then at last when I was nearly four, hallelujah! The boy was born! Grandma Annie liked me no more than before but at least I was promoted to second-best instead of worse than nothing.

Grandma Annie was born in the Klan-ridden flatlands of America, a little alien delivered practically in hiding, a pretty girl but not strong in any lasting way, widowed before her mid-twenties with no alternative then but to return home with her baby daughter and live with her own warring parents. Meagre family lore had it that Gay Gammaw and her husband spoke not one word to each other for the last twenty years of their marriage; instead they gave the child, my mother-to-be, notes to carry from one to the other in scabrous Hungarian. Mother told me when she was little her grandfather had locked himself in a room containing a barrel of pickles and there he starved himself to death, or so she had been told. Grandma Annie, poor soul – still young, trapped in a house of silent rage – would never be made love to again, never be caressed and never admired, least of all by her clever daughter, her only child, her only hope. And what does the bright, beautiful daughter go and do? Barely twenty-one with an honest-to-God Master's degree from Indiana University, she goes and marries for love a handsome older man from the East, a man who then proceeds to let both mother and daughter down when he turns out not to be what he never said he was: not to be what they thought he should be. He transports them, not to the bright lights of New York City, but to a slummy trap across the river. And who cares if I, a little girl, their first-born, by standing tiptoe on a chair at my bedroom window can just about see the Statue of Liberty? Why, that man's parents do not even speak proper English.

'Never analyse love,' a London pseudo-counsellor recently admonished his radio audience.

Love for him and his listeners is a sexy romance he quite rightly says cannot sustain much examination. But there are many kinds of love; there is love in retrospect, too, love that is the gift of finally understanding better and understanding more. Grandma Annie, poor woman, in the confusion of encroaching senility, aware only of what little she had ever had and all she was losing, thumped her addled pate against the rigid past. Grandma Annie, dependent on people she had not chosen, people who would never have chosen her. Grandma Annie, let me try to love you now, inspired, I hope, by humane compassion and not by pity for my own diminishing self. Yes, I will love you at last, Grandma. I will.

And a fat lot of good it will do either of us.

Mother was a gifted show-off well into old age. Ever daydreaming above her station, beautiful to look at in her youth, she could have been a spectacular actress. When I was a little girl she told wonderful and scary stories, traditional as well as made up, for a weekly audience of children at a community centre in the city: 'Auntie Myra's Story Hour'. And during the summer holidays she organised local kids and led a band of us in frolic and make-believe. Sometimes on sunny mornings Mother had my little brother and me link arms with our chums and then, shoulder to shoulder, she steered us slowly down the steep, grassy hill beside our summer house, chanting her words: 'Old and crippled and crippled and old; old and crippled and crippled and old . . .'

Faster and faster we went as irresistible gravity grabbed our ankles, dragging us to the foot of the slope and jumbling our words, 'Oh, and, crip-crip-crippled, oh-oh-oooold,' finally tumbling us into a breathless heap. Mother's game, as childhood games always are, was both metaphor and rehearsal for a fact of mature life. Ordinary time flows downhill and passes with increasing speed when there is less of it ahead. Have young and old ever seen eye to eye? How can they? How will they ever? Increasingly these speedy days, the generations barely brush shoulders in passing.

When Mother was sixty and my father was in his mid-seventies, they sold up both city and summer house and moved to a gated, guarded, retirement community near Princeton, New Jersey. While Mother could still see to read and before arthritis deformed her fingers, she used to type long letters to acquaintances in California where my brother was resident and my parents wintered every year. In Mother's wide correspondence, cherished by its chosen recipients, she referred to the ersatz retirement village as Geriatric Gulch where, she said, reality was considered so tactless by its aged residents the local ambulance rode out disguised as a Bloomingdale's delivery van. After her ninetieth year, although Mother continued to manage her own accounts thanks to an enlarging machine for degenerating eyesight, she began to spend most of her waking hours curled up in a corner of the big sofa under a wall hung with African masks she had collected for their sheer incongruity in that place. She never watched the eternal television, but neither did she switch it off. She barely noticed visitors for she was deep in a process more demanding than society: she was rejecting life point by point before it rejected her. When she ate from a tray on her lap, she chewed the food reluctantly and critically, showing particular distaste for any dish that once had been a favourite. My mother's geriatric defence against the imminence of death was to dismiss and ostensibly to despise whatever she depended upon or had once loved. Once when we had been sitting alone in silence for an hour or so, she turned from the television and snarled at me: 'I don't like you!'

The words return now as a perverse endearment.

Mother's disdain, always palpable, was directed finally against death itself. She died early one January morning just a few hours before I was scheduled to fly from Heathrow Airport for what had become fortnightly visits during her last months in and out of hospital. I must assume she did not want me at her deathbed for my sake and her own, and so let go of life before my arrival. Upon my landing at Newark Airport, one of her hired carers who had come to collect me told me Mother had secretly arranged to be cremated without ceremony or witnesses, immediately and expensively, too. My first act as an orphan was to rob the local bank. The carer kept the engine running while I went in to do the business before Mother's demise became common knowledge in the community, whereupon her current account would be frozen and my power of attorney rescinded.

'How's your mum doing?' asked the friendly teller.

'Never better,' I said and faked a cough to cover the break in my voice.

I rang the crematorium, arranged to pay the bill, and asked them to send the ashes to her house – it was still hers – but, please, not to deliver them until the following Monday when my brother was scheduled to join me from California. Then I set about making myself busy, too busy to think, sorting out jam-packed cupboards, stacking battered pots and saucepans for local charities, skimming books unread for decades. I was surveying a dresser drawer full of stockings, pre-war girdles, and garter-belts when the doorbell rang. The young man was there to collect Mother's hired wheelchair, was he not? No. No, he had come not to collect but to deliver. When I closed the door and turned back to face the empty, over-furnished rooms once more, I held a parcel wrapped in brown paper and addressed to me. My hands shook; small bones rattled. It was the farewell performance of a born actress. Right to the last act my extraordinary mother transmuted fear and disappointment into the scornful laugh her script required. The young do not imagine how sly can be the craft of senescence.

Long before my father's death in 1981, Mother had begun to leave the house only to shop or for doctor's appointments. Go out for a walk with 'Dad'n' and me? What for? A woman with a Master's degree in Sociology from Indiana University; an author who had published a dozen of her short stories in niche literary magazines: what could possibly interest such a woman in a community centred on a golf course?

'A hole in one,' she said, 'distracts fools from the hole awaiting one.'

So my father and I walked out alone. We did not speak much; we never had spoken easily or often, apart from when I was a child and we used to sing together in the car; his tone was true, mine tended to sharp. Side by side we sat on a bench and watched the incomparable colours of October in northeastern America: golden oaks, evergreen conifers, red maples close to combustion under scissors of wild geese cutting through an azure sky that buzzed with early hints of snow. A white-haired woman passed us pushing a trolley towards the community grocery store. A car drove by very slowly, the female driver hunched over the steering wheel like an aged seamstress at a sewing machine. A crone wheeled her Zimmer frame out of the front door of a nearby house and onto the porch; she sniffed this way, then the other, as old sailors test the weather; she turned and wheeled herself in again. Curtains twitched where a stout woman watched her, them, us, and everything.

'You see how it is here, Irma?' said my father. He sighed: 'Only the men die.'

Nature is not politically correct: men and women are not

alike, not yet. The sexes have different priorities and strategies right to the end. The menopause is a first signpost pointing towards decrepitude for women, as impotence is for men. The end of possibility for one, the end of action for the other. HRT replaces; Viagra enables. But neither tricks nature for long and nothing fools time, not in the long run. How different was my father's befuddlement and sorrow in old age from the blame and bitterness of my mother. When he looked back on a life of lost music and rejected love; he saw his own failure; Mother looked back and saw only treachery and the betrayal of her promise. The day after my father's final consignment to a rest home, I watched her weeping and enraged as she ripped out his dedications from all the books he had given her as love tokens in their youth. While she was distracted for a moment by a stubborn binding I rescued a book from the stack and hid it from her tearful wrath.

'To Myra,' reads the dedication dated 1930 in *The Works of Epictetus*, 'who has sought light and found it; who can now see the truth which leads to Happiness. May I also breathe in your atmosphere? My love for ever, Irving.'

When I hold the book loosely in my hand it falls open always to the same page containing, among a collection of 'fragments': 'A daughter is to a father a possession which is not his own.'

I was over sixty when I came upon my father's high-school diploma and learned from it that his birth name was not Irving, as I always heard him called, but Isidore.

The lower age limit for admission to my parents' community was set at a mere forty-eight in order to allow for second and third wives of elderly husbands. When the women were finally widowed most of them stayed on in the houses they inherited. Women of my parents' generation pretty much took charge of the ageing process just as they had always been in charge of routine and diet and the home. Meanwhile, the men played games or dozed, chewing their words and their food slowly as their appetite for battle and triumph dwindled into incapacity and grumpiness. Recollections of my old women are clear and verbal; of my old men they are impressionistic and return in the form of feelings, often startlingly pure. Only my paternal grandfather, Papa Joe – a natty patriarch, as befitted a pattern cutter and tailor of the ghetto – so overshadowed his wife that she must ever be the haziest of my old folks.

Grandma Ida was not so much resigned to a life of obedience and acquiescence but born to it as birds are born to fly and fish to swim. Memory must squint to see her, always in the kitchen, her court and kingdom, where she enforced the strict dietary laws and men entered only on sufferance. When my grandfather became very old and especially after the quiet death of Grandma Ida, his sighs seemed to be exhaling life itself. I think he must have died at home while I was abroad; I know only that one day he was no longer there. My father alone of my old folks died in a long-term nursing home; out of the reverie of his final years emerged sighs too but, unlike Papa Joe's orthodox resignation, my father sighed in a grief so profound that he was soon forced by the pain of it to flee into visions from the past as hallucinatory and intemperate as those of some damaged war veterans.

My father returns to me vividly, painfully with certain chords and strains, especially of Gershwin and other old Manhattan music that floods my heart even now at my age, when a woman expects sentimental regrets to be over.

'It's never too late,' crooned an attendant nurse seeing me listen and watch helplessly as my father departed this life via his past.

He alone of all my old people knew how to offer un-equivocal love. But none of us knew how to accept it. And it is too late. It always was.

★

My old people can set me no example of how to pull off my own ageing in a world so changed from theirs. We, the new old of Western societies, are increasingly numerous and relatively healthy, commonly living to an age that not very long ago would have been considered freakish. We are more numerous than our ancestors, more energetic and experienced, in general more educated and, if not always more prosperous, certainly less often hungry. We are pioneers, the first of our kind. So I start out as my own mapmaker in territory where my age practically disenfranchises me among the young, who are not merely contemptuous of white hairs but sometimes downright hostile. According to a recent journalistic poll 40 per cent of the British fear loneliness in their old age; you can be sure loneliness will be the experience of many more of us when the time comes. Old age is lonely for us new aged and the parents of few children. But as the present, and the future, too, are built on the tales and the details, both mundane and dramatic, of the past, I will find established old natives to help me find the way, or at least to entertain me as I go. I carry with me the only tool that can sharpen with age: wisdom – the apotheosis of common sense.

An Old Voice Remembers: Anne Valery

Talking to men and women of my generation, I am struck again and again by how we shed freight from that heavy-goods vehicle, memory, as we age and gently drift back to early events that were the making of us. Growing old, as it separates us from the world, returns us to our original selves. Unless we resist and cling to the ballast – to objects, to money, to sex, to size eight – as if it were the ship itself, growing old means becoming more intensely our essential and singular selves.

From practically her first breath in 1928, Anne Valery led a life of bold colour and independence. Soldier, model, actress, and finally a successful author of scripts and memoirs, Anne retains into her eighties an aura of head-turning beauty. She also to this day deserves an audience for anecdotal memories that are sustaining and amusing. Her listeners can sense too that for all their entertaining and enlightening value, Anne's memories are often the products of pain and early confusion, governed always by the courage and curiosity of a woman rare for her own time and still rare in this one.

I get up every morning at eight. But I sit in bed and read for two hours. I have hot water and bread in bed and then get up about half past eleven. As a child I had to have breakfast in bed because I was delicate. My problems were caused by the nurse at my delivery; she tied the cord wrong and gave me a strangulated umbilical hernia, only back then they didn't know what it was. When they finally operated I woke up with septicaemia and of course this was before penicillin so I nearly died. I had absolutely gorgeous hair then, I can say it now; I had hair women dream of! It was white-blonde and out to there, a bit Pre-Raphaelite with soft curls. And my mother, who cared terribly about outward appearances, had said: 'Don't let them cut your hair off!' It was something they often did in hospital.

I was in a surgical ward. And the screams! Well, I saw this matron whom I did not like coming towards me with scissors and, to the astonishment of the two doctors near by – I can still see them in white jackets with white gumboots on – I sat straight up and shrieked: 'NO!' That was in 1936, when I was eight, and from that moment I started to get better.

In London then the air was full of sulphur. Two million chimneys! We saw the sun a third of the time that children see it now. There was a pall of yellow fog. But even so, London was beautiful; everything looked black and there was a wonderful unity about it. I was born in Eaton Square and all my life slowly moved down the King's Road. When my father and mother separated, Mother got £4 a week. My poor mother had to get a job. She had never worked but she was taken on as a manicurist at the Army and Navy Stores, simply because she was so pretty; she had Titian hair, a cream skin, black eyebrows, and the bluest eyes you have ever seen. She also had a gorgeous voice; a teacher of opera offered to train her for free, but my grandmother wouldn't allow it. Good girls didn't go on the stage. I had the same problem: I was good at painting and maths, and I wanted to be an architect, but my grandfather wouldn't allow me to go to university. Because Mother was working, she had to find me a weekly boarding school.

That poor woman lived under such illusions! She sent me to a convent school in Fulham Road. I was just six. And when the other girls discovered I was a Protestant, I got locked in dark cupboards. I remember the first time the nun took me for a bath. It was winter, and she said: 'Undress yourself. Face the wall and don't look down when you undress.' And she put a bath vest on me because you must never see yourself naked. And afterwards I got into a damp nightdress and slept on an iron truckle bed. I didn't cry. I shared a room with a terrifying sixth-former who wore pebble specs and who said: 'Don't expect me to mother you; I am going to be a nun!'

I loathe religions, all of them. I remember one of the nuns took me into the chapel. I had never been in a chapel. And she showed me a statue of someone with golden locks and big blue eyes, and she said: 'Who is that?'

And I said: 'Jeanette MacDonald!'

One Friday after school I was waiting for my mother in my school uniform when a nun came up to me and said my grandfather was ill so my mother would not be coming for me. Everything started to go a long way away, sounds went a long way away, and I saw black outlines around people. It turned out I had pneumonia. I survived it. But I took all my dolls and buried them in the garden. I would have read the funeral service over them except I have mild dyslexia and couldn't read until I was ten. The doctors said I had to live above the fog line; Swiss Cottage was meant to be above the fog line, so we moved again. I spent the rest of my childhood in a much nicer school until the war in 1939. I still wanted to be an architect. But I also wanted to be like the girl in the newsagent's who wore a crocheted jersey where all the straps showed through. I thought that terribly grown-up, especially the shadow of her cleavage. You see? We all want practical things.

We had painting on the first morning at school. And I got carried away. No canvas could hold me! When the bell went, everyone left and this little girl came up to me. She was utterly round, with mauve-blue eyes and very thick plaits, the kind you could put in an inkwell and use to write. She put out her hand and said: 'Would you like me to be your best friend and take you in to lunch?'

So I put my hand in hers. And she is still my best friend. She married the son of a friend of my mother's and they had a perfect marriage. Serendipity, you see?

My godmother put me down for Roedean because my godfather had left an educational trust. But my mother didn't like the uniform. So I went to Badminton, just outside Bristol, which was considered safe at the beginning of the war because German planes couldn't get that far. It was bombed, of course, and bombed, and bombed. We were all praying they would bomb the Domestic Science block. The school was evacuated to north Devon. The moment I left school at age sixteen, my mother bunged me into a finishing school, although in reality it taught typing and shorthand. I ran away with a friend called Linda and we joined the American army as civilian employees: fifteen officers to each girl. What an eye-opener! I'd never known a boy before in my life. I started to drink quite heavily, only because it was there. I lost my virginity quickly. To an American, a shit as it turned out. Eventually I joined Special Services, with a uniform and all; we could go out in the evening to the fleshpots of Pontefract: one pub! But we used to go to London, too, to the Café Royal where you could put your uniform in a kit-bag and don a dress and shoes.

I had to be an actress. There was nothing else I could do, was there? I wasn't an architect, was I? When I was twenty-two I got a contract with the Rank Organisation. The other girls were all sent to a drama teacher to iron out their cockney accents; I had to get rid of my Oxford accent. I have been in cabaret with Rachel Roberts and Ron Moody. Tip-top! They went on to wonderful things and I went into the brand-new commerical television station. They were still building the studios around us. They actually built me into a studio once. It was 1956; I had done a programme and I went for a sleep in my dressing room. I woke up an hour later and when I went out into the studio, there were these two men. I said: 'Where's the door?'

One man said: 'There might have been a door. In the future there could be a door. But there is no door now!'

I asked: 'Where do you think the door would be?'

'Well,' he said, 'that's what we've been brooding on.'

At last they very slowly removed one breeze block and as it

came down there was the face of a startled man on the other side. We had taken the wall down in the Gents'! I really should write the history of telly because it's disastrous, and it's funny!

My mother thought men were marvellous and only men could do this, or could do that, which drove me mad even as a child.

'You must find a man, darling,' she'd say to me. 'Oh, darling, you'll marry a rich man.'

But I wanted to have adventures. I was beautiful. *Vogue* chose me as Face of the Year for 1952. You know how your eyes fade as you get older? When I was young my eyes were bright emerald-green and I had thick, long eyelashes. I miss them. That's the one thing I miss most, eyelashes. My eyelashes have got thin and short and I no longer have emerald-green eyes. I don't remember when men stopped looking, but I certainly remember when they looked. I'd go into a room and there'd be a sort of hush. The reason my mother still looked so young when she died at ninety-three was that she still had thick, black eyelashes. All our family live for ever; everyone else died in their nineties except my grandmother who was 100; my great-grandmother was 103; my great-grandfather 101; and I had one great-aunt of 107. And yes, they smoked and they drank. My uncle, who was a great fornicator, was a great drinker too and a smoker; he was ninety-something when he died. One of my aunts buried three husbands.

I find being old very interesting. The older you get, the less you have to lose. You can do anything you want to. I eat when I want to. Get up when I want to. Go where I want to. I've been lucky; my hip replacement is the best they have. I cannot understand these old people who say: 'Oh, I'm so lonely. Nobody ever comes to see me!' Do they never go out? Do they never invite people in? I have lots of young friends.

I got married when I was nineteen to a Greek poet. I left

him when I was twenty-five. I should never have done it. He was the most lovely person and terribly grand. But you do silly things when you're young. I married again, but it came and went. No children. No, no children. My friend downstairs has two little girls and I am their 'non-godmother'.

My first book was about my childhood. And for the next eighteen years I wrote and I wrote and I wrote. I wrote and I wrote and I wrote. I wrote fifty-two telly plays and half the series *Tenko*. I did a theatre play, two autobiographies, and a history of Britain in the Second World War called *Talking About the War*. And then I thought: That's it. Done! I am not going to write again! Money and revenge are the only real motives for writing. I don't want to work like buggery. I want to do what I want to do. So ten years ago I bought this flat with my savings. When I had been here two years I sold it on to National Provincial, or Prudential or something, for a sum in my hot little hand, and £500 and something a month until I die. That and my tenant will allow me to live here at least as long as inflation doesn't get too bad.

You really wanted me to talk about getting old and about death, didn't you? All I can say is: how do you know you've gone too far until you've got there?

2

Talking to Strangers

A S WE PROGRESS towards extreme old age, necessity
becomes more and more difficult to distinguish from
pleasure. The pleasurable necessity of sound sleep, of familiar
food and good digestion, of walking in the open air and being
able to see what is before our eyes; the necessary pleasure of
a cup of tea, or a tot of vodka; and the pleasurable necessity
of communicating with others: the vital and affirming delight
of speech. Less than ever these days are we the aged sheltered
among related generations in big families or small intergenerational communities; less and less do we grow old as part of
any family or any kind of community who will listen to us
with genuine attention, or at least with respect, or at the very
least with patience. Less and less do youngsters care to try to
understand what the hell their old folks are blathering on
about, let alone how it might pertain to themselves, to their
history, and to their future. Even meals-on-wheels teams often
forbid 'carers' when dropping off food trays to chat with recipients lest it delay deliveries.

We the old and ageing must nowadays take an audience
captive whenever we can; otherwise, if we wait for ears to be
loaned instead of grabbing them on the run, many of us will
have no occasion from one day to the next to speak a word,
not one word, to another human being. A necessity as well as
a pleasure of being old is the freedom to talk to strangers in
the street, on public transport, and in the queues that keep

urban lives in order. To make our presence felt, we old gasbags talk to strangers, to each other and, now hands-free mobile phones have removed public soliloquy from the stigmata of lunacy, more than ever we talk aloud to ourselves.

True enough, thanks to nutrition and medical science the numbers of aged are increasing, while at the same time our families shrink and scatter. Furthermore, every day another neighbourly point of contact vanishes into cyberspace or is given over to distant strangers with exotic accents and alien frames of reference. Twenty years ago – even in the midst of this vast city, London – familiar and friendly faces were encountered on both sides of transactions at the local bank, for example, where tellers as often as not greeted customers by name, admired their children, and expressed worry about old regulars not seen for a while. A Christmas card from the bank manager to those in the black used to arrive every year back in the 1960s and 1970s; an invitation to join him for coffee – or even, so I heard tell, for lunch – meant you had arrived fully-fledged in the new meritocracy.

Until recently a group of customers waiting around in banks and shops might start spontaneous seminars on politics, finance, family problems, or love: convivial exchanges that have been made redundant now by do-it-yourself checkouts and holes in the wall that require our backs to be turned to the breathing world and to each other. Surely talking to strangers is much better than keeping an imposed public silence; talking to strangers must be better than nothing. There is often something to learn or relearn from impromptu conversations. Whenever I find myself in Paris, for example, I stop passers-by to ask for directions to a nearby street or metro station, just so I can hear again how many reply: 'Oh, it is much too far too walk.' And thus I confirm my observation of the disdain in which a true Parisian holds areas beyond his arrondissements.

According to a sad little item on Radio 4 this morning, postage stamps could soon be supplemented and no doubt in due course will be sacrificed to payment online. Some day only rich eccentrics will collect those sticky bits of history and artistry that once served as a beautiful geography lesson to children of every class in our society. Soon only the very old will be able to remember when the post was a pipeline for news and friendship and love. In my youth, thank-you notes and letters of sympathy to the bereaved, and of course love letters were all scripted from heart to hand with a pen and ink; businesses alone used chilly typeface. More than half a century ago we American girls – and it was only girls – no matter our gifts or dreams, sat side by side in classrooms adapted to the 'secretarial course' where we learned to type to a professional level. The other day while queuing in my local post office I heard again in my mind's ear the orchestral clatter and ping of our typewriters that in its way made ingenious music. Around me stood a few young people, distant and bored, glued to their own portable sources of digital racket while we old people stood invisible among them to receive our handouts. In front of me was a bent white sparrow of a woman. No old lady worth her salt is seen out and about without a carrier bag; hers contained a bouquet of perfect white lilies, too perfect, too white, and devoid of scent.

'Your flowers are very pretty,' I said, for preamble is not required when old strangers meet and chat in passing.

'They're to put on a grave,' she replied.

Her solemn face betrayed no sudden crease or spasm; evidently her grief was ingrained and habitual.

'They steal the real ones, you see,' she told me. 'Too cheap to buy their own flowers for their deceased folks, you see,' she said and then added thoughtfully: 'Or maybe too poor.'

'I wonder why they don't steal flowers like yours? Silk and plastic are nearly everlasting.'

'Real ones are nicer under the circumstances. Real ones are more appropriate, you see. I would love to take real ones, but I can't go very often these days. And they steal the real ones, you see, so I take these.'

Walking home with the application form to fill in for my 'freedom pass' entitling over-sixties to free public transport in London, I thought about what the stranger had taught me. Graveyard etiquette apparently requires real lilies to decay and leave behind only stalks, stems, and scraps of ribbons; real flowers are the Christian equivalent of living retinues sealed into eternity with embalmed pharaohs. We Jews, on the other hand, when we visit our dead leave on the grave a pebble, as enduring as loss and as imperishable too, should our circumstances prevent a return to the burial site.

During the early part of my grown-up working life you could say I talked to strangers professionally; as a magazine journalist I was often sent out to interview the celebrities of the time. Among the titles on my imagined shelf of books I never wrote is one jotted into a notebook from that era: *People I Have Almost Met.* The tale begins in Manhattan in the 1940s: a bearded man dressed in deerskins leans against a skyscraper and frowns at the passing traffic.

'Irma, I want you to go up to that man and say hello,' my mother urges me, pushing me forward.

'Hello,' I say.

The man looks down, takes a moment to collect himself, and says: 'Hello, kid.'

'Never forget,' says my mother, squeezing my little hand, 'you just said hello to Ernest Hemingway.'

Ten years later a friend at Columbia University invited me to a gathering in a downtown bedsit; it was being held by a poet he knew. I sat on the floor, an arch and cultivated din ringing over my head, while I gazed speechlessly at a coffee cup holding a culture of green mould under W.H. Auden's bed. Of course, Hemingway and Auden and all the others I almost met never almost met me; why should they? Marlon Brando, sitting on a swing in the park outside my junior school during a break from filming *On the Waterfront* near by, certainly never nearly met me, never saw me gawping. Nor did Peggy Guggenheim meet me when she cast her avid eye over those gathered at a dinner party where I was a minor guest. And there was that old film star, what's his name? The one who always played a good guy despite his bad guy's aura? He had an Irish surname and Latinate colouring: what was his name? He was the only inter-viewee to make an opportunistic pass at me, not counting Norman Mailer. But the writer wasn't serious; his pass was just a habitual tic; how could he have meant it with his then wife patrolling outside the room where our interview was taking place? Tennessee Williams barely noticed meeting me; I would certainly not figure in his biography. Nevertheless, the play-wright saved my life. Had he not postponed an appointment for our magazine interview more than four decades ago, I would not have changed my reservation on a plane that went down with no survivors in the English Channel.

And so our memories date us and put us out of fashion. My droppable names are slipping every day a little further beyond their use-by date; already even the best of them have no impact among young listeners. Mind you, the young do not listen as well or even as politely as we used to do before the invention of mobiles and iPods, and the young have never talked well to strangers. For a start, young people venture out alone in public much more rarely than we oldsters and it is tricky even for an old hand like me to instigate a conversation when I'm out-numbered, unless it is with a couple grown old together, moving as one, each talking to the other as to himself. Even then, in my experience, it is the woman who enters into the exchange while her husband listens with bemused tolerance. When young-sters talk to strangers it is as a first step towards something they want, probably sex; so the little egocentrics simply cannot comprehend that chatty oldsters merely need to hear and to be heard, to emerge from invisibility and validate our continuing presence on this busy planet. The young are suspicious of what appears to be a dotty old lech of either sex who tries to start an ad hoc conversation. And besides, youngsters now lack historical vocabulary; they have more trouble than any previous generation knowing what on earth old timers are talking about.

'Have you no black ink?' I asked the young salesman.

The big stationery shop sold books, magazines, sweets, toys, soft drinks, and computer accessories, but no ink could I find.

'It's for a pen,' I explained when he finally located a bottle of black ink behind a rack of ballpoint pens. 'A real pen, I mean: a fountain pen.'

'How does that work?' asked the lad. 'Like a quill?'

No glimmer of wit or sarcasm enlivened the earthling's plump young face, although the querulous old man to come was already furrowing his brow.

'Is this your first freedom pass, dear?' asked the middle-aged woman who was issuing it to me. Her tone tut-tutted; I had long been eligible for my free ride and had left it unclaimed for more than a decade. Only recently among the twinges of old age have I counted the financial pinch of taking frequent taxis.

'Well, you see, I live in the centre of town,' I explained truthfully. Trying to coax a smile, I added: 'And if it's too far to walk, I don't go.'

Eyes behind glasses, smiling mouth raised hopefully against gravity, Semitic nose becoming bossy in its advanced age: within the worn face on my new freedom pass I saw stashed the many faces of my youth.

'Now you be careful not to lose your freedom pass, dear. And if you do, you be sure to let us know right away,' she said in the cooing voice of a grown-up addressing a toddler. 'I know you're going to find your freedom pass useful for future travel, dear.'

Fuck the future. There is hardly enough of it remaining to enthral someone my age. Then and there I decided to initiate my freedom pass on a journey into the past. And I wondered – I still do: why is there no such word as 'matronising', dear?

The number 12 bus has evidently ceased its journey from the centre of London into my outlying history. The closest stop to my old one is on a parallel road aboard a number 94. Allowing myself the 'harrumph' demotic in the nation of the old, I gave thanks at least that I was not boarding a so-called 'bendy' bus made for cities built on a grid, and posing a real threat to the pedestrians and traffic of London's antique curves and roundabouts. I touched the new document to a yellow disc beside the driver and was granted passage with a beep that produced in me a frisson, not precisely of freedom, more of power almost royal. Rush hour was over and the bus a lot less full than buses ever were back when I had to swim with the tide. Making for the stairs to the upper deck, I had to brave the sniffing disapproval of an old man seated near the entrance. He held a copy of the morning paper I had already read; it carried an article about elderly bus passengers being trapped when doors were closed carelessly by drivers, and being jostled off our feet, too, if we did not hurry to be seated before the bus started. While narrowing our own choices, the passage of time also makes us old ones quicker than ever to disapprove of the choices of others; we grant no leeway where we ourselves have none left to spare. The old man snorted and shook his head at me.

Upstairs and still upright, I took a window seat midway port-side that would allow me to look into passing windows; I am a genteel peeping Tom on the sly. After a moment I regretted not having gone for the front seat instead as it commands the most magnificent view of London available from the road. But I was too intimidated to move, thanks to a deplorable innovation, yet another witless distraction from each other and the journey: a television screen suspended over the stairwell. Its hidden camera was panning over the upper deck where a few youngsters sat plugged into other channels. And who was that twitchy old bird looking back at me with disapproval? I realised with the little shock attached to aged reflections: she was me.

Looking down at the multicoloured torrent of humanity in the wide shopping street, I was surprised by sudden delight. I was having fun! Riding on the top of the bus was fun! Oxford Street, despised though it may be by retail snobs and urban aesthetes, is stunning from where I sat. Sculpted cornucopias, mermaids, and warriors – unknown and unseen at street level – bear witness to Mr Selfridge's mercantile aspirations. As we skimmed the green edge of Hyde Park, moving towards the outlying neighbourhoods where I used to live when I was newer in London, memories began to fall into place, some sharp as splinters, others feathery as vanishing dreams from the night before. Feathery and sharp, indeed, for suddenly I remembered trying frantically on this very street late one afternoon to find a shop selling pillows filled with polyester rather than real feathers like the pillows in the local hotel I had booked for my parents. They were visiting London at last to see how I was doing and to disapprove. It was only forty years later, from the height of the number 94 bus, I suddenly realised my father's new allergy to feathers and butter, as well as several other everyday things, was a diversion invented to camouflage the onset of terminal confusion. My poor father had become a lone and weary foot soldier struggling against surrender, trying not to lay down his arms as dementia advanced over the horizon. Whatever his loss of intellectual faculties, he did remain to the end in possession of teeth befitting a retired dentist. On what was to be our final visit to his nursing home, my young son and I watched 'Grand

Paw's' rapturous concentration as he chewed an apple, man's first wicked fruit and his last.

'I didn't want to tell you,' said my mother two weeks after that visit when I called her on a crackly transatlantic line. 'Dad died yesterday.'

She didn't want to tell me? My mother did not want to tell me of my father's death? It was only decades later, using my freedom pass for the first time on the top deck of a London bus and remembering feathers and fathers, I understood suddenly how my mother must have felt, a little girl hardly older than the century, when she was told her daddy had died in a Colorado home for consumptives. Of course. She had not wanted to be the messenger who caused me even a shadow of her own recollected terror and despair.

The bus approached the roundabout that separates my simple past from my past future; it was on the far side I bought my first house on a full mortgage of £5,000. Measuring time by house prices as Londoners do nowadays, that was nearly half a million pounds ago. Uncertain where the new stops were, I moved again, this time downstairs where most of the seats appeared to be occupied by freedom-pass holders like me, but too prudent or too frail for the adventure of top-deck travel. Had so many old folks always travelled on off-peak buses? Or can you see the aged only after you yourself have become a member of their invisible legion? A venerable Chinese woman shifted her carrier bag onto her lap and smiled to show me she did not mind; on the contrary, she would be pleased for me to take the seat next to her.

'Thank you. I'm getting off quite soon.'

'You live here?' she asked, her bell-like accent one of the most difficult to tame.

'I lived here a long, long time ago. I used to take my son to the circus every year right over there on that green.'

'No circus there any more. See? They are going to build a shopping mall.'

She nodded towards towering cranes where once stood Victorian homes and a warehouse for camping equipment, I seemed to recall.

'Yes,' she said, 'it was camping equipment. Old family business.'

Seeing me glance up towards the television screen, she said: 'It advertises too, sometimes.'

We both sighed and clucked our tongues.

'My son will be among the last to remember how it used to be,' I said.

'Lucky boy. Many more will not remember. How remember what they never knew?'

We passed a moment in silence.

'American?'

'Originally.'

'Go back?'

'Not much. Do you?'

'The nation I left,' she said, shaking her head, 'more familiar to me a century ago, more familiar then to me than it would be now. All adult life I live here, far down this road,' said the stranger, my companion on the bus. 'I arrived in this country on a ship.'

'I did, too. I arrived here on a ship, too, from the opposite direction to yours.'

'And see? Only see how we two meet now here in the middle of our opposite directions.'

Born a world apart to cultures and languages that must have divided us in youth, we were united by the weight of our days and by memories in common not many young people will ever make again: the rasp of a lifting anchor, the tearing swish of a big ship's wake as it departs from its home port for ever. Then the engines begin to drum, day after day like an army on the march.

'Not all changes are for the bad,' she said. 'We must not allow ourselves to think all change bad.'

It was my stop. We two, who had never met before and would not meet again, clasped hands for a moment before we parted as friends: two new friends – two old friends.

I have said it before; however, being over seventy I am entitled and, indeed, practically required to repeat myself, so I say again: the young are welcome to their efficient short-term memories and the hectic enlargement of them. Only in us old people can memory achieve its art and its apogee. Veterans of war-torn fields, lifetime lovers, virtuosi whose fingers, now arthritic, once commanded masterpieces, solitary travellers of leafy footpaths now swollen into motorways: in us weary adventurers memory can become a new emotion, fierce, unedited, and sensual. The moment I stepped into the shady street that had once been my own, memories captive in my cells began to rattle the bars and clamour for release. They gathered against reason to overwhelm me and to sweep me back, to where I was forty years ago, full of passions and energy. Memories triumphant and quintessential transformed me there and then into the ghost of myself.

I felt the street itself, Ellingham Road, summoning me back and remembering me. Again I brought my baby home; again I watered the garden and prepared food for guests; again I bled, I smoked, I made love; I stroked the cat until he rumbled. And I dreamed of a future open to good luck and surprises. I cannot say how long I stood there being remembered. But I knew I must not hang around too long lest I melt altogether into the past, losing all use of the present tense as I have known my father and other old people do. So I did not knock on the door of my old house, or even wait to see if I recognised the woman walking towards me, pushing a pram, or if she knew me from her childhood when

31

I had been a neighbour on that street. I turned and left my past as it had found me: alone.

On the number 94 travelling in the reverse direction, the last available window seat was upstairs. All around me were only young people until we reached a posh stop across from Hyde Park where a couple well into their prosperous sixties boarded. The woman, tawny and stout, emerged from the stairwell, huffing and straddling the aisle, leaving her husband stranded behind her as the bus started to move forward.

'It is illegal to stand upstairs. Please be seated,' commanded a disembodied voice from below.

'I can do no such thing. My doctor says I gotta stand with my feet braced when on a moving vehicle,' the woman shouted back in broad American.

Talking to strangers is like any other comfort or painkiller: it can turn into a mindless addiction unless the dosage is controlled and the nature of the stranger balanced against the length of the journey ahead. When the bus stopped at a red light and the American eyed the empty seat next to me, I immediately faked a melodramatic cough. She hurried past me, barely inhaling, her husband shuffling behind her. Fortunately, they made it safely to a pair of seats before the bus started again, so there would be no need for a law suit. That no defunct American has managed to return from beyond the grave to bring a suit against the medical profession must be accepted as evidence against an afterlife.

Wanting only passing company, not a relationship, old chatterboxes like me soon learn that the safest stranger to talk to is one moving in a different direction from one's own. So it is that tourists needing directions get a lot more than they bargain for when they choose to stop me. I have even been known to offer my services to puzzled visitors huddling over their maps long before I am asked.

'This area is Soho,' I told the transfixed youngish couple on the corner. 'It's an old hunting cry, you see. Those were once the green fields of a private estate. And where do you come from? Seattle is a great town, one of the best in America! Where are you going, I mean after London? Oh, Australia! Perth! The definition of a suburb to my way of thinking. If you can, take the train from Perth to Sydney, one of the great rail journeys on the planet. Herds of camels run wild beside the tracks. Alien creatures imported to Oz proliferate, you know, especially flies. And I was told that great suburban room divider, the privet hedge, is overwhelming local flora, too. Sorry. Sorry, mate. Where was it you said you wanted to go? Oh yes, the Royal Opera House . . . Straight down that way, then left.'

My neighbourhood, Soho, was unique among raffish urban centres for containing long-time and old-time residents whose churches and schools prospered right next door to bars and brothels with pretty fair tolerance from all. Old locals could not walk further than a block without a neighbourly encounter. Nowadays our numbers are diminishing and the area is becoming less amiable as newcomers buy up flats as soon as they come on the market when someone dies. New owners then either let them for outrageous weekly rents or use them as occasional pieds-à-terre when they cannot make it home to the shires. Every time I see yet another Flat for Sale sign on a neighbour's building, it strikes me that there can be no counsellor or prescription for antidepressants so effective in alleviating the grieving process of new orphans as an estate agent.

Walking home that late afternoon, I bumped into Michelle, no stranger, though indisputably strange. She sat on a bench on our local green, scattering crumbs to a scramble of pigeons. Her outfit was layered with her usual flair, culminating in a red turban on top of her long white hair and rhinestone earrings, glittering despite several missing bits. Michelle generally camps on the green or in a nearby doorway and she thoughtfully watches passers-by, deciding which one to stop for a chat about the weather, about love and about human nature. The first time she stopped me and introduced herself, we chatted for a while and then I gave her a pound coin, which was gratefully accepted, though she rarely asks outright for money. Ever since, whenever she spots me she rises to her full towering height and offers me a hug. As I approached now, she lifted her head and cried, 'Hello, darling!' in husky, cultivated tones.

I composed myself for her embrace. Two girls passing on the path slowed their pace and sniggered.

'Gross!' said one to the other in a loud voice.

'I like to feed the pigeons, darling,' Michelle said, returning to her bench. 'Poor dumb little birds!'

Her look included the giggling girls leaving the green.

Michelle, undoubtedly christened Michael sixty-odd years ago, laughed and cooed and scattered more crumbs from an ancient Harrods carrier bag, her bracelets jingling and her emergent white beard showing clearly in shafts of late sunlight. The winged vermin scrabbling at her wide feet raised the dust in a frenzy of hunger and gratitude.

'They love me, darling.'

'Sure they do. As long as the crumbs hold out, Michelle.'

'Ah well, darling, *faute de mieux* as the Froggies say.'

'*Faute de mieux*. You know, Michelle,' I said, 'that would be a good book title: *Faute de Mieux* – the story of a life.'

'Dedicate the book to me, darling.'

I slipped a coin into her hand and a legion of small beaks aimed my way.

It required a detour from my homeward route to buy an evening newspaper. A ragged man in his late twenties was scavenging outside the local supermarket, examining discarded food containers. When he found a crust he mumbled it at the corners of his toothless mouth, his eyes closed in bliss. Then he entered the small supermarket ahead of me at a stooping lope, whiffs of misery in his wake.

'Biscuits?' he asked the middle-aged Asian woman behind the counter.

While I studied the headlines of the papers he examined packets of biscuits in a nearby aisle, imagining their taste, or looking for the cheapest, or possibly weighing up his chance of shoplifting.

'Hold on a minute,' I said, handing my paper to the woman. 'I want to buy some biscuits for him.'

She showed her surprise, despite having come from a land of ancient charity, the bankrupt home that she had traded for starless nights in London.

'Thank you,' the vagrant lisped when I paid for the biscuits; his eyes were blue and mad and there was tragedy in his empty smile.

'I hope things get better for you,' I said, as if things could.

'I don't drink, you know. I've been in hospital. Oh, thank you! Merry Christmas! Thank you!' he said as he loped away, and again over his shoulder: 'Thank you!'

Acts of charity resemble crimes in that both victim and perpetrator both soon wonder whether there might be more where the last lot came from. Already I was berating myself for not adding a pint of milk to what was probably the young man's only nourishment of the day. Even if we the aged are still possessed of teeth and remnants of fortunes, we must sympathise with beggars, deprived of status in the community and thrown on the mercy of strangers. As I grow old, I make charity in the street my rule. And just then, along came the exception to prove it.

'I saw you,' said the crone advancing on her canes. 'I saw you,' she quavered again accusingly, 'talking to that good-for-nothing and giving him food, too! Are you so desperate then for male company?'

According to a young medical friend of mine, the failure of

self-censorship that makes many of us oldsters brutally outspoken is due to shrinkage of the brain's frontal lobes.

'Nope,' said my scientific friend when I suggested that senescent tactlessness could equally be due to our having less time left to pussyfoot.

'Nope,' he said when I offered the notion that geriatric bluntspeak grabs attention our aged observations would be denied if delivered tactfully.

'Nope,' he said from a height of half my age. 'Sorry, but it's shrinkage.'

Just now science rules supreme. Either way, the old bat on her Zimmer nearly had a point. In one day's encounters with talkative strangers, women outnumbered the men about five to one; they usually do. Practically from childhood, we women are readier than our brothers to spill our thoughts and feelings as fast as they occur, without rehearsal or editing; it is a characteristic that leads to big trouble in youth, especially between the sexes. However, our spontaneous loquacity means talking to strangers is one comfort that comes more easily to those of us condemned to the increasing loneliness of old age in our materialistic and selfish society.

An article in the evening paper tackled 'fears for the elderly' as energy prices rise and stretch tight budgets. On another page a headline read: '"Scrooge" policies of public transport anger the elderly.' The word 'elderly' certainly annoys me. 'Elderly' is on the way; 'old' has arrived. 'Elderly' is running for the bus; 'old' is on board. 'Elderly' is passé; 'old' is now and for a little while longer. 'Old' can be foolish, but never as foolish as 'young'. 'Old' can be disruptive and mad, but never as bad or as mad as 'elderly'. Why has 'old' become a dirty word? What comes before sixty or sixty-five these days may be called 'elderly' by prudes; seventy is old, damn it. Certifiably old!

I crumpled up the paper for the bin and turned to look out

at the view. The sunset over London cannot be seen from my window, only its broken reflection in the glass of an overbearing office block on the far side of a shabby vista of roofs and chimneys, punctuated by the tarnished aluminium smoke extractors of local restaurants and bars. Defining an address in the old-fashioned way as the place to which one's letters are sent, I have had fourteen addresses so far in four countries as well as a peripatetic one at sea. Never before have I stayed at one address as long as this. Do I talk to strangers more than many other old women because I myself am a stranger? An expatriate is always a stranger, even after decades. Is it time to move on again? Is it time to change the view from my window? Is it time to dye my white hair blonde? Time to start afresh? Is there time?

'Do I dare to eat a peach?' I said. I looked around. 'Have I been talking to myself?'

There was nobody else in the room, no other stranger apart from myself.

'It is sure enough time for a drop of vodka, I think.'

Turning from the window with careless haste, I lost my balance and banged my knee.

'Oh dear, I am so clumsy! Forgive me.'

No sooner do we assume that all the words we will ever need are in place than we start to lose them one by one, largely through neglect. It is heartening, at my time of life, when a brand-new word comes along to make itself useful.

'Hylozoism,' I said. 'An amusing word I came across the other day. Like oxymoron and adiaphorous and hegemony, hylozoism makes a chuckling sound while keeping a steady grip on human pretensions: foolish lapses, and mediocrity, and power that comes oh so rarely, so very rarely, through merit. And hylozoism: it means imbuing matter with understanding. A cute word, don't you think? Oh, what am I saying? Of course you don't think!'

How long had I been talking to my standing lamp?

A Very Old Voice: Rose Hacker

Rose Hacker is immediately captivating for she possesses curiosity, toler-
ance, and wit. We met recently as strangers; however, to meet Rose is
to want to meet her again, and often. The daughter of a Polish immi-
grant father and a London mother, Rose has not merely dabbled in
more than one profession and persuasion; she has gone deeply into
them and climbed high, too. Designer, sculptress, political activist,
marriage guidance counsellor and agony aunt, journalist, wife and
mother and granny and great-granny, Rose is a committed Socialist of
the old idealistic school. She travelled to the Soviet Union as a fellow
passenger of Beatrice and Sidney Webb and was an elected member of
the Greater London Council in the 1970s. Her accommodation, in
sheltered housing, is a delightful studio room chock-full of books and
art created by her offspring and her gifted friends. Having written several
books on social issues in the past, Rose now contributes a crystalline
column to The Camden New Journal. *Often in attendance on Rose*
is Bernard Miller, the son of one of her old friends, who is now her
good friend too and her amanuensis. Although her eyesight has badly
deteriorated, Rose's vision of the world remains alert and encompassing.
Oh yes, and by the by, Rose is 102 years old.

This is my second century so I think of myself as eighteen
months old and when you are eighteen months old you learn
so much, so very much, without words. Thoughts are things
too. The things you learn as a little baby imprison you for the
rest of your life, and sometimes they free you, too. These days
I find myself remembering very early things. For the past twenty
years or so when I have tried to learn something by heart it
just won't stay in; the things I learned in early childhood,
however, suddenly come back, or have been there all the time.
Recently I went to hear *Aida*. Now, that is the first opera I
ever heard, in Paris with my father. I have heard it since, yet

somehow the other night from the first chord, the first bar, I knew it all and it had a strange, new power.

My father came here at eighteen from Poland. He had been a bookbinder and he did beautiful tooled leather bindings. He lived in the most terrible, unthinkable poverty; he was determined to get out. Poland then was divided. Whenever the Poles rebelled against the Russians, the Russians said: 'It's all the fault of the Jews, so go have a pogrom, have a little fun: rape the women, smash their homes . . .' I have never known that kind of fear. I lived through the First World War and whatever my mother did with me and my brothers and sister then, I did with my children in the Second World War; mostly we hid under the kitchen table.

My grandmother raised all her nine children as good Jews. Her eldest son fell in love with a non-Jewish girl and would not give her up; by the way, he had a wooden leg, they said from the Boer War. He was a jolly man. I was brought up as an orthodox Jew but the orthodox only go through the motions, they don't think about God; few orthodox of any faith think about God. I love religious music and paintings, they are marvels of imagination. But then they become articles of faith, mixed up with power and nationalism. Why say: 'This is truth; believe it or I will kill you'? These symbols all stand for just one thing: one god, the god of love. And love is God.

I am lucky. My sons are seventy-one and seventy-four, and they both live within walking distance. I have two lovely sons and two lovely grandsons; sometimes I get them muddled up: four bald-headed men! And both my sons are with the same wives, more than forty years. Isn't that marvellous these days? Mind you, part of my generation, just a very small part, started to be wild and free; they read Bertrand Russell, they read Proust. We were all supposed to be virgins. Men were raised to think good girls were virgins and you married one, but you had as much fun as you liked with a bad girl, and there were lots around, especially poor girls who would do it for money. And then there was the religion thing: 'I love you, darling, but I couldn't possibly marry you; it would break my mother's heart.' That was very much the case among us Jews, and other faiths, too.

When Hitler came into power my husband and I decided to join a synagogue, to stand up and be counted. We were not religious, we were humanists; we joined a reformed synagogue. The orthodox Jews did not speak to the reformed Jews. As if Hitler would make such a fine distinction between them! As if we would not all go to the same gas chambers! I joined the synagogue to help refugees. There was a woman there, the daughter of an orthodox rabbi, a marvellous and open-minded man; we lived a few doors apart. She became my great friend and we began to help the refugees. Then when my husband was in the reserves, I had to be evacuated to different places with my toddlers. Finally I saw an advertisement: 'Rooms available: any race or religion.' Back then people could still specify 'no blacks, no Jews need apply.' So I found accommodation with a Canadian woman, very rebellious and modern, and she was not just renting rooms, but building a community; we looked after each other's kids and took in other people when the bombing got bad. And I did everything for her at the end, the funeral service and all. Her daughter is now a famous art historian.

You know, I am sometimes afraid of what is happening politically. Once we had ideals; a hundred years ago Socialism started, Communism started, the world was full of ideals and those who held them were wonderful people. Don't let us pretend they weren't wonderful just because there was also Stalin and people like him who only wanted power, as has been happening for thousands of years. Among idealists politics was never a job; it was a voluntary thing, a calling to make a better world; it was a Greek ideal. But of course we must not forget that the Greeks had slaves. And the Victorians had maids and servants.

My husband was an accountant, a good accountant, and I mean that in the moral sense. He and his partner were two poor little schoolboys who did not go to university because they wanted to help their families financially; they both got free articles and built up a good business. And then in the 1970s we saw the transformation from – how to describe it? – from a time when accountants, solicitors, and lawyers helped people look after their businesses to a time when it changed into buying up businesses that failed. Bankruptcy? Jolly good! Now we take over! My husband retired in disgust at the way things were going.

Just one quick story: I met a lovely young man at a concert recently; I had known his mother. That's what happens in my life now, many of my friends are the children of dear friends who are dead. I have watched them grow up and now they are grandparents, and they are my friends.

'Oh,' this man said, 'you gave me a job once! With the local Association for Mental Health.'

'Did you enjoy it?'

'Oh yes,' he said.

'And are you a social worker now?'

'No,' he said. 'I'm a financial advisor.'

Now, that's the story of today, isn't it? Get on the ladder, make money, buy a house.

I used to fall madly in love when I was young but I was very virginal. One boy, I remember, said I talked as if we should go off for a naughty weekend in Paris together but he knew that if we did I wouldn't even let him kiss me.

I was an avid reader; I have always read a lot. I can't see any more but I can think. My father encouraged me to read. I was a horrible child, the eldest of three. But I learned because my father encouraged me. He wanted me to go into the business and for a while I was his right-hand man. My mother used to say: 'Don't ask so many questions and do what I tell you . . .'

(*Bernard, Rose's friend and amanuensis, seated near by, laughs and says*: '*That will be the day!*')

I loaned my mother *The Well of Loneliness* to read and she refused to believe it. 'Women don't do that! No! Women falling in love with women? Rubbish.' I believe Queen Victoria had the same reaction as my mother. I cannot read now. But I listen to everything. Thanks to Bernard I am acquiring gadgets. But then I press the wrong buttons and mess it all up.

(*Bernard: 'Then she tells me she's stupid. But she is not stupid at all. The machines are badly designed.'*)

I feel stupid surrounded by machinery and I cannot see what to do. Technology could change the world; everybody could know everything without formal education. But unfortunately mostly rubbish is available. You know, I drove until I was about ninety-six. And I drove without a licence, I never passed a test. I have driven all over the world. I was stopped only once for speeding when I was about eighty and doing about ninety. Oh, please forgive my going off at tangents.

(*Bernard: 'Rose's tangents beat the hell out of most people's dissertations . . .'*)

The position of women has changed immensely. But everything contains elements of its opposite. We must keep the balance and balance is what has gone in the past few years. You know, I have been meeting more and more women recently of about fifty-odd who decided not to have children, and there is a depression underneath. They seem well and on top of the world but they are not. Because nobody cuddles them now; nobody loves them. They have the internet and they know hundreds of people, more or less, but nobody who cares. I remember realising when I was forty and training for marriage guidance how we all want loving arms. That is one truth that holds pretty generally. Of course, nowadays everything has to have an answer. What I believe is that nothing has an answer. You expose the problem, you think about it, you talk about it, and you find your own answer. I think I must write an article about that: fitting the theory to the client rather than the client to the theory. These days one size is supposed to fit everybody. And it doesn't, you know. You meet people where they are, not where you think they should be.

I was a sculptress; I was never two-dimensional; I saw everything in three dimensions. Now, I see only a shadow. I don't dream either but I wake up with all sorts of things going on in my head. My day is busy even though I don't get up unless I have an appointment and in this sheltered housing they help me get my breakfast. You have to be able-bodied; it is a residential and not a care home. You have a latchkey, a front-door key; you can go out and stay out as long as you like. My eye was removed soon after I came here; my son bought me a microwave and a toaster. I can manage what I need. I don't mind whether I sleep or not. I have studied the Alexander Technique and learned to relax. Sometimes I fall asleep in my chair, wake up around two in the morning and go to bed. It doesn't matter. I learned about sleep; my husband was paralysed for two years and I nursed him at home; I learned a lot that way about care and our bodies. I never smoked but I like a drink. If I've had a bad day or I'm feeling miserable, I like to have a whisky or a brandy. And yes, I do feel miserable sometimes; in despair about the world. Things must change. The majority of people in the world are poor and starving. They will not put up with it. They will fight. Even here, top-class education and medical care used to be free to everybody; we built a real welfare state. And only look what is happening now!

I like people; I make friends everywhere all the time, and that is lovely. I talk to strangers too, all the time. All new friends begin as strangers. Not long ago at a Labour Party meeting I encountered a boy who asked me why I joined the party, so I told him about the terrible time people had during the war. And he said: 'Oh, they don't teach us history like that at school.'

And I saw that when I spoke, he did not hear me speaking; it was not me, it was history he heard speaking to him.

Rose Hacker died a few months after this interview. My only regret about our meeting is that it had to be the last.

3

Old Money

THE VERY RICH girls among my young classmates at university in the early 1950s were distracted and gloomy, seeming always to have something worrying the backs of their minds. Yes, they were different, really different from the rest of us: mainly middle income with a sprinkling of *nouveaux pauvres* from families ruined in the Great Depression three or four years before we were all born. Old poverty of the sort my father knew, and his parents, and their parents, right back to the Exodus, is another woeful inheritance, marking its descendants in ways that can lead to paralysis and paranoia for their children and their children's children. Generations after the heirs of penury achieve prosperity at last, as many of them did and do now in our promised lands, pleasures still remain distant and diminished by their price-tags. Love, even love, is a burden when it first blossoms in a space too small for dreams and privacy. My father was endowed with gifts too outlandish and expensive for his folks to recognise or cultivate; even after he finally did well enough financially as a dentist, it was the memory of having no money to spare that held him back from the delights his soul craved, while the dread of poverty nagged at him as the wasteful drip of a faulty tap or scraps left on the plates of his profligate children.

Mother was pregnant again when she finally prevailed upon my father to leave the street in Jersey City where his family had settled earlier as a step up from their decaying Manhattan tenement apartment. He agreed at last to move out of the four rooms where we lived behind his dental surgery and directly across from his parents' home. As soon as the baby was born, my father promised we would move to a nice house in a nice area where cars were parked in garages and children played in gardens, not in the street. And then, having made his promise, he suffered what Mother later told me was 'a total nervous breakdown'. For weeks he lay in bed unable to speak or to earn the money that was our sustenance and his poison.

One rainy morning Mother sent me toddling in with a glass of orange juice to where 'Dad'n' gazed out from his pillow at the grey sky. He turned his head towards me; I dropped the glass and ran away. Whenever I hear old people say, as some do, how they try not to remember, how they refuse to remember, or when they scorn remembering and call it 'jogging backwards', I think I recognise their fear of retrospective understanding. To understand too late is an existential defeat more poignant even than remorse. Only now, much later, much too late, I understand how cruel was my involuntary flight from my father's tears of pain and apology. Mother told me later he had been under threat of receiving ECT, the panacea in those days, as Prozac became later for all mental distress, whether malady or symptom. Only when the plan to move home had to be abandoned did my father more or less recover and resume work not long before my brother's arrival. Dad was barely forty; his depression – and his senescence, too, which was already under way – were rooted in old poverty.

Mother, arriving as a bride in Jersey City from a poky Midwestern town, rued her new home even before she rued the marriage that installed her in it. She hated living within tantalising sight of Manhattan to the east, on the edge of marshland to the west where mosquitoes bred and rats were trapped for bounty. Mother assured me often while I was growing up that I hated Jersey City, too. Honestly? No. I felt nothing more profound about the place than boredom. Once I discovered the Hudson and the Manhattan tube, it was not hatred of Jersey that put wings on my heels, but the thrill of emerging from a tunnel under the river straight into the colour and jazz of West Greenwich Village in those pre-Beatnik days. Too young for the bars, I listened to poets hold forth in cafés, and I began to imagine my future in a place where art ruled, where men were handsome, and endings happy ever after. An older friend, Leah, accompanied me on my daredevil crossings to the Big Apple. Her family thought she was learning Latin verbs from me; mine thought I was swatting up on algebra with her. Fortunately for adventurous souls back then, both subjects were still part of the ordinary high-school curriculum.

While in New York recently to attend my fiftieth class reunion I made an impulsive pilgrimage under the river for the first time since my parents asserted their hard-won prosperity and left Jersey City thirty years ago for a genteel retirement community near Princeton. Our old green door has been painted red and now requires a code to get in; I did not need it to see the old staircase, more clearly in my mind's eye even than the page now in front of my bespectacled eyes. It rises steeply between yellowing walls embossed with shields and fleur-de-lis. One day half a century ago I dragged my burden of schoolbooks up those stairs and suddenly there was Mother, storming down past me and out the front door where I saw her stamp and rage at a strange man; she had evidently seen him following me from the tram stop. So my mother must have watched at a window for my return from school; for the first time I wondered if she was really as blasé and immune to conventional concerns as she liked to make out. On the ground floor below our flat was a candy store; next to that my Uncle Max owned a dry goods store, selling haberdashery and clothing over wooden counters where coins rattled through a chute into a hidden till. The shop's windows are darkened now and how

Mother would laugh to see its new sign, advertising 'pest control and extermination'.

When I was a little girl our neighbours were mostly Sicilian and Polish; these days black men lean in the doorways. The three-storey, red-brick flats built over the ground-floor shops are unchanged; they continue to bask in a seedy American propriety as captured by the artist, Edward Hopper. So untouched is the architecture, so redolent of my childhood the riverine miasma from the nearby Hudson, that it seemed natural, not surprising at all, to hear my name called.

'Irma! Oh, Irma! I thought it must be you! It's me! Remember me? Marie! Marie!'

'Marie! Marie!'

Marie, the fishmonger's daughter, was one of my long ago playmates. In the dark moods of my childhood I used to envy Marie her cheerful anticipation of a future untroubling to herself or her family.

'I wish I were Marie!' I cried to my mother when she embellished my essays with phrases of her own, or chided me for misspellings.

'You haven't changed a bit!' said the plump and pretty ageing woman, lying sweetly.

'Nor have you,' I replied.

But she had. And so had her father's shop. A new Italian name, presumably Marie's married one, hung over the door. Where once blue and silver fish lay in dripping crates now stood gilded lamps, bejewelled frames, and broacaded occasional chairs.

'It's my place now. I'm an interior decorator.'

We both turned to look towards the corner where my family used to live upstairs behind a big front window on which were printed, in letters of gold that memory can only portray in mirror image: NOEGRUS LATNED ZTRUK E.I. ROTCOD.

'I remember how your mother used to call you to come in every fifteen minutes. She really made you work hard.'

Mother, by no means financially rich in her own heritage, had the determination, bred into the heirs of poverty, that her children should make good and better than she but, and heed this well, with not the least lapse of pride in their antecedents. That is to say on their maternal side, of course. Mother did not want me to play with the children of our impoverished neighbourhood and did her best to prevent it. One snowy day when I was twelve the local kids pursued my brother and me, pelting us with snowballs and shouting: 'Dirty Jews! You killed Christ!' A puzzling accusation if less alarming than the snow-balls packed around pebbles and shards. Therafter Mother could justify as more than mere snobbery an edict forbidding us ever again to play on local streets, and reluctantly my father agreed to it.

'I guess it paid off,' said Marie cheerfully. 'I saw your picture in that what-do-you-call-it magazine. That's how I knew you.'

A group of black boys passed, wearing baseball caps and baggy trousers.

'The old neighbourhood is going downhill fast,' sighed Marie.

Back into the Hudson and Manhattan tube, bound eastward once more. The stout blonde across the aisle scalded me with suspicion when I took out my camera to photograph an ad on the wall of the subway car, put there by something called Reproductive Medicine Associates.

'Be an egg donor,' it read, 'and become a dreammaker. Women who complete the programme are compensated $8,000 for their time and dedication.'

Dedication to what? Presumably to $8,000. My interest in the offer was academic; egg donating is another stab at 'dream-making' and the big bucks from which age excludes those of us who long ago completed that programme.

'I will not sacrifice my youth to my old age.'

Thus I explained to my parents why I would not continue

on to graduate school for a further degree in sociology and then become a social worker as my mother had. Social work and teaching were two of the few professions to welcome educated girls of my era and underpay them too. At that point in my young life 'old age' meant around forty; nevertheless, I had the right idea. My impassioned refusal comes back to me now whenever I hear parents agonise over what on earth their son or daughter is going to 'do' with a degree in the arts or humanities or pure sciences. 'Do' with it? Let me tell you what they will 'do' with it. They will be with it and see with it, sing with it and fly with it. They will keep it as one keeps faith. And in due course they will have to make ends meet with it. Unless youth sacrifices its ineffable hope and energy to making little more than money out of this life, then, yes, youth will probably end up poor in old age but not necessarily, not by a long shot, end up poorly.

The fact is that every old or ageing woman I know, and a number of the men too, if they led their youth as adventurous free spirits are now worried by poverty or the threat of it. We who were off-beat, we who are still dealing with the here and now, every last one of us old originals is leading a life hobbled by a lack of funds unless we inherited pots of the stuff, or struck it lucky or, of course, unless we wedded it. To this day, as always – and probably even more so now that status and money have become synonyms – parents continue to hope their daughters especially will find a rich mate. Good girls have always been expected to fuck up. So what would happen if we aged eccentric spendthrifts now falling on hard times had it to do again? We would do it again. We would embrace life and each other before joints ache and stiffen; we would see the world and hear it for ourselves, not polished and catalogued by tour guides or framed in the porthole of a floating hotel.

★

Here in the big city I do not recall ever before seeing so very many old men and women shuffling in the supermarket aisles, studying labels, looking for bargains, all unattended, without a carer or anyone near by who seems concerned that their budgets cannot stretch to fresh food. One daily paper says, yes, British old folks are generally in bad financial trouble; it quotes a Help the Aged spokesman saying that a recent increase in gas bills could create 'a nightmare choice for older people between heating and eating'. On the other hand, a Sunday-paper pundit a few days later points out that over-sixties 'own four-fifths of the nation's wealth' and goes on to predict an older generation spending its money to 'make itself feel younger while the younger generation grows old before its time'. He puts so-called geriatric wealth down to the soaring value of property the aged inherited or bought long ago. Indeed, it was in that very paper that I saw my former London terraced house advertised for sale again for exactly one hundred times the price I paid for it in 1970. But when was the last time he tried to eat a brick?

A new trend appears to consider food, heating, and medicine to be among those things that make the aged 'feel younger'. Only a day later I read that lenders are selling an increasing number of mortgages to 'want it all' pensioners who then have trouble keeping up the payments. What, I wonder, is the 'all' the pensioners want? Have the lenders noticed, or do they even care, that a house can heat itself only by burning to the ground? Have they seen as I have how many more ancient smiles are showing ugly gaps since the deteriorating National Health Service disinherited its dentists? Have they reckoned that a roof will cover medical bills only when put in extreme jeopardy as collateral? And doesn't selling so-called 'equity' in a family home, as so many old folks must do nowadays, mean that acres of desirable property will one day soon belong to banks and loan companies with a vested interest in keeping prices astronomical?

'For money you get honey,' my paternal Grandma Ida used to say, her Yiddish cadence giving the word more rhyme than reason to young ears. Money in my lifetime is credited more every day with being the sweetest aspect of life. Money buys safety. It buys power. And money buys time. Statistically, the rich live a lot longer than the poor. Wealth, according to Legal & General's new guideline for their pension annuity rate, 'is a good proxy' for life expectancy; postcodes are therefore being included in their calculations. Those who live in Kensington and have a life expectancy of 82.2 years will not be supported as generously as those who live in Glasgow and peg out on average at around seventy, saving the company a decade of payments. No wonder even the well-off can become notoriously penny-pinching and cling desperately to their wealth.

But not all of us age as Scrooges. I, for example, have never loved money. I have never been able to afford to love money. I can barely afford to like the stuff. And my indifference has been soundly reciprocated. Needing money, earning it, owing it and chasing it has dominated most of my life. Especially after my baby was born, stinking money drained my energy, ruined my sleep, and soiled my few innate gifts. More perfectly than my beloved son's first words, even now I recall the daily thud of yellow envelopes on the mat: which to open, which to postpone, which to ignore? Money has clouded memories that I would now pay if I could to have returned to me clean and bright.

And what is money, after all? It is the effluence of commercial life as shit is of feasting. There is no poetry in the crap. No force in history betrays honour and love as effectively as money. When money is used as metaphor, especially for love, the result is grotesque. I can reel off the top of my head the names of ten people I know in a state of enmity with their siblings. It is painful to consider how many ageing brothers and sisters there must be who no longer speak to one another after a graveside dispute ostensibly over their inheritance. And those bitter quarrels about the detritus left by their parents are always really about which brother or sister received more when the parents were alive: which was more loved, or more admired, and which a greater disappointment. Squabbles over inheritance are a camouflage for the final battle, not with each other, but with Mummy and Daddy. It is a tragedy, and increasingly a modern one, to enter the last lap of life at odds with one who shares a unique conception, the only person whose memories can inform one's own. Filthy money destroys families more effectively than poverty.

There is a cute little irony in the fact that anyone over seventy has probably thrown away a small fortune in their lifetime.

'Oh my God! Look at that, would you?' muttered the old man next to me.

We stood in front of a stall in Covent Garden Market selling antiques and bric-a-brac now where some of us can still remember flowers and fresh vegetables. The old chap's clothes were shabby and frayed; he smelled of tobacco mixed with disinfectant. He had been addressing the air or possibly the deity, then, seeing my interest, he spoke to me.

'Do you see that thing?'

He pointed a shaky finger at a big black telephone with a dial the colour of old ivory.

'She wants £100 for that phone. And you know what? I had one! I had one just like it. I threw it away! I threw away £100! God! My telephone what I used every day is an antique now.'

The young stall-keeper looked up from punching text into her mobile.

'That is not an antique,' she said. 'That is a collectable.'

The old man scowled and sighed; antique himself though never collectable, he would notwithstanding be a hundred quid to the good, had he not jettisoned his big black telephone.

'They used to make a sound,' he said to me. 'Do you remember that sound: chk-chk-chk?'

'Like the tap of a typewriter, music for collectors,' I said.

We both watched the stall-keeper punching the keypad of her mobile.

'I wonder,' the old man said, 'do they still call it dialling?'

The pronoun 'they' rang out of a lonely place where old men take shelter from the derision of the young.

More than twenty years ago, when I first moved into my Soho flat I used to look down practically into the ground-floor flat of the building next door where lived a stocky old solitary rarely seen out and about. A neighbour told me that the old chap shuffling to and fro behind his windows had in his time been a celebrated actor and the author of books on Edwardian theatre.

One afternoon I was alarmed to hear cries from his apartment. Evidently, he had gone to open his sash window and it crashed down, entrapping his hands. Pinned in place, he was calling for help into the empty courtyard between us. Fortunately, my son managed to gain entry and free the old fellow, who in gratitude inscribed one of his books, a rollicking reconstruction of the very first production of *Pygmalion*, and gave it to us. Only a few months later the ailing old actor was taken by ambulance to his penultimate resting place. Within hours an officious landlord had cleared his possessions unceremoniously onto the pavement and soon a swarm of collectors, who must have gathered telepathically from all over London, arrived to feast on piles of theatrical memorabilia, some of it signed by Tree or Beerbohm, abandoned in the wake of an intestate and discarded old life.

I don't speak Finance. I am neither proud of being financially illiterate nor contemptuous of those with expertise. On the contrary, I always found humane and interesting people to interpret finance for me, precisely because I had no idea what they were talking about. I therefore relied on intuition when choosing accountants and financial advisors as I would not have trusted myself to do in any other area of life, least of all in love where intuition can be easily misled by hope. When my friend and primary finance-translator Kate Nathoo speaks, as she does always with eloquence and style, I listen. And sometimes I feel I can almost begin to understand.

'For what you call "old money",' Kate said, 'there is still the influence of the global slump of the 1930s, and the subsequent conflict that haunts them. They have inherited fear and even if some of them have also inherited capital they cannot enjoy it. I often see old people worth a lot of money – if I drew up the balance sheets, maybe a million pounds – but they are trying to survive on £8,000 a year because there is a fear, almost a moral stipulation against touching the capital. Bear in mind, the old people I see are only calling on people like me because they have capital in the first place. Yes, property values have risen. This flat, for instance, is worth a lot more than you paid for it,' and like a good consultant Kate did not then pull her punch. 'But the day will come when you stop working – it is rare enough to be still working at your age – and you will have to think: I can no longer afford to go to the theatre or do all the things that give me pleasure. If you tap into the internet and check sites like Age Concern, you encounter a huge raft of old people who live in truly impoverished circumstances. Mind you, the upcoming lot, the post-war baby boomers, may turn everything around. They have money, confidence, and spirit. Watch out, youth cult! Your ground is about to be challenged! This lot now in their sixties are the first to inherit property big time; they are also the first and the last to have decent pensions from their employers. Both income and capital! A new kind of old person could be on the horizon. But go just ten years earlier than that and, I'm afraid . . .' Kate shrugged.

One day in early spring a few years ago my brother and I flew from our two sides of the world and met in New York. We were going to scatter Mother's ashes. Michael hired a car and we drove to the retirement community where she had lived during her last three decades. Our eerie package, sealed and sealed again within a small suitcase, had been left with one of Mother's friendly neighbours.

My father had been buried next to his parents; his surviving brothers and their families were in attendance at his funeral. But Mother had no living relatives and anyhow she purported to despise reverence of bodily remains. She told me, in one of her fearless declamations not long before the end, that she did not choose to rest her bones next to my father in his family's plot.

'All the other wives will be buried there, Mum. Dad would have wanted you next to him, too.'

'Your father is dead. The dead want nothing.'

She arranged for a cremation and left a request for her ashes to be scattered at sea, a romantic finale that turned out to be scuppered by red tape involving the United States Coast Guard. Mother had been no seafarer or even much of a traveller. I could not recall seeing her ever go out alone, not even just under the Hudson on the tube to New York; she certainly went nowhere more distant unless she was accompanied or had someone waiting to receive her at port or station. So my brother and I decided to scatter her over the familiar waters of the inland lake where we once had a summer house and where we used to swim and fish as children.

'It's not a betrayal is it, Irm?'

'Of course not, Mook. Think of it as taking Mum's last request without a pinch of salt.'

Even after forty years in southern California my brother continues to drive as our father did, in priestly engagement with the highway, anticipating turn-offs miles ahead and braced for disasters. I barely drive at all and have never owned a car. My generation was born to families who believed women could not and should not drive cars. Women drivers, like mothers-in-law, used to be classic butts of jokes. Our mother had driven only from the back seat where now her ashes reposed.

'You are an unmitigated liar!' she snapped once at a bored highway patrolman with nothing better to do than stop my preternaturally cautious father en route to the very place we were bound now and accuse him of speeding.

'Do you remember, Mook, how we had to go straight to a local court and Dad had to pay a fine? And, you know, it was all because the cop didn't know what "unmitigated" meant.'

'Do you remember, Irm,' my brother asked a minute later when we stopped for a traffic light, 'how we used to visit Grandpa Joe at that kosher hotel in the Catskills? And how he always asked Dad to drive down the road and wait so he could join us on foot? He didn't want the others to see him in a car on the Sabbath.'

I had no recollection of my grandfather's mild hypocrisy. But two children of the same family do not have the same childhood; it requires tuning and adjustment of more than one memory to restore a semblance of the past. I was going to ask my brother whether he remembered the lined and powdered faces of the old ladies rocking on the porch of the hotel, talking together, in a cadence of complaint and resignation, in Yiddish, a dying language. But we were moving again and concentration on the traffic prevailed on the highway for the son as it did for his father.

My brother carried the little suitcase to the rocky end of a sandy area we called the Big Beach, though it was shrunken mysteriously from its expanse in my memory and looked now no bigger than any urban playground. I stood guard at the gate for we were undoubtedly about to break the law. Not a soul of the summertime community was in evidence; not a boat on the lake, still chilled and wintry. I watched my brother walk out onto a flat boulder that extended into the water; we used to moor our boat next to it in olden days after we rowed to the Big Beach from our house at the distant end of the lake. He unlatched the case and removed an opaque plastic bag. After struggling for a moment to open the sealed package, he raised it, turned it over, and shook it into the air. Small fragments of bone plashed into the lake while a flurry of dust rose and trembled briefly. A handful or so fell on the water to drift for a while before dissolving into the elements.

'How old was she?' was the first question put by those to whom I reported my mother's death. And every one of them responded: 'A good age!' The younger ones in astonishment; the older ones relieved she had been a decade or two or three ahead of their own next birthdays. Ever the disappointed actress, the undiscovered star, my mother outlived her great tragic role; she could not be keenly mourned; no injustice attaches to death so late in life; there is no cause for rage, no threat of apostasy, among her survivors. As greatly as Mother had been admired and even adored, especially by younger women, her passing at ninety-three was only natural.

As I stood on the Big Beach I was overtaken by a new emotion, neither as rending as bereavement nor as hot as anger. Deep? Permeating rather, a mist in my heart. There was something in it of resignation, and quivers of fear too as even the bravest old soldier remembers feeling when first he stepped into the firing line. My brother joined me and I saw in his eyes the same strange, graveside emotion. It is a feeling that accumulates with increasing age; the young are too quick for it. It grows in a field of desires gone to seed; the young are too juicy for it. This new keynote of old age is in fact profound and permanent, and it is practically mute except among poets. William Butler Yeats as he 'withered into the truth' was one of its great masters. The feeling stirs in me now painfully, mournfully, when certain music plays or when I find myself out of pace with others on a busy street. Say love is a peacock and anger a crow; this old feeling is the raven of our emotions, crying 'never' and 'nevermore'. Geriatric melancholy came home to roost in my brother and me as the ashes of our mother sank, for the descendants of fish that had escaped our childhood hooks to make of what they could.

'We had better go,' my brother said. 'The lawyer is expecting us.'

Up until a year or so before the end, Mother cherished her investments. When time began its slippery slide, she set kitchen timers to ring and remind her to take medication, to make a shopping list for her carers, to pay her bills, and to call her stockbroker for consultations. My brother speaks Finance pretty well and used to chat with her about it while I sat as dumb as our father would have been, like him longing to be listening to music. Talking about your money with anyone but a professional consultant is as uncouth as discussing bowel movements. So I will say only that from Mother I inherited my first ever unearned income, paid off the remains of my mortgage, and set aside a nest egg to help my son with the debts of modern maturity. Yes, I know surveys show that baby boomers, whom I consider merely middle aged, do not trouble to leave their money to their kids and would rather use it to enjoy a pleasant, prosperous retirement of their own. But I am of an older generation more directly descended from poverty and perhaps more communal, too; we did not work for ourselves. There is money trouble ahead for me, of course there is; money trouble always awaits improvident old life-lovers.

'I'd die for you,' Mother used to say when my brother and I were little, and her voice trembled as she imagined herself persuading a homicidal maniac to take her instead of her babies. Supreme sacrifice is a common melodramatic maternal fantasy, probably connected to our deepest past when parental love must countless times have saved the human race. Under the current law of this land, concrete evidence left of devotion to the lives sprung from our own is heavily taxed. Leave a sizable inheritance to those we love and damn near half goes to the state. How long will it be, now that getting and spending is the only significant power, now that medical treatment and thus life itself can be withheld if it costs 'too much', now that thinking about money occupies most of our brain power and loving money pre-empts human love: how long will it be before an old life is of less value to its community than the room it lives in?

'When an old man dies,' they say in Senegal, 'a library burns.'

How long will it be before our libraries are put to the torch because, like, why waste space on books nobody reads any more?

'Don't get me wrong. My parents are great. I love my parents,' I overheard a youngish man in his cups saying to a mate at a local bar. 'But it will sure solve my money troubles when they die.'

An Old Voice of New Poverty: Judy Dainton

'Pensioner' is not a glamorous word: on the contrary, it sounds dreary and dismissive. Pensioners are relegated, in the inner geography of their juniors, to a flatland where they shuffle, stooped and cranky, towards the next cup of tea. And of course, the young cannot imagine pensioners ever being adventurous or sexy, or anything other than old and dowdy. The young hardly think that they will one day in their turn be pensioned off; nobody is ever pensioned on.

Judy Dainton, well travelled and bohemian, would strike most people as an unlikely pensioner. Her history and attitude are reminders that there can be as much variety, eccentricity, and flair in a bunch of the aged and ageing as is to be found in any mob of younger people; moreover, the older people are naturally bound to be more experienced and some of them will be more philosophical. Educated to doctoral level, Judy, a former journalist, has a striking, smoky voice that is never far from laughter. Her council flat in central London is welcoming, arty, and idiosyncratic without obvious extravagance. Extravagance is a part of Judy's past; she neither regrets it nor misses it.

I'm sixty-seven soon; you could say I'm in my sixty-eighth year. My father was a clergyman and we lived in the country. My mother was a Roman Catholic so I grew up in what was in their terms a very liberal household where people discussed one another's religions without trying to kill one another. And it was extremely non-commercial. It wasn't a house where we talked about money. I was the only daughter; my mother lost two children before me so there was a nine-year gap between me and all my brothers. My mother was a crypto-feminist and absolutely determined I would have the educa-tion that her parents would not give their daughter. Honestly? She was not a woman I liked particularly but she was extremely helpful to me and sought every possible scholarship, angle, bursary, whatever, to get me educated. It was a practical lesson, by the way, that I repeated with my own children in due course. My parents had money back in the 1930s but they'd run out of it by the time I was growing up. And a clergyman's stipend was less than I earned at my first job. When my father died at ninety-six, we all divvied up, without fuss; I inherited a chest of drawers, I think it was. My mother worked for a Catholic publisher until she was in her seventies and finally went off to live with the nuns; she chose nuns with sister houses in France and vineyards and such things. Mother was no slouch.

When I arrived in London with my shiny degree I had absolutely no idea about the world of commerce or how it worked or about climbing ladders. I went into my first job in journalism thinking: My goodness! They're going to pay me! It was lovely because I met fashionable people and I interviewed artists of the day: the dreaded Yoko Ono, for example. I was good at interviewing people because I was still in provincial mode so I would let them talk, genuinely fascinated by them, a trick that always works: show interest in people and they will be interesting. The trouble is I'd come to London with a vision of the life I wanted: a false vision. I was about seven when I decided I was going to live in London in a Georgian house and be a writer. I did end up living in London, not in the grand Georgian house I'd envisioned, but in a Georgian flat around the back of Charlotte Street. And indeed I did always turn out a good bit of journalist's copy, but I discovered I was absolutely no good at writing, no good at all: I have in some bizarre way no imagination. Although I had ideas, I could never be a storyteller. It is disillusioning to find out that the one thing you'd decided on when you were young you were ill-equipped to do. But it was glossed over by a job on Fleet Street and, quote, 'interesting' bohemian friends. I wore black as an intense writing person; I played the part. It was about falling in love, and going to parties, and having fun, and staying up late and going into work with a hangover. I lived the stereotyped image of a London person in the 1960s; I wasn't posing, I believed it all. I worked on a women's magazine and then on a Sunday national; I was literate and reasonably ambitious, but not dedicated. I look at girls in journalism now and think: I couldn't have been you in a million years! Although I thought I was probably going to live to be old because it was a genetic likelihood for me, I did not imagine myself as a pensioner. My friends and I all had the same theory: earn money while you're young, enjoy it, give it to your children or not, depending on circumstances, and be prepared to be poor when you're old. Besides, I'd had good early training for future poverty: the children of clergy in those days grew up in lovely houses with all the attributes of gentry but no money. I grew up with poverty as a fact of life.

I met Roger Dainton, one of the people who built that funny ziggurat tower on the Hayward Gallery. An electrical engineer, a born deconstructor, a natural artist. We fell in love and married. Then he got a contract with a demented, third-generation billionaire in Texas.

'Ah have just stayed at the Savoy and ah saw this tower. Can y'all come on over and build me one, too?' he said.

So we went to Amarillo where there was a very hippie scene at the time.

'What shall we do today, honey? Oh, I know, let's sink a piano in the pool; it could be real conceptual!'

So I said to Roger, if I had to listen to that every day I'd throttle someone. A job came up for me in Sri Lanka through a London national paper, a very post-empire sort of job to train up staff for a local paper. So while Roger worked in Amarillo I worked in Sri Lanka. Then out of the proceeds of the tower we bought a shack in Gloucestershire for £850. It turned out to have lots of land attached, which was a surprise to us as we hadn't read the deeds properly. Roger loved it. But I could not stand it in the country. I stood around in wellington boots and buses never came. I had to take driving lessons and I could not do it, I simply could not do it: the eye-to-brain distancing just does not work. I was employed in London part of the week and we kept on our flat there too on a regulated rent. So suddenly, we were rich; we were so rich! Flat in London, house in the country! Eventually, we separated for a few years, got divorced, then after the divorce we went on holiday together to Greece. We are still friends.

Roger took me on with two kids I had before we met. I have eight grandchildren now. My daughter lives in Ireland, my son in New Zealand, but I have never been to see him there because I cannot get my act together to raise money for the fare. I loved the theatre in my twenties; I haven't been in ages. I have a friend my age who goes every week but he's still working part-time and he's richer than me. My pension status is pretty miserable; I get less than the full state pension due to a patchy employment history because of the kids and taking time off to do two further degrees. My state pension is £63.49 a week plus some sum they've done that brings it to around £75, and a small occupational pension for a job I had in market research when I stopped being a freelance journalist. I can claim state benefits, and I do, for I paid a lot of tax in my time. And I'm in a council flat. I did some sums the other week and if I turn the heating off I can live on about ten pence an hour. But it is chilly.

'If it's cold,' my other half used to say, 'put on more jumpers': that's how I grew up.

Yes, I've done crap jobs to put food on the table, and pay the rent, but the absolute horror of doing a gerbil-like, wheel-turning job was a spur to get something better; I don't mean money, I mean something I felt happy doing. Surely that motive-force remains in the young in spite of the need to sell themselves in terms of their degrees, their willingness to work ten hours a day in the mills and kiss ass every time they move! Surely the desire to do things they want to do and like to do must still shine through! I've kept that hippie attitude: I am not that interested in money. Either you've got it or you haven't.

Only this morning I realised: Shit, I haven't got a penny in the house! I get my pension on Monday. I have a friend who takes me for a drink on Thursday because he knows I'm always broke by then and it's his day off work. I have another friend near here and we have drinks on Sunday. Then I take them out on Monday when I get my pension. It's a demented little local network. We know the cheap stalls in the local street market; there's one that sells things spot on the sell-by date. One of my friends who is equally poor rang me yesterday and told me to get to Tesco's fast; they had a cheap deal on pork loin. Because, yes, it does matter. But I have decided to look on it as an old-age challenge; otherwise it is just too boring and would get me down. Pretty soon I'm bound to be one of those little old ladies in the supermarket pushing my Zimmer frame, looking for bargains. Oh, I intend to Zimmer around! Just you watch me! Only I won't have the attitude.

My failing is I still love eating out. There's a restaurant up the road and if you go before seven everything is cheaper. Whenever I get a little money I say to friends, let's go eat! One boring thing about being old is that you feel sleepy after you've eaten and some of them are even older than me so they like an early meal. It's silliness. But you must have some fun in this life.

The bishop gave a dispensation for my father to marry a Catholic and I was raised as both Anglican and Catholic. I went to Anglican church services every Sunday because my daddy was taking them but we had to go to mass first. Catholicism is now the religion of my choice. I am not a good Catholic but I am a believing Catholic. I believe in God as in the Bible;

I believe He will judge and He will punish. If I fear death, it is for the fire and judgement to come. Perhaps that's why I don't complain about my economic condition now. It seems to illustrate the principle of just deserts: I had the money and I did not want to save it or invest it in some complex scheme. I earned it and I spent it. It is the sowing and the reaping.

4

Reunion

H EAVEN MUST BE a reunion. Lost relatives, siblings, and spouses gather again in welcome at the pearly gates; childhood's hamsters and puppies scamper around their ankles once more while canaries, free at last to fly, sing celestial airs to goldfish born as carnival prizes and toted away in plastic bags, now swimming in crystal lakes. To be old is perforce to be an orphan; rest homes differ from orphanages only in the age of the residents and the manner of departing them. So we who arrive late in paradise will see our parents in the throng, smiling in angelic calm, ready at last for apologies, explanations, and forgiveness. In the afterlife, former lovers and friends eager to pick up where active life left them appear as in the photographs over newspaper obituaries, in their prime and not a day older. A lot of old enemies must attend heavenly reunions too; they cannot all go to the other place. And besides, most enemies, especially of women and politicians, start out as friends. Free from bathroom scales and tape measures, bank balances, dance cards, electoral votes, bylines, and scoreboards, they are ready to be friends again and for ever in an eternity without comparisons. If there is an afterlife, then similar reunions must perforce be happening too in hell, where the persecutors of the blessed have their suffering exacerbated by one another's damned presence.

What possessed me to attend the fiftieth reunion of my graduating class from Barnard College for Women in Columbia

University? God knows, I am no believer. If I hoped to renew old acquaintances, then the list I was sent of the others planning to attend was no help at all. Back in the 1950s the lock was still firmly in place on wedlock. My classmates could hardly wait to cover their own tracks into posterity under their husbands' monikers; I recognised only one or two maiden names among the multitude of old wives planning to reunite. On what extravagant and unlikely impulse did I dispatch my enrolment fee and buy a plane ticket? Was it simply curiosity as usual? Was I curious to see how the girls who had started out with me were growing old? At my age, chances to meet coevals en masse diminish; we long ago stopped going out in bunches on the hunt for one thing or another. Codgers who continue to join classes and teams in pursuit of a supple frame or a new frame of reference are likely to find themselves the oldest in the crowd. When gangs of old-timers do join up purposefully, it is with no common aim beyond the next meal, the next game of cards or golf or bingo, the club's next book or the ship's next port of call, the next TV soap instalment, the next breath.

The Big Apple may be a far cry from heaven but that does not mean crossing over to it from London is without agony, certainly not in economy class.

'I was on the inaugural transatlantic crossing of this airline,' I moaned to the plump American dowager jammed in next to me. 'Would you believe this trip used to be a celebration? It used to be fun.'

An air hostess, tired and fretful behind the fixed rectangle of her smile, plunked fodder in front of us biped cattle. It was faintly fluorescent and highly perfumed.

'I wonder how long it is since Mr Branson has flown economy,' I grumbled, picking with a plastic fork at something green and gooey on my tray.

'Oh, Branson's rich,' replied the American. 'He's got to fly first-class. Why, he probably has his own plane.'

After so long abroad I need to be reminded every time I return to America that for Americans in general – as for the very young and the very, very old – no question is ever rhetorical; all must be answered. Literalism is a childish defence against confusion in this troubling world.

Let an expatriate depart in flight or in exile, or let her leave as I did as a sailor before a following breeze, home remains bright and indestructible among memories even as we shed others made more recently. But while we expats are slowly growing accustomed to our adoptive countries, the lands we left behind are changing too. I left America for the second and final time before 1960 and for almost twelve years had neither money nor inclination enough to go back. On the contrary, at my lowest – especially at my lowest – in Paris in the 1960s, broke and broken from my childhood roots as well as my native tongue, adrift alone with nothing more than fragile dreams: even then I knew an obedient return to my homeland would end in humiliation and a lifelong chorus of 'We told you so!' Only over the past three decades have I been able to visit New York regularly, and by the time I returned for my fiftieth class reunion, the changes had become more than affection could bear. The hotel where I always stay was undergoing 'refurbishment', according to a sign in the lobby. Oh yeah? Sez who? Anyone over sixty knows 'refurbishment' means 'destruction'. Sure enough, idiosyncratic rooms suited to bohemians on the hoof were renamed 'pods' and 'refurbished' to the sensibility of frozen peas. A short walk showed me that the whole city of my youth was in the throes of heartless refurbishment. What has become of the smart-ass hoyden, Manhattan, and her watchful henchmen? What have they done with that gorgeous sleazy broad who raised children from countless fathers to be poets and jokers and villains? Even the guttural savvy of her old accent has given way to a Californian shrill of girlish astonishment and the carrying tenor gargle of boys. Barely two years since my last visit, established neighbourhoods had been levelled and the old burg surgically lifted, made stunning to be sure and more photogenic than ever, but a steely anorexic now, all bone structure, too tight-faced to laugh, devoid of the recklessness and fantasy that used to give her shadows and a soul.

'Geometry and anguish,' wrote Federico García Lorca of New York in 1930 when he arrived from Spain to be a student at Columbia University.

Geometry has triumphed; anguish is enshrined at Ground Zero to be photographed by tourists.

Those of us who grew up before 'to Google' was a verb will be the last generations to die surrounded by sacks of paper printed with words, words, words: of love, art and mystery, words of wisdom, naughty words, threats, recipes, treatments, spells and numbers. A few carcasses are yet to be discovered behind bulwarks of paper covered with words collected to defend their old lives from loneliness and protect memories from loss. Born long before a 'delete' button was added to the keyboard, I too maintained a ton or two of paper and words until twenty years ago when, in the process of moving house, I gave away a thousand books and threw out batches of correspondence. Into the bin too went all the scrapbooks I had kept of my journalism.

Nevertheless, despite radical culling, my shelves still bowed under totem classics of literature, recherché histories, albums of undated, unlabelled photographs, and a hefty inheritance of Mother's papers that to this day I cannot sort through for long before small scars start to weep. But wouldn't you know, my 1956 Barnard College yearbook was nowhere to be found; I had to tackle the reunion without its essential guide-book.

The afternoon before our reunion I came down to the lobby early for a meeting arranged in a brief exchange of emails with Rachel, a former classmate. Hers was one of the few unwed and still familiar names on the handouts from our alumnae committee. Nevertheless, I kept an eye on the street door; I was fearful of giving offence. Yes, I knew the name, but would I know the woman when she appeared? How many times in how many places are we gregarious survivors greeted by unknown passers-by and swept up in their embraces? How often do I fumble in my leaky memory for the name and provenance of an ecstatic old bloke with whom I evidently, once upon a time, had cordial, possibly even carnal, relations? In general it is harder to recall the youthful version of old men than of old women; to this day there are fewer cosmetic props on the market for men. Besides, having less to lose in terms of looks, hardly more than hair and waistline, men lose it more substantially.

Since the days when we were chums and classmates, Rachel must have greyed and altered shape: fat or skinny, there is no natural alternative for old women. Mouths purse while jowls slacken; eyes become unfamiliar that years ago shed their tears. We old ones complain, grieve, and suffer, not always in silence, and, God knows, we can despair; tears, however, are another of the bodily fluids that flow more plenteously in youth. As it turned out, I need not have worried; the moment Rachel walked into the lobby, I knew her. I would have known her anywhere. The handsome girl had grown up into a hefty and handsome old woman, dressed with touches of youthful flair, her hair discreetly coloured to almost its original shade. Rachel knew me too on sight.

'I hear you're quite well thought of in London,' she said as she sidestepped my proffered hug. 'Over here nobody would take the kind of thing you write seriously.'

Her tone was matter-of-factual, not sly or bitchy. Evidently Rachel had become one of those old spinsters who bestow opinions as if they were cast-iron facts to be accepted uncritically by anyone wanting a good mark at the end of term.

Rachel turned and strode out the door ahead of me on our short walk to a pre-reunion cocktail party given by a married classmate whose name rang no bell with me. She walked straight and tall and fast. She was stunning, epic, downright biblical, as she raged passionately and steadily en route against former friends, teachers, colleagues, and relatives who had done wrong or done her wrong over the past half-century. Anger is an underrated cosmetic emotion, more enduring than happiness and flashier than love. At last we entered a slick high-rise building of condominiums. The lift, swift and merciful as a guillotine, opened into a big apartment milling with people. Without a word of farewell, Rachel disappeared among them. Our reunion was finished.

One old Barnard girl had evidently made it right to the top. I accepted a glass of champagne from a liveried waiter and looked out at a dollar-millionaire's vista. Abstract modern sculpture in every corner seemed little more than scraps left over from the masterwork below: Manhattan, marching towards her river boundaries and beyond on every side. How could an apartment, towering as this one over common humanity, be a home for people, for mere people? This was a fortress, stern and impregnable, built as if in a desert or a forest. I wondered what the master and mistress did here day after day at their long desks facing sky-high windows. What could any feather-less creatures do so high above the clamorous city except perhaps plot the passage of stars while they waited for wings of their own? And how did they sleep up here suspended over shoals of electric lights, already beginning to prickle below? Dreams had to be pretty thin by the time they stretched so far above ordinary desires and regrets.

'You'd never catch me living up here,' I heard Rachel's cranky voice near by. 'Not since 9/11. Not since I found out fire engines can't get above the fifth floor.'

I turned and looked around. I did not know anyone in the room, was not even sure which pair of superannuated girls and boys were my host and hostess. I deposited my glass half full, and not a soul noticed me leave to return to the streets, down there where my sort belongs. Once upon a time popular songs told complex and subtle stories; back then, snatches of lyrics or tunes inadvertently hummed could betray unspoken thoughts. Listen to what old-timers hum and, if you are old enough to have seen the same Broadway shows and sung the same songs, you will know what we are thinking. As I walked out again on terra firma, I heard myself humming Cole Porter:

> With a million neon rainbows burning below me
> And a million blazing taxis raising a roar
> . . . Here I sit, above the town . . .
> Down in the depths on the ninetieth floor.

To the sly satisfaction of this long-time European, the Manhattan subway was on strike the day of our reunion. The arrival of a not very prodigal daughter to her old haunts was going to be in a taxi.

'Take me to Columbia University, please.'

'Downtown? Is correct?' asked the dark-haired young driver.

'No. Sorry. Uptown, way uptown.'

'East Side? Is OK?'

'No. Sorry. West Side.'

As an expat myself I am always curious about the lengths to which hope will travel. I asked: 'Where do you come from?'

'I am coming from Colombia,' he replied.

And so an immigrant homonym finally dropped me outside the familiar green gate of Barnard College. The gate used to be locked every night after ten when good Barnard girls were required to be singly abed in the dormitory. In these days of urban dangers, the gate is manned twenty-four hours by a uniformed guard; in these days of strident equality, the dorm houses male students, too. I noticed immediately upon entering the campus that my rigorous old school has sacrificed its tennis

courts to a featureless new building; much of the secluded green
that we used to call 'the jungle' is gone too, along with its colony
of overfed squirrels. Nevertheless, Barnard College remains part
of Columbia University; gowned and aloof and brainy, she keeps
her distance from the prancing verticals of lower Manhattan.

Graduated classes other than my own were reuniting that
weekend; in the milling crowd of women, I was surprised to
see many older even than I. The undergraduates in charge of
the sign-in desks were scrubbed and bright; no chi-chi refurbishment was in evidence; their smiles showed teeth of a human
hue, not the spooky shark-white in current dental fashion; the
girl who gave me my programme and goodie bag had short,
clean nails rather than the ten lurid finger-puppets currently
the rage. We ageing women define beauty in terms of our
youth; for us old girls, beauty is as beauty was. And wistful
bereavement of our own former allure expresses itself as disapproval of whatever passes for sexy now.

'What are you majoring in?' I asked the undergraduate.

I had already pegged her abstracted air as suitable to an
English or American Literature major, or just maybe Art History?
Her eyes were too fanciful for Political Science or Economics;
she was too merry for Physics or any other pure science.

Did I actually hear her reply as she was turning away: 'Film
Studies'?

That is what I thought I heard. And my favourite professor,
Eleanor Tilton, her bony hands holding a copy of *Walden*, rolled
over in her grave with a sob.

The canvas bag the film buff gave me was embossed with
the Barnard shield; in it I found a programme of the day's
events, a pen and pad, and a tag printed with my name under
the photo of a girl with flowing dark hair, eyes more ardent
than dewy, set in an oval face free of crease or blotches. She
was a pretty girl, very pretty, prettier than she would ever know.
With the incriminating tag around my neck I skimmed the

programme and wondered again why the blazes I had come to this fiftieth reunion. Obviously, it was neither for the Alumnae of Color Dinner nor the Lesbian/Bisexual Alumnae Tea, the latter at least saved from an absolute contortion of political correctness by the addendum: 'All are welcome.' As for lectures scheduled on Immigration and Protecting the Rights of Children, and a VIP tour of the Museum of Modern Art, worthy though these entertainments might be, they seemed hardly pertinent to a clasping of old friends and the pooling of memories I had imagined were the point and purpose of a half-century reunion. At the bottom of the goodie bag was an atomiser of 'foaming hand sanitiser', labelled 'anti-bacterial, alcohol-free, fragrance-free', and redolent of 1950s propriety.

'I remember you,' said a total stranger, eyeing my name tag as I turned to descend the steps of the building.

Dressed schematically, as almost all the others appeared to be in a white blouse and dark summer suit, she stood grey and stout in the sunlight.

'You were one of the girls who always wore blue jeans,' she said, her tone accusing.

To say anonymity has ever been a sexy virtue in womankind does not mean every girl has not always aimed to look her best; but when I was young for a girl to look her best meant, as it does now and as it ever will, the best of an established order, not of a different species. My distaff generation was uniformly tweezed, permed and, from the age of puberty, squeezed into girdles offering plenteous curves without discernible seam or wobble. These truncated iron maidens, combined with the off-the-shoulder evening wear fashionable in the 1950s, curbed male lust while simultaneously encouraging it, only, however, above the waist. A stylish silk sash or cummerbund used to mark the line between what was known as 'petting' and 'heavy petting'. As the stranger walked away I remembered saying to one of the other girls in my class after our first year at university: 'I will never marry a man who cares more about how I look than how I think.'

And so, barely seventeen years old, this Barnard freshman consigned her trousseau to the sale rack.

When everyone trudged off dutifully to a lecture on Barnard Today, I slipped away to see whether I could find my Barnard of yesterday. A few streets down on Broadway was the West End Bar and Grill, the first of the nine great bars I have known in my lifetime, nor would I have recognised the subsequent eight had the West End not accepted me as a neophyte and taught me what a bar needs to be great: sawdust implicit on the floor; oak in evidence; music infrequent or, better yet, altogether absent; and, most important, a proprietor neither ingratiating nor jolly but ideally, whether male or female, cool, even suspicious, and barely welcoming. Complaint is the muse of urban banter and the atmosphere of a great bar must stimulate communal moaning. Three or four of us Barnard girls, the ones who wore blue jeans, used to foregather at the West End to moan about life, education, politics, and each other, shoulder to shoulder with a gang from our brother college, Columbia. Most of the boys at the bar were homosexual, an orientation that did not discourage us from falling for them. Rejection can be a sexual attention too and a fierce one. They called themselves 'queer' back then; the survivors to this day prefer it to 'gay'.

'I'll never be gay,' one of my West End friends cried when closets everywhere were being thrown open. 'I'm queer, damn it. I'm a queer. And a queer queer is what I mean to remain.'

The queers of the West End were irreverent, witty rather than wise, and they were brilliantly well read, qualities not generally evident among the wholesome fraternity lads our parents favoured for us. In the 1950s it was not just girls but boys too who were still being instructed from puberty that every man wanted only one thing from a woman: the last thing a good girl should give him, and never, never before they were married. As soon as a guy got what he wanted from a girl, we were all taught in so many words, he would want her no more. How this dictum of the day sorted with lifelong married love was never explained to us. Meanwhile, for virgins in jeans to fall for men who wanted something altogether else, who kept us around for our words and our laughter, was liberating and risky.

The old hangout has a new name now. Foreground music is favoured over palaver, smoking is forbidden, and the new pavement terrace is another innovation that would have displeased habitués of my day; we liked our murk to begin before dusk. Evidently I was not the first veteran to stumble through the door and mournfully survey the refurbishment of our dear old dump.

'But hey, look,' the young manager said, his tone one of practised conciliation, 'I've kept the original floor.'

I looked down and echoes returned to me of laughter and words, words, words, back then before young people plugged themselves into diverting machines, so fearful have the young become of being bored. They are too distracted now to observe that boredom is one consequence of being boring. Not one word or phrase emerged from my memory of our old loquacious torrent; nevertheless, I knew, knew in my very bones, that it was there, right there on those scuffed tiles of the West End Bar and Grill, a girl in jeans learned how to think on her feet.

Barnard incomers used to have a compulsory class called Modern Living, which sounded pretty silly even then, especially to a freshman newly mad for John Donne, a girl whose round earth had begun at last to develop imagined corners. The professor of Modern Living was a beautiful Russian sociologist who had nice things to teach us about marriage and purity and 'family values', institutions under early threat in the 1950s thanks in part to the emergent vogue for psychoanalysis with all its blame-laying and sex-talking and parent-bashing. Many of the richest girls in my class were seeing shrinks every week; one posh New England women's college required all incomers to undergo analysis.

Youth was relatively brief in those days and we the young were instructed in our duty of continuity, not innovation, thank you. And please, girls, no weird ambitions either. Many of us were the offspring of disappointed idealists, lefties, and lapsed Commies like my own parents, who kept a thumbed copy of *Das Kapital* on the bookshelf, hidden behind *How to Win Friends and Influence People*. In my final year at university a few of us campaigned for the patrician Democrat Adlai Stevenson against the military fundamentalist, Dwight D. Eisenhower. Ike won. Stevenson was divorced, which made him less likely even than a woman or a bearded man to be elected to high office in America then.

Poisonous McCarthyism nudged girls in blue jeans towards liberal thought, too. But genuine rebellion among us was not overt and political; it tended to be private, even lonely. Girls in jeans of my generation went for art rather than politics. We listened to Juliette Greco records and daydreamed about left-bank Paris, the bohemian epicentre of free thought and creativity. We believed art to be a vocation and true artists no more in it for fame and money than angels were on a salary. Young bohemians of the 1950s knew that asceticism enforced by poverty was absolutely necessary for Art with a capital 'A'. And you know what? Looking at what is out there now, we were right.

Strolling back to the reunion from the West End, I worried about why my specific memories of four years at university were oddly few: a number of poems and passages, a few names of respected professors and a few more of old friends, but not much else, just a tidal wave of amorphous emotion – like trying to collect debris after the turbulence and beauty of a storm at sea. On the corner of 116th Street and Broadway, opposite the dormitory where I lived as a freshman, there is still a coffee shop as there used to be, although it is no longer called Chock Full o' Nuts. On the brisk autumn morning my parents delivered me to Barnard as a freshman, we stopped there for coffee and doughnuts. Mother kept an eye on the mirror behind the counter as she reminisced about her own student days. My father frowned, his chronic pessimism made worse by imminent farewells, to say nothing of serious misgivings about the expense and purpose of higher education for a daughter. Dad paid for the coffees and when we stood outside he slipped a sugary five-dollar bill into my hand. Then they left me alone right there where now I stood, old and alone again.

At that moment, suddenly, my heart soared and danced within me precisely as it had more than fifty years earlier, on that very same uptown corner, when I understood in a flash that I was born not to one place but to earth entire, her history, her peoples, and all her oceans. Once again I felt the youthful thrill and joy, there where first I embraced the thorny gift of freedom. Just as I had done decades ago I then turned a little breathlessly to enter the university of higher education.

I stopped. How long had that old crone been keeping an eye on me from the window of the coffee shop? What did she want from me, the dotty old trout, with her bemused smile and her eyes full of crooked affection? She resembled my mother, only slightly taller, and Mother would not have been caught dead – as it were – wearing trousers and trainers in Manhattan. The old woman and I made an involuntary move towards each other. We stopped cold. Then we shrugged in the ancient way, widely, hands outspread. She tapped her forehead significantly as I was tapping mine. We winked and smiled. I walked away; she disappeared.

Back on campus, in the lounge reserved for my class, a group of fifty or so well-dressed dowagers was taking it in turn to give a précis of their lives over the past half-century. Rachel was sprawled in an armchair at the far end of the room addressing a smile of showy nonchalance to the toes of her pumps; when I saw her I was surprised by a surge of kinship, almost love. Otherwise I recognised not one among these educated virgins of my day, now matronly. A former classmate ensconced on a sofa near the door deigned to slide over to make room for me.

'I was married in my junior year,' a solid old lady was saying. 'Then I took a further degree in Sociology. We had two children and now four grandchildren and my first great-grandchild is on the way.'

'I took my Master's in Political Science,' said the old lady next to her. 'I married a lawyer. We have a daughter. I am now on the Wisconsin state legislature.'

'I met my husband, a doctor,' said another, 'while I was at medical school. We had three children. I took a further degree in Psychology.'

When I told friends in London that I planned to attend the reunion, they warned me to brace myself for Botox and boasting. But on average my friends are a dozen years or so younger than I; they are barely beginning to slip out of the midst of things. Their retrospection does not yet measure up to mine and what is a reunion if not a celebration of retrospection? The prevalent look of my classmates was post-post-menopausal, unadorned, untreated by knife or chemicals; their jewellery was low-key and their style owed more to propriety than fashionable designers; the prevailing tone was matter-of-fact and hardly boastful. On the contrary, at the end of each recitation, before the next voice picked up the theme of further degrees and husbands and children, there hovered for a moment the unspoken words: 'Is this then all? Is this really all?'

And what if I should be called upon for a précis of my past

by the classmate who was all but waving a ruler and evidently in charge? My autobiography could be delivered here only as a stand-up comic's routine.

'After graduation I served as the most over-educated waitress in Manhattan. I finally made it to Paris, soon to be sacked by the Berlitz School when caught elaborating fancifully on the prescribed lesson. I hitch-hiked to Istanbul, lived in a Moorish watchtower on Majorca, drifted around the Med on a sloop as its cook and mate to the first mate, neither his first nor my last. I was busted in Paris for smoking pot, I have learned to say "thank you" in twenty-three languages, which, as you clever girls know, is a pre-emptive form of apology, and Hubert de Givenchy, when persuaded by a mutual friend to hire me for no ostensible job, kept me in the basement of his *maison de couture*. Once I answered his phone to the breathy *bonjour* of Jackie Kennedy. Finally I left Paris and went on to master a further degree in pontificating as a London journalist. I survived Women's Liberation, countless Greyhound buses, heartbreak, and a war zone in Vietnam. Realising at last that marriage was not strictly required – *pace Modern Living* – I gave birth to an English baby boy. I make a skimpy living now telling girls how not to do as I did, and nobody here would take a word I write seriously . . .'

Quietly, I rose to slip out as I had entered: unheard. But even while the comedy goes on, tragedy waits in the wings.

'I took a further degree in Education,' a small, greying classmate had started her spiel as the door was closing behind me. 'Twenty years ago my husband killed himself. Our son was very depressed after his father's death and five years ago he committed suicide . . .'

The crowd on campus parted and coming towards me at last was a dearly remembered friend.

'Thank God you're here!' we cried in unison and flew to each other.

'What are you doing here?' we both asked and she replied: 'Fifty years! Now or never . . .'

Andreina's hair had become a cloud of perfect snow, a new setting for her Italianate dark eyes.

'Sometimes, Andy, do you start to think never is preferable to now?'

'I guess our kind just doesn't reunite.'

'And do you get the feeling Humanity and Arts majors are outnumbered here about fifty to one by boffins?'

'Puffins?'

'Boffins: English–English – practical ones, the ones who count on their fingers; they seem to be the ones who like to reunite.'

'Yeah, I know what you mean, the girls who did what they should,' said Andreina. 'Tell me the truth, Irma, did you ever wish you were like them? So sure?'

'When I was a child I did. But I finally saw that to be so sure was a life sentence, with no remission, no time off for good behaviour.'

'Or bad,' said Andreina.

Whereupon occurred the miracle of reunion: Andreina and I laughed away fifty years. We stood there as girls again, the girls we had been, a couple of unwrinkled, untried, unadulterated young brunettes, still ready to let ourselves in for life.

I had been home for a fortnight when an email arrived from the Alumnae Committee, attaching class photographs and offering prints for sale. My returning classmates had been too many for a single group shot; we needed two separate photographs with fifty or sixty women in each, standing in rows on the steps of Millbank Hall. I was beginning to wonder whether I had accidentally joined the wrong bunch of women, to be immortalised with some other class of Barnard graduates altogether, when I recognised the glittering spectacles of a pale dot in the second picture: there I was, not notable even for bringing up the rear, two in from one end of the penultimate row and six rows behind Rachel, who leaned out to the edge of the frame, smiling as frantically as an ageing movie star. Seeing her, I understand at last why I had felt the need to attend my fiftieth class reunion.

Time is distance too; minutes are as measurable as miles and as erosive. We lose bits of ourselves as we travel through the years: some we give away, some wear out and others we outgrow. We desert dreams and abandon hopes en route, subduing or satisfying appetites as we move further from where we began. Old, really old, old girls reunite, neither as young women do to show off how slim they are and how well they are set to do, nor as those do in middle age, to show off how well they have kept, how well they're doing. When aged classmates reunite it is not with each other, not really, fragmented as we all must be in due course by due course. Each old girl reunites with herself. Upon seeing my image so firmly put in place among my old classmates, I knew I had attended the fiftieth of our class reunions for evidence that I was, I really was, that I had been, have been, and that for a happy while I am. So my reunion had been a success after all. Memory stormed the present when an old friend and I each returned to herself as she was once upon a time. And I would never forget how on Upper Broadway, for a moment rare enough in any aged life, on the very spot where my maturity had begun half a century ago, I was all there again and reflected in the window of a café once known appropriately enough as Chock Full o' Nuts.

An Old Voice of Academe: Richard Langton Gregory

Academics are cherished in old age more than most professionals; they accrue respect denied these days to the very old in general, and as long as their mental faculties remain respectable, their scholarship continues to bring them work and recognition. It could be argued, too, that the protective world of academe allows those within its shelter to keep their prejudices untried and their emotions unaffected by mundane observation and experience.

Professor Emeritus Richard Langton Gregory, CBE, DrSc, FRSE, FRS, was born on 24 July 1923. He served in the RAF during the war, then read Philosophy and Experimental Psychology at Cambridge. Professor Gregory — Richard — is a scientist, an inventor of scientific instruments, and a prolific writer in his area of human perceptions: the extraordinary way we see things. He has received many honours and honorary degrees, and has been a teacher in Britain and the United States, as well as an investigator of scientific phenomena. He is a contributor to journals, has written important books in his field, and has edited the estimable The Oxford Companion to the Mind. *Richard has been married twice, and has two children and two grandchildren. Recent surgery for a back condition has slowed him down physically. However, his chief frivolity — he calls it 'a hobby' — is a penchant for puns and nothing slows that down. Richard's vast intellect can be mischievous and his eminence is all the more admirable for being often seen to twinkle.*

When does old begin? I think when you get to eighty you're getting old. Think of people of eighty and you think of them as old. So that means, objectively, anybody in their eighties is old. How does it feel different from being young? There are stage posts. You start to think about your capacity to do things that when you are young you take for granted: things like running. The first time you don't feel like running any more, you are getting old. And when you get into your eighties you don't want to walk that much either.

However, I do not think intellect is attached to any specific time. The mind can develop into a time machine that lets you whizz backwards and forwards; you can whizz through forty years, fifty years, even sixty years just by switching on your mind. That is one of the good things – the best thing – the only benefit I can think of about getting old: your internal reference library is extensive. Of course I reread the books on my shelves that I read as an undergraduate. Say, Bertrand Russell I read as a student and now I read him again in the very same actual book. Russell was one of my teachers. The young can generate a huge halo effect, and he could do no wrong. I revered him. Mind you, although I continue to think Russell was a super person, I don't think what he actually wrote is all that sensible really, certainly not about perception, which is my subject. Most philosophy is total rubbish; there is very little I care to read now of classical philosophers; mostly they talked delightful rubbish.

It's terrible to think of friends I have lost and I miss. They often come into my mind and they are a tremendous loss. I do not live in the past. But I quite like comparing past and present. I've got an awful feeling that if time suddenly ran back, one would feel optimistic about it. There has been dissolution of society that is quite scary. I liked England when life was stable, when you could shoot off everywhere in your imagination but always from the basis of a secure society. Now your mental apparatus gets worn out questioning things that are essentially boring and require no imagination. Getting worked up about politics, for example, is amazingly uncreative because you cannot do a damn thing about it. There are so many more important things, such as science – how to form a good hypothesis and how to test it. The activity of science is wonderful and it is truly important to have an effective empiricism that encompasses people's needs and aspirations, and does not get bogged down in metaphysics. As technology advances we will be able to answer questions that were once metaphysical; we will reframe them and think of tests that decide what is true or not. Technology is urgently important, not just for living standards, but also for thinking. It is brilliant to live in a world with all this advancing technology, with wonderful instruments that can answer questions once impossible to answer, questions that were metaphysics not long ago and now are part of physics. Technology won't destroy poetry. The trouble with poetry is it's so damned fuzzy! Technology brings greater clarity and precision.

Time has taken some things I am glad to be rid of. It is great one no longer has to play games in old age. I used to play cricket but I was bored out of my mind, fielding, waiting for the ball to come, and I'd be thinking about something else, so when the ball did come of course I missed it. As for games with women, when you're a young man and good-looking you get a sense of a reflexive, autonomic turn-on in women. I find women more interesting now I am old; at last I can have a proper talk with them. I admit it was only in age I learned to credit women with intelligence. I used to think most of them were pretty goofy. There were not many women you could have a discussion with equally. Now there are more because, first, I've got stupider and, second, they've got cleverer. We've met in the middle. I am not referring to wisdom here, by the way, women have always been rich in wisdom; I mean women with whom you could talk about your work. In age women become attached to the next generation. Men still want to steer their own path, set a goal and try to get there. Most women do not feel the same way. The young ones say they do, but I don't think they do. I may be out of date. Figuratively speaking I am certainly out of date.

★

One of my best memories was starting the Exploratory in Bristol, a hands-on science centre for the public. That was exciting: to have a dream that was very hard to sell to backers. And yes, the businessmen abandoned us in the end. But it wasn't a total failure because some of those young people who went there had a spark struck within them and developed a lifelong interest in science. You know a successful firm always issues its glossy brochure? Well, I had a matte brochure designed for the Exploratory; it was called the Matte Brochure. That is an important principle. Glossiness is something I hate in the world at the moment.

Just for the record, my father and I built a mechanical television together before the war; it had spinning discs. That is fun to look back on. And we built an aeroplane that could actually fly. That was fun, too. Of course I get grumpy. They've actually given up Physics in the University of Reading! And I don't believe any Welsh university has a chemistry department these days. Only technology remains wonderful, increasingly magical. I have two grandchildren. I like them. But I am not particularly involved with them. Basically, I am bored by children. I have never spent a whole day with a child and I don't think I want to, not until they can ask questions; when they develop curiosity, that's when I like children. But you want a pun from me, don't you? Well, here's one: do you know what to say when an alcoholic dies? The unfortunate man has been delivered.

5

Old Salts

TIME IS LIKE passing a mirror. To see your image you have to slow down – and slowing down is a natural process of ageing – then look back. Looking back at myself, I see a doer rather than a dreamer, a girl and then a woman more sharp-eyed than imaginative, more adventurous than contemplative. My very first memory is of sunlight slicing through slats in our venetian blinds to fall in weightless strips on me and on the floor under my high chair; on the spot I was enthralled by the wonder of the real thing. In the mirror of hindsight, it is clear in spite of admiring poets to the point of worship, I could not have accomplished my journey by voyaging within. Some of us are born seamstresses, not spinners: we require bulky material to do our job. As soon as I had my first and only university degree, I waited at tables for more than a year in a frenetic midtown Manhattan restaurant; I needed money to begin my design. Working in uniform ten hours a day, shoulder to shoulder with a dozen valiant older women, not only earned me more money in the short run than a conventional secretarial job, but it also made rare memories to graze on in the long run.

'Bread 'em, kid! Water 'em!' I can still hear the redoubtable Helen shout over the heads of our hungry herd, and dutifully I put a basket of bread and a pitcher of water on each table.

It was a good while before Helen and the others trusted the Ivy League smarty-pants among them; when they did, it was with the absolute trust of companions-in-arms. To this day I find it hard to have confidence in the valour of any woman who has never, not even as a summer job, waited at tables. When I look back on my education it is not an image of gown and mortarboard that comes first to mind; it is a blue satin dressing gown with rhinestone buttons, my going-away gift from 'the girls' when I finally collected enough sticky dimes and quarters for my voyage to Europe.

'Are you still working?' asked the chatty young Polish woman behind my local London supermarket checkout the other day.

'At your age!' The words hovered unspoken between us; nevertheless, her question did not perturb me, not as, almost four decades earlier, when I was nearly thirty, unmarried, un-settled, and penniless in Paris, I winced to hear myself addressed for the first time as madame instead of mademoiselle.

'Yes, I work,' I told her.

Next to her till a sign requested proof of age from anyone buying alcohol and 'lucky enough to look under twenty-one'.

'I thought maybe you were retired,' said the young Pole.

'No. I used to be retired. I retired in my early twenties. But I didn't like it much. I'm not retired any more.'

Retirement, if no longer strictly compulsory in all jobs, is certainly expected at a certain age and, like as not, required by company policy. Among the self-employed and freelancers, retirement comes about through an increasing neglect of older contributors in businesses scrabbling for the 'youth market'. One way and another, retirement is enforced in a way that democracies would tolerate for no other restriction of an adult's free choice except imprisonment for a crime. The crime of growing old? To retire whether you want to or not at a specific age from work, and thus from so-called 'active life', is a rela-tively new concept in prosperous Western nations and it is altogether absent elsewhere in the world. There are many nations still where a man works until he dies or until he can work no longer and, exhausted, he becomes the responsibility of his extended and extensive family; its aged distaff side, however, never retires and ends up as granny-carers. The old women barely notice when their old men become full-time residents of the mob. Among us, however, when our husbands are kicked out of work to take up perpetual residence at home, it does not generally do much for marriages that have long since become reliant on habit and routine.

Middle-aged media 'feministas' have lauded a growing statistical trend for sixty-plus women to sue for divorce; they take it as a sign of independence and high spirits among ageing New Women – the WOWs: Wonderful Old Women – and the baby boomers. The truth is that old wives are being driven to go it alone not by adventurous inclinations; on the contrary, it is more often than not the ruination of their established routine, and the sheer boredom of having the grumbling old fart suddenly installed in front of the TV all day and every day, that can make single life preferable.

'I would have said we had a good marriage until now. We chugged along pretty well,' says a sixty-plus former teacher of her husband who has recently retired from banking. 'All he does now is mope around and give orders. My day has gone to hell. The bloody sports channels are blaring all the time. The only time he speaks is to shout for a cuppa during half-time. Think about leaving him? Of course I do. You bet I do. I think about divorce at least three times a day, I kid you not. Both our girls are grown up with families of their own. I've worked too, you know, and I've made a home. I could manage perfectly well on my own. The trouble is, I don't think he could. The truth is, I know he couldn't.'

An awful lot of people swept up in the daily rush hour do not relish the way they have to make a living; it pleases plenty of new retirees to stop work at last; they wanted to chuck the grind years ago. However, as surely as those who were fortunate enough to have enjoyed a true vocation, even the trudging legion will overnight find themselves no longer welcome or valued in the area where they have spent most of their waking hours; suddenly they are evicted from a place and a job they know inside out, more profoundly and intimately than will any of the eager new recruits jostling behind them. Ask men in midlife, 'Who are you?' and they tell you first their names and then what they do for a living. Men define themselves by the nature of their work; they always have done. And young urban women are determined to follow suit and put up with retirement too when the times comes, just as their own mamas endured what used to be called 'the empty nest syndrome'. So when a man retires with nothing but a name and empty hours to call his own, is he half the man he was? Who is he? What does he do?

Who will I be when work dries up altogether? What will I do? I don't play golf.

Out of the million or so Britons who take their annual holiday on a cruise ship, the larger percentage are retirees seeking an 'at last' experience. When I was invited to give four lectures in exchange for a fortnight's room and board on a cruise for the over-fifties, I accepted with eager curiosity, my lifelong weakness and delight. Where better to learn about life when it has ceased to be what we commonly call 'useful'? Where better than a cruise ship to learn how to be comfortably useless?

I contracted to join the ship in Miami on the last lap of its journey around the world. Miami, it so happens, was the first lap of my own life's travels. Every winter from the time I was five my parents used to drive down the coast from New York to spend a fortnight in the Florida sun. The sun was believed good for the skin back then. My father regularly plunked me and my little brother in his dental chair, then pumped it up high with the foot pedal so we could bask for twenty minutes under an ultraviolet lamp with only our eyes shielded from its rays. Thus we conspired against immortality as fast foods, and high frequencies, and radiocative fallout do now.

The plane bringing us new arrivals from London to join the cruise was late in to Miami, which meant we had to race straight to the ship, with no time for sightseeing as I had hoped. I could only lean on the rail as we put out to sea and peer landwards in vain.

'Never forget this, Irma,' Mother commanded me sixty-five years ago.

I had to close my eyes to verify obedient memory and see again the opalescent sand under Mother's sandals, before us an orange sea, behind us art deco buildings looking as perfect and stylish as they had on the drawing-board, while we danced at sunset around the palm trees. From where I stood on board the ship, our old holiday destination was hidden behind the new skyscrapers of Anywhere: Everywhere.

'There's so much noise on a ship,' said the English woman next to me.

The roots of her bluish hair showed white in the sun. She was talking to a plump companion of her own age.

'And I have a bad ankle. And I've done more talking in the past six weeks than in six years. And I've done more eating, too. Isn't the food rich? And it's good, I guess, but enough is enough.'

'I love playing bowls,' the plump woman replied. 'But people don't take the game seriously on this ship. Seven out of ten people don't take playing bowls seriously. They just throw it. I get fed up with that. They don't even learn the rudiments of the game and that gets me very irritated. They shouldn't play at all if they can't be bothered to learn the rules.'

'I do wish they wouldn't put so much whipped cream on

the cakes,' said the other. 'I just know I've gained ten pounds since Southampton.'

'Heed well, Irma,' I admonished myself silently. 'I do not want to hear you kvetch or cavil or carp about anything, not about skyscrapers, not about sportsmanship, not about the food. Remember, old girl, the depredations of great age are not all merely cosmetic, not by a long shot.'

My immediate reward for restraining the aged urge to grumble was a witty fly-by of pelicans.

Scouting around on board, I found a hairdresser, a cinema, many shops, a library, a vast dining room as well as a smaller posh one that required reservations. There were several bars, smokers' areas, a computer centre, a games room, a ballroom, a café, and a gym where the seaborne could simulate terrestrial biking and jogging. Pilates classes were on offer, as well as yoga, line dancing, art classes, computer classes, and aqua-aerobics in an indoor pool below a smaller dunking pool on deck. The daily newsletter, slipped under cabin doors, announced a morning mass and a vicar too, available for ecumenical chats. In one bar a cool jazz pianist was at work, and classical concerts by a resident string quartet were scheduled in another. There were evening variety shows, and fashion shows, and cocktail-hour dancing with 'Gentlemen Hosts', presumably for the six or seven women travelling alone and those whose partners could not or would not dance. 'Lady Hostesses' were not on offer. Television in the cabins kept us up with earthly news, detective series, soaps, and sports. There were telephones, and beauty treatments, and food was available at all hours; there were crosswords, sudoku, bingo, whist, and daily general knowledge quizzes. The medical centre below decks offered professional staff and treatments ranging from an enema (£20) to 'high dependency care' (£180 for twelve hours).

'A morgue?' exclaimed one of the Philippine cabin staff when

I asked. He leaned on his mop and lowered his voice. 'Passengers do die. One died earlier on this trip. They can be frozen. Usually they bury them at sea if so wished.'

He looked around and dropped his voice lower still.

'One man on one ship I hear about, he goes over the side, dead. And his younger wife, she moves into a cabin with another guy.'

One way and another, on board was every first and every last thing any old-timer could want during his or her four-month tour around the world. Only one essential item appeared to be missing. It was a cruise, after all: where the hell was the sea? What had they gone and done with the mighty Atlantic? Wild water was visible through the windows of the café where I was sitting over a cup of coffee, plenty of it, and behind us our wake trailed, pale jade, to the horizon. But the sight was so disconnected from my other senses it could have been a film. There was barely any surge under us to feel; I could not smell the ocean's tang nor hear its swish and thrash. The only sign was the coffee slopping into my saucer, until I put a teaspoon in the cup to break the surface tension, a trick acquired half a century earlier on board the sloop *Stormsvalla*.

Have I mentioned that in my twenties I lived for eighteen months before the mast? A real mast it was, too. Tall and made of wood, it supported the most inspired and beautiful of all mankind's inventions: a sail. When the weather was rough we took quick meals standing up; with our backs braced against the bulkheads, we passed plates from the galley down a chain of hands. En route to Gibraltar, two days into the Bay of Biscay and out of sight of land, *Stormy* sailed into a ferocious gale. We brought in the canvas before it was ripped away. Our engine was kaput. The wind and sea were in charge; they roared and deafened us. Spray filled our eyes and drenched us to the bone, and all around our rearing, plummeting wooden hull raged the element from which life had emerged, dead set on having us back again. We huddled our combined weight to starboard, trying to bring up the top of our mast that was scraping white caps to port. And it was then, our teeth chattering and our reason blown to smithereens, a calm suddenly descended on us seven young sailors. We surrendered. The sea had defeated us. Our fear and our very selves were made insignificant. When the sea rises it can lick anything on earth.

'Please for your own safety, ladies and gentlemen, do not move about the ship,' the captain said over the loudspeaker.

He spoke aptly for there were Zimmer frames and wheel-chairs in use on board, and I had noticed here and there casts on aged wrists and ankles. Through the window of the café I watched grey waves lolloping to the horizon, our big ship rolling gently, flirtatiously, with their swell. I finished my coffee and went to draw another from the perpetual machine. The only other person in the café was a handsome woman in her late seventies or early eighties. She sat tall and straight on a banquette, her ivory-tipped cane to hand.

'You are appalling,' she said in a clear, clipped tone as I was passing. She pinned me with her icicle eyes. 'You are absolutely appalling,' she repeated. 'You are disobeying the captain. To disobey one's captain! What abominable behaviour.'

'But . . . but . . .'

I nodded towards the cutlery lying pretty much in place on laid tables and then towards cabin staff going only a little cautiously about their business.

'Your behaviour is abominable,' she said. 'Appalling!'

To the end of the journey, even after I learned her patrician name, the lean and blue-eyed dowager was going to be 'La Generalissima' to me.

A balmy morning ushered us into the port of Charleston, South Carolina. Waiting to disembark I eavesdropped all too easily. A small spry old dear addressed her circle of three or four listeners in a carrying voice, only her consonants blurred by the stiffening jaw that gives late age its unique drawl.

'I thought I was going to drop on that coach tour of Miami. I was so exhausted that I had to buy myself a cold drink. I didn't mind, I really didn't. But it was just too much. They must stop more often on those tours. It is too much. Not for me; for everybody. I'm going to tell them on the tour today. You can't make right what was wrong before. But I am going to tell them that from now on people on tours must have a drink. And I needed to go to the toilet. Have you noticed they call it the washroom here? I said to the lady sitting next to me, "Oh, I feel really uncomfortable!" And she said, "Well, Jessie, make him stop the coach!" So I did. I called the young man over and I said: "I'm very sorry. I need to go to the toilet or whatever you call it here!" And then didn't everybody else say, "That's a good idea!"? They all needed to go too, but they were too embarrassed to ask. So we stopped and went inside this garage place. And the man in there said, "What's the matter, don't you have any toilets on your coach?" Only he didn't say "toilet", he said whatever they call it. And I said, "Where's your toilet? I'll buy it! We need it on our coach!"'

Arrive by ship to see an old port city as it should be seen and is meant to be seen: its back to the common highway, its important face towards the sea. I nipped swiftly past the bus waiting dockside, presumably without a toilet, for passengers registered on the tour. Land swayed slightly under my sea legs when I crossed the bridge and walked as I have always walked best, alone, into the streets of Charleston. Browsing antique shops and sizing up cafés and bars, I chatted with locals, and soon found myself raising covetous eyes to high windows, framing views I would never see over this town full of grace and history.

With only enough time in hand to visit just one of the many museums, I chose the Confederate Museum of Charleston, owned and operated by the United Daughters of the

Confederacy, and installed in small rooms over the central market. Its racks of Civil War uniforms and cases of worn memorabilia make a domestic jumble of history; I felt I had stumbled into the attic of an old auntie, not my own.

Local accents are disappearing everywhere in the anglophone world, overtaken by monophonic sounds resembling the moos and squawks of lesser critters. But the women attendants at the museum were not young, and their inimitable Southern American accent, with its extravagantly long vowels, dispatched my memory back to my family's annual crossings of the Mason–Dixon line in the 1940s. When the townspeople in those days talked to us Yankees, 'y'all', their tone of voice held traces of animosity, albeit faint. The little grey grannies and grandpas in rockers I saw on front porches in those days were not much more than my age now.

There in the museum of what had once been everyday, the thought struck me for the first time: oh my God! Those ancient people, with whom I exchanged curious and suspicious glances when I was a child: some of them must have been alive when Abraham Lincoln was assassinated. I had to lean against a case of flintlock rifles to catch my breath. History can lie. But arithmetic? Arithmetic is too simple to lie.

It is rare for a traveller of my age to find a brand-new place she wants to see a lot more of. While we were pulling out of Charleston's beautiful harbour my heart was pulling me back to the land; I had fallen in love with Rhett Butler's home town. I longed to jump ship and stay there for a long, long time, maybe for ever. But a cruise ship waits for no pining old lady. And besides, how well I know that the pain of separation is infinitely more intense for the one left behind on land than for the sailor. Before we had outrun the gulls the ancient mariner's agony had passed; by the time we made open sea Charleston had taken its place among my memories of charming places.

★

Onboard spiels were listed officially in the newsletter as 'lectures'. My first was on the topic of writing an advice column for young women in a national magazine. I entitled it: Who Do I Think I Am?

'Your jokes weren't bad,' said a fellow speaker at dinner the evening after my debut. 'But you should never laugh at them yourself. And don't wait for an audience reaction either.'

He appeared to be in his mid-sixties; he was with his spouse of about the same age. Lecturers' spouses could travel too as part of the deal. The two other speakers at our reserved table were middle-aged women, academics accompanied by their husbands. I was the only tyro; my colleagues undertook this gig regularly as a holiday from writing and researching treatises and books.

'You have to remember on a ship like this the audience are slow reactors,' said the expert.

And that was fair enough. It is not easy to electrify an audience averaging considerably more than sixty-odd years of age; a ton of memories keeps them grounded. Out of their vast bases for comparison they can always come up with something more compelling than whatever is on offer. When I had asked for questions after my palaver, a few men raised their hands to complain about the salacious nature of modern journalism. Then one wrinkled and leering old chap asked a question about telephone sex; he was going to pose similar enquiries after each of my lectures. Women accustomed to an archaic gentility are by and large not keen to speak in public; they preferred to corner me privately with questions and sharp observations, too, on the nature of modern youth.

'I teach public speaking, you know,' my fellow speaker summed up for me as he poured himself more wine. 'I would give you an eight and a half for today's effort.'

'I must say,' said a bleached and superannuated spellbinder the following day as we found ourselves side by side, circling the lavish cream tea on offer, 'whom you sit next to at dinner on these cruises is make or break. You don't want to spend months or even a couple of weeks in the wrong company.'

I sidestepped quickly and asked about an earlier stop the ship had made: 'So how did you find Samoa?'

'Fabulous! I bought the most beautiful straw sunhat you have ever seen!'

'Wasn't the shopping in LA spectacular?' said a bespectacled dark woman near by as she served herself a slice of Madeira cake.

'Pricey though,' the blonde replied. 'I thought Sydney was just as good and it was cheaper than LA.'

Sydney, Samoa, and LA could have been names of high-street boutiques. The women were bound to be thrilled when we arrived in Manhattan, that nirvana and training ground for world–class shoppers.

'Did you enjoy Sydney?' I asked the woman taking up her place behind me in the informal queue.

She and her husband made a good-looking old couple. They were usually to be seen reading side by side in easy chairs in the library, rarely exchanging words, only smiles quick and vivid. She had told me in an earlier impromptu chat that he was a retired doctor and they were both soon turning seventy. To watch them cross the ballroom floor in a moderate swell and see the way they linked arms, supported and supportive, was to admire the embodiment of a good marriage. I hope I was wrong to sense in him the distracted and reckoning air of a man in perilous health. Did the occasional labouring of her smile presage bereavement?

'Sydney was wonderful. We flew in early and then joined the ship there, you know. We spent two whole weeks with our son and his sons who live there now. That was just perfect.' She smiled, then said softly: 'Only too short.'

Of the five hundred or so passengers who had started out on the cruise months earlier, almost half had already dropped off en route; quite a few more were going to leave at the

American ports, too, most of them to spend time with their expatriate children. For many passengers of advancing years, a cruise ship serves as a luxurious maritime bus, taking them to visit friends and relatives they have not seen, sometimes for a decade or more, and grandchildren they may be meeting for the first time.

'Why are you wearing that awful grey? Too dreary! Show some taste. You really should wear bright colours,' snapped La Generalissima at me on her way into the dining room.

The dress code for that evening as announced in the newsletter was 'formal'. She herself, in purple with her ivory-tipped cane in hand, looked more military than queenly; her pearl brooch could have been a decoration for bravery. A young string player from the quartet was next in her line of fire.

'Your hair is a disgrace. Have you never heard of a brush and comb?'

The girl turned to me, and passed a hand over her Pre-Raphaelite ripples. 'If that old bat goes on at me one more time, I don't know if I'll be able to control my temper.'

'Keep out of her way,' I said, 'and think about her daughters and granddaughters ashore who perhaps can't.'

The approach to Manhattan by sea is part of every old New Yorker's family history. I peered hard at the Jersey coast as we passed but the new skyline was jumbled, jagged and unfamiliar. I could not spot the riverside cemetery that used to double as a playground for kids of my neighbourhood.

'A little island all its own, this ship,' grumbled the stout old man near me on the deck.

He was one of the few smokers on board, and I had noticed him often out on deck, puffing. 'I've been away from England for a long time. Months. Never been away so long before. Homeward bound soon. It'll be nice to get back to reality. I guess.'

'Oh look!' I cried, and pointed.

Through the wrong end of memory's telescope, the Statue of Liberty appeared smaller, much smaller than when we used to peek out and see her while we played hide-and-seek among the tombstones. My companion merely grunted and drew hard on his cigarette.

'Do you have children?' I asked dutifully, for it is a question that rarely fails to animate despondent ageing women, who usually then produce photos of grandchildren, or launch into vigorous critiques of their children's lifestyle and choice of partner.

'My sons lead their own lives,' he said.

We moseyed in silence towards Manhattan.

Then he said: 'I lost my wife last year.'

His even tone suggested he had merely misplaced her, except that his eyes of washed blue were suddenly mortally puzzled. But I could not even try to distract or console him for at that moment he lost me, too.

We were coming in to Pier 92 on the Hudson River. And on the dockside in the crowd stood my parents, precisely where they had waited to greet the ship bringing me back after my first trip to Europe half a century earlier. Mother still wore her long hair in a crown of braids; she called it 'her trademark' and would not cut it short until she was well into her sixties. My father was looking worried, I could tell even from that distance, until he spotted me on the deck and he smiled with heart-rending tenderness. I was moved and happy to see them. They both waved. But I did not wave back, not this time. One does not have to believe in ghosts in order to see them; to wave back at them in greeting, however, requires a faith I do not possess.

After an unscheduled extra day in Manhattan due to rain and high winds, we set sail at last for Boston. Barely out of port, the skipper announced that because more storms were forecast ahead our scheduled last stop in Halifax would have to be scrubbed; furthermore, there was a strong probability of a late arrival back at the home port of Southampton. I heard a few subdued grumbles from the passengers around me, nothing comparable to the wailing of students aboard my first storm-tossed crossing of the Atlantic. Too much cream with the cream tea and too few loos on the tour buses would always irk us, but no matter how much we oldsters complain about our comfort, our joints, our bladders, and our digestion, we ceased long, long ago to expect the titanic forces of nature to be on our side.

'In Sydney you think you've got a long time ahead,' said Jessie. 'We have been travelling a long time. I always travel alone. But I am never on my own.'

Jessie and I had been seated next to each other at the Singles Lunch as there were not enough single men to go around, only five or six of them, all taciturn, embarrassed, and concentrating on the food that came their way rather than on the wistful female company. We single women ended up chatting among ourselves and laughing a little too loudly lest anyone imagine we had really dreamed of meeting an antediluvian Mr Right on our world cruise. Jessie was far and away the most engaging single of either sex among us. A young Philippine stewardess waved to her and called out a sunny: ''Ello, Mrs Jessie!'

'They are so friendly on this ship, darling. That's the girl who cleans my room. The sad thing is she has a child at home. But she must earn money so the child is being cared for by Granny.'

Jessie was in her mid-nineties and beautiful as very few very old women can be, and rarely is it one who was a beauty in her youth. Late-blooming beauty is not stiff with vanity; it is unique to its age, never an imitation of what has passed. Even when animated by a strong intellect, the allure of an old beauty is mothlike and feathery. Jessie's hair was white as a halo, her skin as thin translucent velvet, sagging only slightly over a slender bone structure; her eyes had turned an antique colour, not green nor grey nor blue, and not quite brown. She was small and compact.

'Still dancing, Jessie?' called a woman passing the table where we sat, and then with a wink: 'You were on the tiles last night!'

'I like to dance,' said Jessie and waved briskly and rhythmically to a steward who waved back and shuffled a neat two-step. 'I must go now. I must get some of my things together. It's not long before we're in Southampton, is it?'

'Six or seven days,' I said.

'I don't think that's a long time. I can't sit around. I need things to do. I don't sew. I don't knit. I don't do much any more. But I have done lots of cruising. Sometimes when you're not well and you get on one of these ships you forget you're not well . . .' She stopped, and shook her head gently. 'Did I ever tell you, darling, we were bombed on the first day of the bombing? We lost our home. Did I tell you? My mother built an air-raid shelter in the garden. But the bombing was so bad we moved out of London. And that was it. That was the end of everything. A different era. Another season. Do you have children? Children, that's what it's all about, darling. We can't go on for ever. And I wouldn't want to, either. I get tired now. I had a son. He died when he was eight. I cannot speak of that. I have a daughter. And grandchildren. And two great-grandchildren, too. They call me Gran-Gran. But now I really must start getting my things together. It's not long, is it, darling, before we're in Southampton? My daughter is coming to meet me. But I will be staying on this ship when it continues to the Mediterranean. That's where it goes next, you know? I don't know why they will all tell you here that I'm in my nineties, darling. I am seventy-seven.'

Another passenger explained to me later that seventy-seven was Jessie's age when her husband died.

'Sometimes she gets confused and just stops there,' said my informant, gently smiling, one of the majority on board who found occasional episodes of confusion in very old fellow travellers no more worrying than the passage of a sea breeze.

★

Later, after a month or so ashore, I read in my daily paper that cruises restricted to the over-fifties are under threat, ostensibly due to political correctness, for they are deemed discriminatory to the young. Could there be a financial interest too in cruises for younger people keen to push out their glitzy boats? To pour out money at the bar? And shell out on more than just aspirins and toothpaste in the on-board shops? Under-fifties, forty-somethings, and probably some well-heeled under-thirties, too, if they are still unencumbered by kiddies, are bound to change the shipboard daily schedule to something a lot raunchier. They will dominate the computer room where now silver surfers take their time. And who needs all those books? How about games and videos instead? And, by the by, where's the porn channel on the TV? A string quartet! You must be joking! Old people are OK but so totally sad. We're on holiday. Like, give us a break. No matter how good their intentions, the young must soon impose upon the new minority of the aged on board these purpose-built ships the very same patronising and unwritten stric-tures ashore from which the old folks longed to take a holiday.

'Is it a Generation Gap or a Chasm?' was my last scheduled talk. When I asked for questions one of the young stewards raised his hand.

'I don't understand,' he said. 'In my country when we grow old, we live with our children.' He looked around and shrugged. 'I don't understand.'

'Treasure what you have,' I told him. 'And brace yourself. This is your future.'

My single cabin, not quite below decks, lacked the rarefied luxury of my married co-speakers' quarters. Although I had everything I needed, there were no extras; no easy chair, for instance. Whenever I tried to read stretched out on my berth I soon gave in to the atavistic cradling of the deep; the book fell and I dozed off. Finally, after a quick check to make sure there were no members of my lecture audience in evidence eager for a chat, I found a seat in a corner of the library and opened a collection of Somerset Maugham's short stories.

'For no day is so dead as the day before yesterday,' said the stylish Mr Maugham.

I sighed. I closed the book.

Whist or bingo, a worthy lecture, an old film, a game of darts, jazz in one lounge, and choir practice in another: loads to do. But nothing for me to do; nothing I needed to do; nothing I wanted to do. I stood and watched a line-dancing class in the ballroom for a while; the nonchalant grace of the young dancer in charge lifted the exercise out of absurdity. He happened also to be the only black man I had seen on board. And there was one Asian couple among the passengers. My English-born friend, Mona, who is of Indian origin, could not afford to stop working and finally had to put her gently dementing eighty-five-year-old mother into a London rest home. One day I stopped into Mona's shop for our usual chat and found her frowning and teary. She had decided she must bring the old woman home again.

'The other old folks in there treat her with contempt. And what is worse, they seem surprised she expects anything better. The Raj generation, you see; the British empire generation. There is racism in these old people's places; it is just a more subtle, old-fashioned variety than what the youngsters get up to.'

Out on a secret and secluded corner of the lower deck recommended by an understanding steward, I sat behind a stack of deckchairs. With but two days left to go, the sky had brightened at last and there was the Atlantic again, sparkling as in the long ago dreams of explorers and immigrants. But those adventurous transatlantic dreamers had not been going our way. Our way was back to what every passenger I spoke to, even Jessie who practically lived shipboard, called 'real life'. Back to a familiar diet and TV sitcoms, back to doctor's appointments and public transport, back to family feuds, to children and grandchildren, back to grass and pavements.

Earlier I had been down to check my emails in the computer room where a young geek in a state of tense boredom was teaching his kindergarten of crumblies how to surf. Now in the sunlight I unfolded the printout of a long email from my brother. It contained an email he himself had received from one of his retired colleagues; in it were laid out six reasons relatively well-heeled old folks often choose to live out their lives on cruise ships rather than in residential homes. First, the service is always polite and friendly because the resident is a customer, not a patient. Also, there are more activities shipboard, swimming pools, games rooms, workout rooms, films and music. And the faces are constantly changing as passengers disembark and newcomers join the cruise. There are exotic ports to visit. And with discounts available on board for subsequent cruises, permanent residence can work out a whole lot cheaper than the ever rising price of many a private nursing home, some touching £600 a week.

Finally, said my brother's friend, 'When you die they just dump you over the side – no extra charge.'

I am a dedicated rough traveller and I travel alone. For me a cruise to safe ports on a floating hotel full of nice people affords no special pleasure, too much constraint of every kind, and no excitement, certainly none greater than the one that surprised me there on deck: the giddy urge sweeping over me or surging suddenly from within – the longing to be back on city streets among strangers. I felt a need, a must so strong it hurt, a lust for languages and music, for solitude and spontaneity. I wanted my son and his wife on the end of my phone line; I craved brown rice and honey in my cupboard: I was dying for real life. I closed my eyes, my old body flooded by desire overwhelming, gasping, and fierce – unexpected, and probably unwholesome, too, at my time of life. Thank God! I was homeward bound! Then I laughed out loud and opened my eyes. There in the salty field surrounding our ship a seamark bobbed by: if not at this very point on the nautical compass, then certainly not far off was the place where, more than half a century ago, I had lost my virginity.

It was my second transatlantic crossing, a journey that was to change my direction definitively, and finally expatriate me. Virginity was treasured back then in the 1950s, or at least it was guarded, if not quite as a treasure, certainly as an asset in the marriage market. Like patriotism and climbing the ladder of a conventional life, I'd had enough of it. We were outward bound on a cheap ocean liner, four or five women or men to a cabin. Not very long at sea, I cheerfully abandoned my maidenhead, appropriately enough in a lifeboat suspended beside the deck and covered with canvas. He was French. His name was Jean Something-or-other. Was I in love with him? Not much. He was handsome and older. And he was Parisian, for crying out loud. The Frenchman knew what he was doing. Except afterwards in a state of post-coital apprehension, he purported not to believe I had in fact been a virgin before we did the deed.

'Maybe it's because I used to ride horses?' I suggested, though I thought it was more likely due to the use of what our mothers warned us about: the newfangled Tampax.

It had started raining again on my grey head. I rose to go below. Perhaps I'd take in a game of whist. I had no idea how to play but I liked the nineteenth-century literary sound of it: whist.

'Curiosity was the making of me,' I called out into our following breeze. 'And by that token has it been my undoing.'

A Salty Old Voice: Jeffrey Smart

To travel in the first half of the last century was to change a lot more than language and climate. Even nations that used the same tongue did not say the same thing with it, back before television and later the internet spread the word. Arguably – opinion is always arguable – there was a lot more variety of taste, flavours, and entertainment on the planet in those days when it was still a big place; certainly you needed to travel fewer miles when I was young to turn a journey into an adventure.

Jeffrey Smart was born in Australia and was bound to leave it in pursuit of his star. Refusing the prosaic destiny to which he was born in 1921, Jeffrey has held many jobs from chief bottle-washer on board a ship to serving as a popular commentator on matters artistic for the Australian Broadcasting Company. In recent decades he has been a dedicated painter, an artist celebrated both in his homeland and abroad for his crisp, haunting style. He attracts friends for life, many of them figures of renown. His book of memoirs, Not Quite Straight, *is a sprightly and peripatetic romp. For the past thirty years he has made his base in Tuscany where he lives and works in a splendid revamped farmhouse with his companion, Ermes de Van, who is also a painter, a gifted gardener, and an occasional shepherd.*

We are the only species on earth that knows we are going to die. That's why I love my dogs, you see, because they don't know; they're immortal; they live in the Garden of Eden. But I try not to think about that. Do you realise it is fifty years almost to the day since Humphrey Bogart died? Now that is hard to believe, isn't it? What, you're only seventy-odd? You're still young! I'm eighty-five and that is not funny. The work at the moment is going well. Not particularly the picture I'm working on, no, never that, but the work generally is going well right now, yes. But it might not last, you know. One is always facing inspiration or bankruptcy. Is painting satisfying? Not really. I will paint something and think: Good, then look at it again . . . Well, now and again you can bring off something, but it is still not very satisfying. I've got very high standards, you see. I'm aiming for the top! I work every day if I can but that's not discipline, it's just giving in to one's natural bent. Mind you, sometimes I think one's natural bent is just to lie around and go into a daze. Doing nothing is a nice way to live, I imagine, until you get bored with it.

Admirable? No, there's nothing to admire about it; it's what I like doing. It's like stamp collecting; you can't admire a man who collects stamps because he loves stamp collecting and goes to all sorts of trouble to get just the stamp he wants. You can admire his collection but not him for collecting it. Nabokov went butterfly catching and that was a great joy to him, to go out with his net, catching butterflies and mounting them and making his collection. Admirable collection! But that is not what we admire Nabokov for. That is what I am doing: doing what I like. I could not have stayed in Adelaide through fear of boredom, yes, but also through knowing the field was too limited. You've got to be near the masters, you must see the masters; you have to stay close to the masters. I meant near the real thing. Just as you cannot live on canned music. Mind you, I have good speakers in the studio and we can play Wagner in the car. I'm lucky with Ermes: he likes Wagner, he loves pug dogs, and he's a painter, too. I am lucky. I am very, very lucky. I suppose that makes the process of growing old easier, because I don't get bored. I think a lot of old people get bored; they've got nothing to do, nothing at all to do. The retirement age of sixty-five is ridiculous. Just as we are learning about things, how they work, and what to do to make them work better, we are put out to lie fallow.

I don't know that I had a calling to art. I wanted to be a pianist and I also wanted to be a writer, and I really, really wanted to be an architect. You see, I'd like to be a dictator, telling people how to live, and architects are dictators, aren't they? You will have your kitchen here, your dining room right there; I'd love all that. Remember André Gide wrote at the end of his life that it was a shame he took up writing. 'I am not born to be a writer, I should have been . . .' I've forgotten what he thought he should have been. But I am a frustrated architect. My parents couldn't afford to put me through university. I went to art school in 1940; I became a teacher of art in 1943 in what they called in Australia back then 'the technical education department'. And people working in that department were spared from being called up to go and be killed in New Guinea or Thailand or England. I had no real urge to do anything about the war in any case; I just wanted to get on with painting. But I always liked mathematics so they persuaded me to teach navigation in the air force. And then later, when I went to see Dresden and other cities in Germany, I thought: I just helped to destroy these places.

I am not a superstitious person at all. I just know there is another real world; we are in the effectual world, not the causal world. I have had spiritual protection all my life. I think I have a guardian angel; as a matter of fact, I know who it is. But I am not allowed to say. It has nothing to do with life after death; I don't know about after death; it is another sphere of existence that is there all the time, and we all live in that other sphere as well as living in this one. So when we die, do we just transfer into another existence? And take our memories along? I don't know. Do not know. I don't suppose we can. The brain rots after all. But I really don't know. The guides who have spoken to me in seances, they were all dead but they were thinking clearly, very clearly. One was an Indian; the other was not. I have been blessed; I have had so many visitations and protections, and warnings too from outside myself, not from within.

What is naive is to believe that when you die, you are dead. I know people who give up their churchgoing and immediately become atheists. It's like someone having a motor car and it breaks down, so they give up all motor cars. Roman Catholicism is a muck-up of a religion in that way: it leaves you no alternative. I was a churchgoer until I was sixteen. But we are not meant to question too much while we are alive; we are here to live. A man called Nicholas Monsarrat wrote a book titled *This is the Schoolroom*: now, that is a good title. This is the schoolroom. One cannot sit here and be a 1920s atheist when there is evidently so much more going on. Coincidence alone when it happens, and it happens a lot, is enough to make you think. And experiments in telepathy and psychokinesis are very convincing.

Oh yes, I have regrets. Why didn't I go off with that person? Why didn't I go to bed with another? Or why didn't I buy shares in that company? Or why was I so suspicious of that estate agent? Why did I think he was a crook when it turns out he was right and I was wrong? There's a lot of that in life. But no major regrets, just little things. If we had it to do again, we'd go on making the same mistakes.

Do you see my fireplace? I am very proud of it because I invented it. That fireplace has seventy litres of water in it; do you see those pipes at the top? And it is sitting on pipes, too, fixed in a way so the hot water circulates and heats the whole house. I invented it. You can call me Leonardo. Yes, do call me Leonardo! I did the drawings, designed it, and worked on it with a local plumber. It seemed such a waste of power to have a fireplace and all the heat going up the chimney. I can't do computers. I've got a low IQ and I cannot do them. It took me two years to learn to work a fax machine. But that heating system? That's a different sort of brain, I think.

How do you know when you're old? A man knows because he can't make love so well. Oh yes, a man knows. A woman can counterfeit. But we can't. I know Goethe had a girlfriend when he was eighty-three or thereabouts and she became pregnant, but I don't know whether he could actually do it. He might have masturbated on the lady and the clever little things clambered up to the promised land. In my salad days I was asked by the National Gallery in Sydney to give lectures in country towns and the women were very kind in those towns; they drove me around to where I was giving my lectures on art so I got to know them very well. Quite a few of them, a lot of them really, told me how unfortunately their husbands were homosexual. I love confessions, you see, so I got them going and I found out most of them had once been very happily married and they had two or three children, but then the husbands stopped making love to them. And obviously it wasn't their fault; obviously, he must be homosexual. But I used to say: 'Look, your husband has a family, he has a cook, he has a housewife, he has a mistress, he has a roof over his head; so why should he bother to make love? He has all love can bring a man.' They could not see it. Just watch animals; as they get on in years they don't continue to make love; why bother?

Ermes and I have just come from Spain, which is hopping with vitality. The young people are marvellous, good-looking, too, and, I'm sure, having it off with each other all the time. They are free of the Church now, absolutely free of it. I have never seen such happy young people. Is it an advance on the way things were? I don't know. Advance and progress are impossible conceptions. People think that because of the telephone and television, things are getting better; they're not. Things are just the same. Instead of the Church it's television showing them how to be these days. Television has changed life for everybody.

My family was interested in politics and I was always helping at elections and taking little old ladies to vote. But I'm not sure I'd be a Democrat any more. I think I could be a Fascist, but only if I am the leader. Until that happens I guess I'll put up with democracy; as Churchill said, it's not perfect but it's the best thing we've stumbled on.

Music is my passion, a real passion; I cannot live without music. I'm lucky that when I have to be without music I can remember whole symphonies, like the whole of Schubert's Fifth I can sing to myself right through from beginning to end: da-da–dat-dat-da! Isn't that a bit of luck? Modern music? I like some Shostakovich. Otherwise, I don't like it much. I don't know about jazz; I can't listen to it. I hate it. In my twenties I used to listen to Bix Beiderbecke and that sort of musician; I liked them. But I've grown out of modern music, I think. Of course, as I said, hearing things or seeing things first-hand makes all the difference. In Madrid where I was recently, I saw the Rogier van der Weyden *Deposition from the Cross* in the Prado. I had completely forgotten it and when I saw it again I was gobs-macked. So unbelievably great! So wonderful that it is painfully appalling to think of what people are doing now. But you have to see the big picture. Painting goes on. Yes, it goes odd for a while as it did in the Dark Ages, but be patient.

If you're a painter it is always a secret joy to find mistakes. Picasso, for example, was really terrified of using colour. *Guernica* has no colour at all, which was wise of him because he couldn't handle colour. Maybe he was a bit colour blind? A lot of good painters have been. Matisse is the master of colour but then he has such a barren soul. I have had reproductions of Matisse up in my studio and they have given me joy, but deep down they are just decoration. I suppose by painting I have expressed myself, yes, but this is to one side; I am not eager to express myself. It is no harder to paint now than when I was young; painting is always difficult. And as you get older it becomes more difficult because your standards are higher. The van der Weyden was such an incomparably high standard! It was shaming. Who am I? What am I doing?

It must be amazing to have children and then grandchildren;

to watch them grow; it must put you through all your own memories of how you grew up and what you did. To be homosexual when I was young in Australia was not easy. It was terrible. But I think I would have suffered as much had I been heterosexual. Now, looking back on it, I think I'm lucky I was born queer. One loves sex, one loves companionship, but if I'd been born straight I would have had several marriages by now and two untidy, expensive divorces. I'd have to have been a teacher and I'd have ended up in my old age as a principal of some art school, painting at weekends. Being queer has given me freedom. I hate the word 'gay' but what can we do about it? Besides, a lot of the homos I know are sad sacks. And we've lost the word 'gay' for ever, which is such a shame. I've just been rereading Somerset Maugham and he uses the word 'gay' such a lot as nobody will be able to use it ever again. But being queer is so different now; much better. I suppose. I preferred it when it was all a secret and you were getting off on the side and nobody knew. It was better then. I don't like all this openness at all. But it is hard to know. Everyone says, look how the Greeks accepted homosexuality. But we forget that Athens had a population of ten thousand free people and several hundred thousand slaves.

What would I change about human nature? Oh, not much. You know, it's their defects that make people lovable. I think this generation has even more chance of joy and success; now medical science will allow them to live much longer and learn more of interest. Just think of teeth and dentistry! People must have suffered terribly in the past; we are lucky now. It is quite appalling the geniuses who died only in their sixties. There are exceptions, of course; Titian went on to a great age. But now there is much more hope for us all; we can live to ninety, can't we? And live reasonably, too. Of course, getting old is physically bad; I've got arthritis. And I've had the hip operation; that's why I walk in this peculiar way.

Shall we have a little more wine, do you think?

6

Old Souls

ATLANTIC CITY, CONEY Island, Blackpool: on our northern shores are towns, now seedy or dilapidated, flourishing only in aged memory banks as the settings for childhood delight. Back when we old folks were young, when air travel was strictly military or esoteric, there were similar resorts, our first resorts, to be found on the coast of every chilly sea. Rich and poor families used to drive to them from near by cities on hot summer days, or they came by train or coach, so that their children could taste the salt sea and thrill to the terrors of the roller coaster. Clowns danced along the boardwalks, magicians under painted awnings pulled rabbits out of hats, and chariots of light and colour flew too high for us little ones to go in them alone; we needed grown-ups to grab us and hold us back in case we bumped into recruiting angels. Old ears, then around adult knee-level, heard the music as a celestial hurdy-gurdy. Tongues for which tastes are dimming these days slurped ice cream melting in the sun; there was salty popcorn, too, and sausages dripping with fat that would polish off our digestion now. Accustomed to a choppy sea reflected, we blinked into sunset as we struggled to keep our eyes open so the day out might last for ever. And from those sandy beaches, strewn with seaweed entangled with shells, we set out on our own odysseys.

Some day an eccentric scientist will invent an instrument to weigh and measure the trace left behind as a mood or an emotion wherever humankind has rejoiced together or suffered greatly en masse. Whatever revisionist historians claim, for example, no birds fly over Auschwitz; certainly on the morning I visited the site thirty-five years ago not a bird was to be seen flying there. No wonder gambling syndicates often consider establishing themselves in outmoded seaside towns where our old childish faith in magic is still in the air. My parents' retirement community was not far from one of these enchanted spots: Atlantic City, once a kiddies' paradise, recently transformed into a watered-down Las Vegas. Despite Mother's fluency in Moneyspeak, and the fact that she relished a flutter on her occasional trips to Vegas and Atlantic City with my brother and his family, she would not dream of joining a busload of retired folks from her community on one of their regular outings to the seashore casinos.

'I have better things to do with my hard-earned money,' she snapped when I suggested it.

During my lifetime I had not known my mother ever work for hire or earn her own money, except when she fictionalised a collection of sad and funny tales derived from her job as a social worker at the end of the Great Depression and published several of them in literary magazines: 'little magazines', they used to be called. Mother wrote with folkloric charm, or so I recall; she destroyed all her writing, published and unpublished, in one of her periodic clean-outs. Why? Why dispose for ever of imaginative history while keeping drawers full of laddered stockings, piles of dented cooking pots, and stacks of old clothes that no longer fit and would never suit again? Do old hoarders hang onto masses of inconsequential rubbish in the hope against hope the rainy days, already long gone, may magically return?

'And I have better things to do with my time than waste it gambling with old biddies,' Mother said, switching on the telly.

She had recently become addicted to the confessional talk-shows coming into vogue in the 1980s, forerunners of today's 'reality TV', a genre Mother would have despised for its absence of a star – a Jerry or a Judy or a Vanessa – to put lesser beings in context and keep them in line. Like most lapsed Commies of her era, Mother in old age developed a very low opinion of the judgement and general behaviour of the proletariat. And, like practically all the very old who more often than not live alone these days, she relied on television for familiar faces and routine, and also for a taste of how it felt long ago to be needed: needed again, if only as a viewing figure.

Shortly before Mother entered her terminal decline, my brother and I on one of our mutual visits drove out to spend a few hours together in Atlantic City. My brother enjoys gambling the way he enjoys wine, knowledgeably and sensibly. As for me, money is not a turn-on, on the contrary I do not like the stuff and never have, least of all when I desperately needed it, and therefore gambling leaves me cold; it is one appetite I enjoy only superciliously, as a voyeur. See men play poker, as I used to do when I catered a game for a friend, and glimpse the cowboy fantasies of their secret selves. Watch how the son of a millionaire will throw in one strong hand after another in his eagerness to lose Daddy's money fast, and know a young man's raging heart. And that guy who consistently walks away a winner? He's the loneliest man at the table. It is rarely a woman who scoops up the chips, and if she does you can bet she is not getting laid. The mature system cannot support more than one kind of game and its climaxes in a night. The pawnshops of Vegas hold trays of wedding bands, engagement rings, inherited wristwatches, and class rings from every American university: evidence of hope addictive and un-redeemed. Passing agog through that neon oasis many years ago, I saw a christening cup, as tragic as a suicide note, in the window of a hockshop.

While my brother did battle with a one-armed bandit in an

Atlantic City arcade, I strolled the corridors lined on both sides
with flickering machines; here and there stood one decorated
with garlands to mark it as having recently poured out its
jackpot. Even though many stations were unoccupied in the
late morning, the vastness echoed with ratcheting and crackling and the rat-a-tat-tat of coins spilling into troughs. People
at play were all of the generations that in times past used to
spin themselves dizzy on merry-go-rounds in that very place.
And all but one or two of the old gamesters in the hall were
women, several of whom I recognised from Mother's community. Each sat on a high stool before her chosen machine, feeding
coins or tokens into it, then pulling its handle in a regular
rhythm without the slightest tremor. It was not hope that kept
the grannies too engrossed to notice me walking back and forth
behind their backs; they were not playing to win, not like the
young who believe in luck and trust to it. These punters were
too old to believe in luck; they'd had their luck; luck needs a
future. The perseverance of the grannies and great-grannies at
the slots was not sporting; it was devotional. Each tended her
machine dutifully; it was her altar, her purpose, her companion,
and it depended upon her.

'I wonder there aren't more men playing the bandits,' I
commented to a passing waitress. She was long-legged, bored,
and already dressed in satin for the younger crowd, due later.

'The guys, they mostly play, like, wheels and cards,' she said
with a nod towards the serious gaming rooms beyond our noisy
arcade. 'Like, you'd think the lot of them was old enough to
know better.'

My brother was signalling me from the exit. It was time
to go.

'The old fools, the silly old coots,' the girl said and then,
with a glance at my wrinkling, aged brow, she muttered, 'Oh,
like, sorry . . . not because they're old, I mean. Like, sorry, you
know what I mean . . .'

Like, yeah, I know, 'old' is an insult and it is bad business to offend a departing guest, especially a crotchety old bat who could report your rudeness to management.

My brother had lost twenty dollars, his absolute limit. I was as sympathetic as a non-player could be. The fact is, were it not for my hyper-rational disposition, it was on the cards for me to become a devoted gambler after a spooky occurrence in my early teens. The arrival of an annual carnival to a field near our lakeside summer house was a hotly anticipated event of childhood. Not a patch on the extravaganza of Atlantic City, the fair nevertheless had a power of its own, especially in the early morning when a little girl could crawl under the fence and walk all by herself through lanes of sleeping magic. There among the painted horses frozen in mid-leap, 'ever after' seemed already to have begun. One evening in late August a week before my birthday, we all went for our annual evening at the fair. My father threw darts with my brother for a prize of salami, my mother was having her palm read by a gypsy, and I walked around, enchanted. Horses were prancing again, lights were blazing, music played, sugar spun, and the crowd surged, laughing and happy. A big wheel of chance was set up high under a canopy. As I was passing, the tout went into his spiel: 'Ladies and gents, boys and girls, try your luck for only a dime! Winner takes all for just ten cents!'

On the instant I heard a woman's voice loud and clear between my ears; she said just two words: 'Red fourteen!'

Next week is my fourteenth birthday, I remember telling myself, and red is happier than black.

'Try your luck for one thin dime!' the shill cried.

Eager punters placed coins on the board while I fingered the dime in my pocket thoughtfully. The big wheel started spinning.

'Last chance! One thin dime!' called the shill.

The wheel was spinning fast, faster. No. No, it was not for me.

I was going to buy an ice-cream cone instead. Behind me the wheel slowed, clicking. I turned back to watch it stop.

'Red fourteen!' the tout called.

I laughed; for the first time in my young life I laughed knowingly. There and then I formulated and have kept to this day one early tenet of what would become my earthly faith: a winning hunch is a miracle only thanks to all the times too numerous to remember when the hunch is a loser.

Coincidence is one genuine delight of old age, at least as long as memory lasts, for coincidence is an exercise of memory. Coincidences are wonderful, of course, but not mysterious; they are bound to occur and even to increase as we accumulate more and more to be coincident with. Unlike déjà vu, a quirk of the individual subconscious, coincidence often requires the enthusiastic participation of another human being. Liberated by age to talk freely to strangers, to question them with impunity and answer them, too, we old-timers woo synchronicity; we encourage it and challenge it on every street corner to present evidence of how small this old world is, and every day becoming smaller. Meanwhile rapturous early coincidences are lost and wasted everywhere on youngsters plugged into distractions or self-conscious silence.

'Where do you come from?'

'Southern California.'

'Really? Where in So Cal?'

'Oh, you wouldn't know it,' said the old American; he and his wife had stopped me out of the passing crowd for directions to the British Museum. 'It's a little place called Carlsbad.'

'But yes, I do! I do know it! My brother lives there!'

'No kidding! Holy smoke! What's his name?'

'Kurtz, Michael Kurtz.'

'Not Dr Michael Kurtz? Why, your brother saved my life.'

Open-mouthed, we squint towards the Pacific rolling in just west of Tottenham Court Road.

'So there we are on our way home from seeing the grand-kids in Seattle and we stop off to take a look at Vegas,' said a retired New York attorney, sitting next to me on a transatlantic flight. 'It was pretty late so we jump in a cab at the airport and ask to be taken to our hotel. I start talking to the driver and, to make the story short, he turns out to be the same guy I shared an apartment with forty years ago when we were both law students. He used to be brilliant. But the guy has developed a gambling habit. And here he is, probably breaking all kinds of laws, hacking at our age in Vegas. And out of all the cabs in that town, which one do I get into? It makes you wonder, doesn't it?'

Any event that inspires ingenuous wonderment in one person is bound to tickle irreverence in another.

'About American lawyers?' I asked.

Coincidence rarely knocks at the door; it is usually found where it has almost always found me: on the road, among people bound for the same port. A group of thirty or forty American tourists, for example, are hanging around in the restive queue for a trans-Channel ferry. When the gate opens at last the middle-aged woman in front of me lifts her suitcase so for the first time I can read the label on its handle: Danforth Avenue, Jersey City. A stranger who happens to be standing ahead of me in a crowd of strangers in a vast European port turns out to hail from not just the same dinky city but the very same nondescript street to which I was delivered more than seven decades earlier and thousands of miles in the past.

'What is life if not coincidence?' said my aged neighbour later when I regaled him with the experience.

Just because men tend to age more gnomically than women does not mean two cannot play at that game.

'Fancy meeting me here,' I said.

Old travellers all have tales to tell of passing through the same place coincidentally with a relic of memory or experience.

Chatting with a bilingual stranger on a bus out of San Ysidro in Mexico a few years ago, I discovered him to be the grown-up son of an Englishwoman I had met decades previously on the island of Mallorca.

'Oh, Jesus Christ!' he cried, young and inexperienced, all but falling to his knees at finding himself singled out for a miracle. 'You're that lady who taught me how to play tiddlywinks!'

Tiddlywinks and Jesus to one side, the coincidence had as much to do with the vagaries of cheap public transport as with chance, let alone divine election. A car-free, carefree style of travelling is bound to entangle the paths of like-minded paupers and eccentrics. So, not long ago I found myself again aboard an ordinary Mexican coach carrying coincidence. This time I was leaving Oaxaca, one of my three favourite places on earth, the closest in air and spirit a traveller can come to visiting ancient Egypt. The only other 'gringo' on board was a slender man in early middle age. It emerged in an impromptu conversation at a pit-stop that he used to be the boyfriend of a man who wrote an astrology column for the same British magazine I worked for in the early 1970s. The stargazer had retired to a Greek island twenty years earlier to live as a sybarite and in due course we heard he had died as a result.

'You have simply got to be an Aries,' the stranger cried. 'This kind of thing only happens to Aries!'

I am not an Aries. And what if I were? Rationally I must subscribe to what Arthur Koestler calls the 'law of greater numbers'. But let no punier law dull the glory of coincidence in adventurous old lives becoming increasingly reliant on routine and sinking deeper every day into ruts of habit.

Only one more, I promise. She was dark and beautiful, not very young, but not yet old. We were waiting in the crowd, this time to board Eurostar in Paris. Thanks to our proximity in the unruly queue and because we were women travelling alone, we naturally began to chat.

'Oh, I'm a writer,' I said with the usual apologetic tremor when she asked what I did in London.

'What do you write about?'

'Oh, you know, anything. Everything. Freelance, you see. A jobbing pen. But tell me,' I said, hurrying to change the topic, 'where do you come from?'

'Bahrain. I'm visiting friends in Europe. Bahrain is where I live.'

'Nearly forty years ago,' I told her, 'a man from Bahrain did me a great kindness.'

Our mob was stalled and shuffling. With time in hand and a courteous listener, I found myself relating how, long ago when I was new in London, I tagged along to a suite in a sumptuous hotel with a friend who was calling on an older friend there, a Bahraini. When our host learned I was American, he asked how long it had been since I had seen my family. I told him though my parents and I exchanged frequent letters, we had not spoken in nearly a year; my bedsit had only a pay-phone for local calls. He surely deduced, too, I was unable to afford what was then still a fabulous luxury: a transatlantic call. Glancing at his gold watch, he asked me their number in the United States; I watched in astonishment as he dialled it on a phone beside the sofa. Then he handed me the ringing receiver and signalled my friend to leave the room with him so I could speak privately to my mum and dad.

'Such unaffected kindness,' I said. 'Such elegant charity.'

'What was the man's name?' asked the stranger.

'Hussein, Hussein Yateem.'

'Hussein Yateem is my father . . .'

Anyone who fears being entrapped next to garrulous old me on a journey should know that, though I am burdened and bursting with anecdote, I do not remember dreams; they return only as wisps of threat or mystery. But one dream returns perfectly, the first and only one I can recall at will. I am a little girl; before me is a turnstile like those in the Manhattan subway, except this one leads into a golden tunnel without end. My mother stands at my side and she is pointing forcefully to the ground at our feet. I look down and embedded there in sparkling letters is the word: 'Mira!' We have been learning a little Spanish at school so I know 'Mira!' means: 'Behold!' Mira: both command and destiny – behold and observe. Mira: an anagram of my name, too, it so happens, which in turn is practically an anagram of my mother's name: Myra. To this day I wonder whether I was not designed by nature, and certainly by nurture too, as half a coincidence.

The young expect a beatific singling-out from their religion; the guarantee of more earthly rewards, of admiration and wealth, do not go amiss either among those still fit and pretty enough to enjoy them, as the sales staff promoting popular cults know very well. Cult hagiologies are sprinkled with movie stars who have nothing much to recommend them except money and a brief moment of fame.

'Oh sure, we get elderly people interested in Scientology too,' said the hulky young American fronting their head-quarters in London. 'I've met Richard Gere,' he told me in a tone of portent.

Presumably he wanted me to return in ecstasy to the noisy street, having taken his encounter with a celebrity as a poor man's epiphany. The card he handed me then as I turned to leave was emblazoned with the question: ARE YOU CURIOUS ABOUT YOURSELF?

Frankly? I'm not. 'Myself' ceases to be a central dilemma for one who has been herself as long as I have.

'Your IQ, personality, and aptitude determine your future,' was printed below, hardly a soul-stirring lure for one whose future is a whole lot shorter than her past. 'Know them and be in control.'

In control of what? What do I need to control? Cholesterol? Knee joints? Fading memories of mistakes made long ago?

And finally I read: 'No obligations.'

But is obligation not precisely what we want our faith to require? And who could want obligation again in life as much as we old folks, who feel ourselves being superannuated and pushed irrevocably out of playing any useful role?

'Oh, I am so tired,' said the white-haired woman turning to me in the short queue at the checkout of the supermarket next door to the Scientology headquarters. 'It's Friday, you see, and every Friday I do the flowers at our church.'

I'd like to see the Scientologists determine her IQ by the radiance of her smile.

Church attendance is generally higher in the US than in any other Western nation. According to American statistics, 'Elders' remain the most constant and numerous group at all services. My guess is that the majority of old people go to their churches not as the young do, to save their souls; the damage is, after all, already done to souls too frail for further sinning. Church is one of the few places old folks are truly welcome and some of them, like the aged flower arranger, can be of ostensible use. The churchgoing aged are at least as much in search of companionship as salvation, and of continuity more than enlightenment.

Furthermore, established cathedrals and churches in urban neighbourhoods like mine have a quality particularly soothing to old bones: they are cool in summer and warm in winter. Now and again I pop into St Patrick's around the corner to sit in quilted silence; there are usually a few other old-timers there too who have the same idea. Unlike the occasional young-sters bent in avid prayer, the ancients frequently appear to be asleep. They may well be praying, too. But for what? An ease to the ache in their old bones? An end to the chilly distance from their children who are no longer youngsters either: grown-up offspring, who look at their decrepit parents these days with impatience and concern not a million miles from fear? Or do the old folks pray for divine intervention in what they have seen for themselves is mankind's inability to learn from its bloody mistakes, repeating them over and over again without thought or mercy?

At the Wigmore Hall's Sunday morning coffee concerts a soothing churchy ambience prevails. Out of the dozen early arrivals one typical winter Sunday, I count ten who are bespectacled like me and three using canes. Only five of us are alone, four women and one white-haired old man whose hand trembles on his stick. The crowd increases, the doors open at last, and in we file, ancient couples totting up almost two centuries between them, who in their time might have heard, if not quite Mozart, possibly Shostakovich tickle the ivories. Next to me a woman seats herself slowly, settling in place with a sigh.

'I've had a complete hip replacement,' she tells me gratuitously. 'There's a piece of porcelain in there now. But I can walk a mile. Better than my friend who had the same op. She's still on her back.'

Younger members of the audience arrive later, the youngest last of all. Then silence settles over the lovely room and lovely sounds take over. To hell with those latter-day philistines who scorn the geriatric allure of great cultural events in concert halls and theatres. The young are a minority at the Wigmore Hall's Sunday concerts, true enough, but they listen knowledgeably, reverentially, rapturously even. It is not long before a few old men start to nod off here and there. The young ones too in due course will achieve the valetudinarian skill of enjoying utter devotion in a state of utter repose. And may they too in their turn have dedicated old spouses to poke them in the ribs before they start to snore.

There is a gathering vogue for atheism. I am an atheist, to be sure, but I'll be damned if I will forgather about it. My family were Jews, and Jews still seem to me a family, albeit extraordinarily extended and no longer mutually respectful. My father, his siblings, and all their scattered family belonged to a 'Kurtz Family Association', derived from a traditional 'burial society' such as were formed in *shtetls* and ghettoes, their aim to groom the dead in prescribed ways preparing them for resurrection when the true Messiah finally turned up. In the Diaspora, our 'Kurtz Family Association' united far-flung relatives for equally practical purposes, among them care of their aged. The Jewish old folks in America back then were sheltered within the family as most aged immigrants everywhere still are, and probably will be for a generation or so longer, in the homes of their numerous children.

Aged Jews of our region used to be sent by their offspring to spend New York's punishingly hot summers upstate in the kosher hotels of the Catskill Mountains, known as the Borscht Belt. There grandmas and grandpas rocked on porches and kvetched amiably, ate, kvetched more, ate more, and kvetched again. Then after the Sabbath they chortled at the performances of young New York comics destined for Broadway and fame, cursory though fame is, especially for funny men. In the morning while the old men debated the finer points of the Torah, their womenfolk weighed the marital potential of one another's grandchildren. Many of the boys were conveniently on hand earning pocket money as waiters and busboys; granddaughters appeared on weekends to be sized up in turn.

Outside the orthodoxy, Jewish assimilation was well under way in America and Western Europe where it continued apace among what were called 'reformed' or sometimes 'enlightened' families. Nevertheless, very old Jews are to this day appalled when their children 'marry out'. The old have finished with assimilating; assimilation is sexy. Until not very long ago there was still a synagogue in my central London neighbourhood.

It makes me smile whenever I pass the premises now to see it has been converted into a theatre specialising in stand-up comics. I am descended from a race never far from the last laugh.

When I was a girl my father was distressed by my forays among the other tribes. His roots, though stretched, were holding and he feared if the Jews were to lose me, then he would lose me too. He could not comprehend that when I accompanied schoolmates to their meetings and churches, it was not a faith I sought, nor friends, and certainly not a future. I was simply curious. Never mind the proverbial cat; her curiosity was fatal only because she was a prisoner of domesticity.

Suitably, in my adopted land I have found the Church most intimately involved in the everyday life of both young and old to be the Church of England. In my area the local branch is non-sectarian to a notable degree. Not only does it give over its beautiful garden to an annual street fair, and provide office space for the neighbourhood paper as well as the residents' society, it offers cheap Thursday lunches for the over-sixties.

'Will you join us?' asked the woman at the door when I poked my nose in to have a sniff.

The old men appeared to be especially self-conscious, outnumbered as usual by the fairer sex in the big room. It was very quiet in there, no hum of conversation, no laughter. Young people, teenagers, and children were altogether missing from the round tables, of a size to accommodate entire families. No doubt the generous cheap meal was as welcome to some of the pensioners there as was the semblance of company. But who in this exclusively geriatric congregation was going to ask Grandpa what London was like during the Blitz? And where were the adolescents who needed their table manners corrected by Grandma? Where were the daughters-in-law requiring the beady eye; the sons requiring haircuts? This was a solemn ghetto. As I grow old my tastes in food are becoming rigid and repetitious: always the same breakfast, rarely much lunch beyond a cup of soup, never any meat, only fish and the occasional piece of chicken. So it was the aroma of cooked lamb I thought I caught in the air, not the exclusive company of coevals, that gave me an excuse to say thank you, perhaps another time.

The ancient nomadic impulse overtakes my old soul even now. As I walked the few blocks home from visiting the Anglican Church, I knew for sure that my days in this 'hood were numbered. The time had come yet again for me to trade in my address for a new one. Why? Do I think moving will fool time and make it harder for death to find me? Nothing fools time, I know that, or not for long; and death is its own boss. Am I angry about changes to the local streets and the loss of an ambience that was once flourishing? No. To leave in anger is pointless; the anger comes, too. True, the area is no longer the bohemia I loved. But bohemia, evanescent by definition, blew into high streets everywhere years ago. It was not as much the urge to leave building in me recently as the old familiar urge to be on the move. Yes, it was time to move once more under my own steam. Where to this time? Retirement communities on temperate seashores remind me of those towns considered 'good places to raise children', boring beyond endurance for a grown-up. They are bored too, and gossipy, and self-contained in ways that exacerbate the loneliness of ancient singletons. No retirement for me; I was going to stay in London, my dear city, near theatres and cinemas, and danger and rainstorms, and conversations with interesting strangers, and adult entertainments for which we are all for one period in our lives too young, but need not ever be too old.

'I've lived on this street for twenty years. That's longer than anywhere before. I feel I've come to the end of it. I long for a new view from my window. Yes, I think – I am quite sure – I'm sure, I think I'm sure, I am going to move again.'

Even as I was speaking to my friend, Janie, with the phone

gripped between chin and shoulder, I continued to sort through books on my shelves. *Vanity Fair* stays; I will read it again. Travel guides for Ceylon, now Sri Lanka, another for Bombay, now Mumbai, a third for Leningrad: I chuck them onto the pile of rejects at my feet.

'I remember years ago when Bernice was thinking about moving house . . .' said Janie.

We were silent for a moment in honour of our gifted friend who had moved yet again, and not long ago, into the smallest space a body claims on earth.

'Bernice told me she dithered over her books for days, taking them off the shelf, then putting them back.'

'How funny! That is exactly what I'm doing as we speak,' I said.

I replaced *The Psychopathology of Everyday Life* on the shelf. Freud may be out of favour, but you never know when he will come in handy again. I weighed in my hand a paperback copy of Kerouac's *On the Road*.

'Dear Bernice,' said Janie on her end of the line. 'Do you know what she told me?'

Would I ever read *On the Road* again? I asked myself. Yes. No. Maybe? No. No. No, I was never going to read *On the Road* again.

'So what did Bernice tell you, Janie?' I asked and I tossed *On the Road* onto the pile of rejects.

'Bernice told me the moment she knew she was old, really old, certifiably old, was when she finally made up her mind to scrap *On the Road*.'

A Reverend Old Voice: Peter Watkins

When it comes to matters of body and of soul, ecstasy is a province of the young; the aged in general are resigned and practical. Before sainthood became a reward for virtue — before virtue and charity were seen as self-denying — saints were by and large youngsters, some of them less devotional in the long run than self-sacrificial on the spot. And not that long ago clerics, including family doctors, were central to their communities in ways practical as well as spiritual.

Peter Watkins, now in his mid-seventies, the long-time vicar of a West London parish, is a worldly and entertaining man who sees humanity with independent eyes. Sometimes he even skirts teasingly close to irreverence, as only a clergyman secure within himself and able to communicate his inner faith would be able to do: as only a tested and experienced old man can do. Peter Watkins was divorced more than two decades ago. He is the father of two sons and a daughter, and has three grandchildren.

I only admitted I was adult a few years ago; it was only then I stopped, when in mixed company with children, veering towards them because I felt really I still belonged among the children. I was very into athletics and went on playing football and so on until a disgraceful age. I used to play a lot of games with my two sons, running around the common with them, and beating them and beating and beating them, and then suddenly it seemed they started giving me a hard time; and finally they beat me. And so I became conscious of the physical process of ageing. It was the other day I was on a boat with a friend who has a little place on the Thames. We went through a lock and had a bit of lunch, and it was getting on and off that boat that made me realise I was truly old.

To go into the Church is a decision you make when you're eighteen or nineteen, so when you are in your seventies you hardly understand the creature you used to be. I just remember knowing that this business of Christianity and its values is very, very important. And I remember thinking, if it was that important I had to do something about it. Then I was scared. How could I commit my whole life to something that might be erroneous in any case? And it was when I recognised I was scared that I knew I had to do it. I put my name forward to a bishop and went before a board for acceptance; I had already been before a board for the army, too, to become commissioned. But I was not a military man. And I remember they said to me then: 'We don't make mistakes.' The Church board was almost the exact thing again, three days of it. And I knew I was going to get through it. They were not sussing me out spiritually; it was the social aspect and I knew that time how to do it. Does that sound awful? I did the army medical first and then I had to have the Church medical. I began to think the whole of my manhood was going to be a process of having my balls clutched and being told to cough.

When I went to theological college we had to do an exam on the Book of Common Prayer. Nowadays young clergymen don't know the Book of Common Prayer; they have never used it. My generation valued the language of faith; yes, it had to change, it could not stay as it was, including, for example, weather-prayers, which are hardly pertinent now. But part of the equation is that you cannot have first-rate music if you have fifth-rate language. And when churches abandon beauty of language, they go happy-clappy with their music, too. Theoretically, it attracts the young. Some people bend over backwards to get the young into their churches by any means; I do not. I feel when the young go off and leave home they need to expand, to think, to experience, and work things out for themselves. Then when they get married and have their own children, they often want to return to community life and its values, spiritual and moral.

That is when some return; perhaps not a great number, but any number is important.

One of the things central in my life, as much by luck as anything else – or perhaps not quite luck – is that we have marvellous music at our church. Last Sunday we had Advent carols and four readings and four poems: the language of the Church is a language of poetry. The Dawkins lot fail to appreciate we use a special language that fires the imagination, and symbols that spark thought. I am supposed to believe in an afterlife. But it is more a matter of hope than anything else. I have seen enough of death to know the finality of all visible signs of life. There is a reading often at funerals, which I do not use myself: 'Death is nothing at all . . .' That is not true. Death is big. It is the last enemy. And perhaps the last friend, too. Symbols do get ridiculous when pushed to their limit. Eternal harp-playing! God! I could not stand it! Let it remain symbolic. The world outside is often a world barren of symbols. That does not mean you haven't got to be critically aware of the gospel narratives as inventions of the imagination. They are. And the Divine Creator? Um . . . um . . . One comes to Him, I think, through one's sense of wonder; it is not as though one has a theory of what happened in the beginning and how it was mapped out in the best of all possible worlds. No. Nothing like that. But what there is is your sense of wonder if you only open your eyes at whatever age. And sometimes as your eyesight gets worse your power to see gets better.

The Church of England and the pub used to be mainstays of the traditional picture but the village pattern is going, gone. Once upon a time when you reached the age of sixty or so, as a clergyman in a huge industrial parish you might go to a rural parish and have one little church and six hundred people; if you go to a rural parish now, you have seven parishes and you run around faster than you would with an urban parish. So the pattern is changing. Another thing about the C of E is that its labels are completely out of date now, originating in the nineteenth century, and that's where they belong: High Church and Broad Church and Low Church. Low Church proselytises and so, too, does High Church, in a way; Broad Church tends not to and that is where my affections would be, though the labels these days are going rapidly out of date.

I have not got a dog-collar; sometimes at parties people learn I'm a clergyman and they come up and say: 'I'm not religious, but . . .' When I was young I wanted to say: 'Look, I'm not religious either,' but I feared that would be too confusing. I used the word 'religious' circumspectly because it implies things I am not: it connotes a certain narrowing of interests into one sphere of life, a ceasing to be enthusiastic about what is exotic, exuberant, and intellectual. I am very anti-authoritarian; I am a child of my times, in the sense of rebelling against public school, the Church at the time, gurus, army discipline and the ridiculous orders; that is, I am not anti-authority but against misplaced and inflexible rules.

There are areas where things remain much the same among the young. Of course, there is a realm – it won't happen in the Arab world for a while – where women take part more and more. But the first interest in sport remains; in playing games; the first time you score a century; the thrill of physical accomplishment remains the same; and dancing, the thrill of dancing. Appreciation of music and dance is unchanging; and of love. But the bit I do not know about is technology, the mobile phone bit, and the computer bit; I feel it makes the young of now so different from us. I often ask people in my parish to please send me a seven-year-old to sort out my television. In age, you can feel lost and lonely in that sense. But you can also become bolder, no longer have appearances to keep up, be less frightened of people, truths, and judgements.

There is really only one interesting thing about me: I should have had to retire at seventy. You can retire from the Church at sixty-five but you must retire at seventy. Except that I entered my parish so long ago the rules do not apply. I am the longest-standing vicar in London. I do the job. I know my parishioners and now I am marrying the daughters of people I married. I make strong connections in my parish, yet never force friendships. I have been there for forty years and my relationships have gone on and on. When I began as a curate we visited people, went into their homes, checked they were untroubled. That is a world away from what happens now. So many younger mothers are at work now or out of the house; I go for a reason and when I know people are in. Clergy are compared with social workers; social workers see only people in need, whereas clergy sees the whole family at different times, including times of rejoicing and happiness. Is that not a more rounded view of family life than seeing it only during crisis? And that view is being endangered. There is a modern trend of moving vicars constantly around parishes; relationships are your stock-in-trade – move parish and you jettison the lot. In the parish everyone calls me Peter. When I first came, some did so because they thought themselves on the same social footing, not to say a higher one. I was not going to have people differentiating in that way so I ask even the children to call me Peter. The business of 'father' is absurd, frankly.

I am in contact with the young; I especially like to write to them. One kid was sent to boarding school and was very sad so I sent a postcard every week. We had a marvellous musician who went with his wife to live in France. They asked me to write letters about my views and beliefs; I like writing letters because they have a date. I don't know what I am going to believe next week. I don't know whether I am going to believe anything. For me doubt is not an enemy; it has been a friend and kept my views alert. As your brain deteriorates you expect to forget things, yet I do not think my writing, for example, is deteriorating. I am a clearer writer than I used to be. And certain artists, true artists, improve and produce marvellous things in old age. They have the courage to be simple. The young feel they must show off in ways to prove to others they are who they think they are; or want others to think they are. As you grow older, it does not matter.

Before public libraries, wisdom lived in the elderly.

7

Grannyhood

ONCE UPON A time in a faraway land of elves and ogres, there lived a little old lady called Granny. Granny's thatched cottage smelled of baking cakes; a fat cat purred on the sofa; and treasures were hidden in wooden chests and cupboards: dancing dolls; and wind-up, wooden trains that hooted; spinning tops; and books with crumpled yellow pages from which Granny read aloud stories both wonderful and scary. There were bigger books too, containing rust-coloured photographs of men with beards, and women with long hair, and children wearing funny clothes. Granny always had something very special waiting for her young visitors to hear and play with. And if Mum and Dad were hanging around, Granny winked at you when they weren't looking so you knew she was your best and first ally, someone to teach you spells that would keep you safe in the big dark forest beyond her garden.

'We won't tell your mum,' she whispered while you scoffed a forbidden second piece of chocolate cake or as she squeezed your hand around a silver coin. 'No, we will not tell your mum, not by the hair of my chinny-chin-chin!'

Granny was magic. Granny was a star. Granny rocked. But that, of course, was before Walt Disney took over the Grimm Brothers' going concern, before playgrounds went online, and long, long before TV and iPods and mobiles replaced old told tales. Once upon a time that was Granny. These days, the chances are she lives in the suburbs with a man who is not Grandpa;

they have a holiday flat in Marbella. And there are no hairs on her chinny-chin-chin, thank you, darling; Granny is on HRT.

It is as well I do not hold with that leftover of early psycho-babble, 'the role model', and its stultifying implication that the young should choose someone to fashion themselves after, rather than each be given encouragement to discover and to fully become himself or herself. But I did not have exemplary grannies; neither was there a woman whom I would choose as anything like a role model or a good example to me, now that I am in my own grannyhood. My grannies did not much like each other; they had nothing in common save their great age and the manner in which both greeted me, the first grandchild to both, with disappointment due to my gender. I was born back when a girl was seen as an expense to her family until she married and became an expense to someone else's. My paternal Grandma Ida had nine surviving children; one son died in infancy, but she could console herself that all but the first and penultimate of the remaining brood were boys. She showed the sorrowful sympathy due a little granddaughter by never hugging me unless it was in private, and covertly slipping me titbits from her holiday table.

'You should only eat, Irmele,' she used to whisper to me and it wasn't long before I understood her to mean I should eat for myself only until the day came when I cooked to feed others.

My other granny, Annie, was widowed soon after the birth of my mother, her only child; she did not even try to hide her displeasure, which ran deeper than disappointment, or her abiding dislike of me.

'That child is spoiled. She cannot even wash a dish and hates to help around the house in any way,' she used to complain about me to neighbours and in my hearing, too, when I was barely seven or eight.

It did not escape my notice that my revered little brother

was not expected to make his own bed or lift one soapy finger around the house.

'It's a girl,' read the announcement Mother sent of my arrival. And in brackets she wrote: 'Drat it!'

Mother was sorry for herself when her first-born was a daughter and she was sorry for me, too, being born one.

'It's a man's world, Irma,' she told me countless times, watching me with pity as well as self-pity while I was growing up.

Hers was a common reaction to girl babies in the pre-war and post-Depression 1930s, not only in families needing sons to help support them financially, but right up to the highest levels of society with money and titles to hand down. The first few decades of each new century are managed by those born in the preceding one and their hold over morality and politics was, until quite recently, firm and unyielding. Wisdom and, just as often, impassioned stupidity could over-turn the status quo only after noisy complaint and outright rebellion. Feminists in our town were still in the closet during my childhood; I would be into my thirties before they broke out, enraged.

'Is it a boy or a girl?' was the first question put by every last person of either sex to whom I announced my daughter-in-law's recent pregnancy. And, oh yes, believe me, I do mean every friend, every acquaintance, and every colleague: every amiable stranger who crossed my path after my son told me a baby was expected. Every last one of them nodded their approval on learning that the young couple did not care to know the sex of their child-to-be. Whether out of shallow political correct-ness or a real improvement on the old sexist ways, not even dotards would dream now of saying, 'May it be a boy,' in the way everyone still did when my mother's generation announced their pregnancies, and quite a few continued to do when I was pregnant thirty-odd years ago. On the contrary, it surprises me – and, as surprises usually do late in life, it alarms me, too –

how many young women I meet these days who declare their strong preference for a daughter.

The stranger next to me on the underground train was heavily pregnant. For nearly twenty minutes we had been stalled between stations: a delay entailing conversation, practically requiring it, in my case. After some introductory chit-chat she told me she had just been sent by her gynaecologist for psychiatric counselling, so distressed was she to learn the foetus she carried was male.

'But why does it make so much difference to you? I mean, doesn't sexual equality have to start in the womb?'

'You can talk to a girl,' she said. 'A girl can be your friend.'

'Don't you think it would be . . . ' I caught myself and stopped before saying 'wise' lest it sound too, well, too wise; instead I said, 'fair, yes, wouldn't it be fair and fun, too, to receive your baby and raise him – or her – as your wonderful discovery rather than your invention?'

Then I told her about my own son and what a lifelong source of joy he has been to me. Her eyes flickered; I almost heard her think: Silly old granny . . .

Nevertheless, after a further half-hour stuck underground she became increasingly happy to talk, even to a nosy old stranger. She was twenty-five, unmarried, living with her partner, both of them vegetarians with a devotional faith in organic foods. Her parents lived in Wales; she had three sisters, one of them a twin. When we were under way at last, I scribbled my email address on a bit of paper.

'Here,' I said. 'Let me know if ever you're in my neighbourhood and want a cup of herbal tea.'

Two months later I received an email from her that justified my having been a meddling old ass.

'As you predicted, he is wonderful, he is gorgeous, a special and' – wrote the once-dedicated vegan, – 'a totally edible baby boy!'

An increasing number of women are starting their families late; over-thirty-fives now account for more than twice as many births as when my generation was fecund. The marked preference expressed by many independent new mothers to bear a daughter, baby, friend and infant ally, hardly seems to me a victory for feminism, merely another symptom of loneliness endemic to the way we live and love.

'Why should the hope of giving birth to a little friend be any less ill advised than hoping to be delivered of Mama's little hero and protector used to be?'

'So you want women to go back to the old ways?' said my friend Janie when I was holding forth over our occasional drink.

'No, Janie, not that! Never the old ways! Good God, no! I want us to find new ways, each woman her own way, her adventurous and creative way, a way not so damned exclusive and judgemental: pre-judgemental, even. As for the business of preferring one gender over another, can we not have one kind of loving at least, the maternal kind, I mean, that is unconditional?'

'Oh, Irma,' said Janie, rummaging in her Prada bag for a packet of Nicorette, 'you are really starting to sound like a silly old granny.'

Because daughters of my generation were often received as second-best, we girls among ourselves regularly used to instigate a competition in mama-bashing during late-night gabfests in the college dormitory. Enthusiastic amateurs like me stood small chance against early analysands of the 1950s who were being coached by their shrinks in methods of blaming Mama to a professional level. Even now when old daughters meet after a glass or two we can often be heard laying into our mostly defunct mamas. Daddy-bashing was a sport too, of course; indeed, it still is, though of a minor league; even hard-line feminists find it difficult to blame Daddy for much more than being distant or absent. Our mamas, on the other hand, were competitive, envious of us, over-protective, critical, hateful to Daddy and, of course, they played favourites.

The girl is mother to the granny, not always, however, in expected ways. The very women who found their own maternal relationships troubling and burdensome often turn out to be the most indulgent, flamboyant, and fun-loving grannies, at one remove at last from the unending guilt and responsibilities of mothering – and of daughtering, too. My own tough and troubled mother was triumphant in grannyhood, though nobody ever called her 'Granny' or would have dared. To my son she was always 'Baba', syllables that must have been bred in his bones; they emerged without prompting the very first time I took him to America to meet her and my father: 'Jampaw'. My brother's children called Mother 'Wicca' as she instructed them, for even as she decried ritual and declared religions to be twaddle, Mother presented herself to the wide-eyed as an adherent of the dark arts. My brother in an affectionate display of maturity shortened 'Wicca' to 'Wick' and that is how he refers to her to this day. As for me, I called her 'Mome' after a childish misspelling of 'Mommy' when I was five. Baba to one grandchild, Wicca to the other two, Wick to her son, Mome to me, Minnie in childhood, and Myra to grown-up friends: had ever honest woman so many aliases?

Mother knew how children love to be scared, and how to mesmerise them, too, with the dark and macabre of which their parents never speak. She surrounded herself with eclectic memento mori – a shrunken head from New Guinea, papier-mâché skulls from Mexico, a broken headstone nicked from a derelict cemetery in New England – and there in the retirement community where she lived as a widow, she cocked a snook at the grim reaper and winked at her grandchildren from behind his back.

'Am I not the most disgraceful little old lady you've ever met?' she used to challenge young visitors.

Naturally I had not known my mother in her own youth; children know Mum and Dad as older beings, powerful and weird. In retrospect – which is how we who are old know our parents better than we have ever known them before – I see that Mome was a frustrated being, born a generation too soon to become her gifted self in the grown-up world: the man's world, as it was. Her escape and joy was in make-believe, and thus she was a divine granny, never more inventive or beautiful than before an audience of worshipful children, as long as she did not have to sustain or understand them, only impress and entertain. Depression descended heavily on her in her mid- to late eighties, in part because her grandchildren lived thousands of miles away to the east and west, and also because they had grown worldly and beyond her genius for let's pretend. At first it was only in the mornings she scowled and stomped and barely replied when spoken to. Soon a full-time carer moved into the spare room; I was happy – more than happy – to stay in a nearby hotel on my increasingly frequent visits. Eventually, Mother was prescribed antidepressants and that was when, whatever relief the medication undoubtedly brought to her carer, her wit and snap faded away, along with the last remnants of her old *joie de vivre*. Feeling bad, after all, is feeling, too, with its reasons and its vocabulary. Do away with feeling bad and the whole personality falters. It was then, about four years before her death, that Mome began to reach the end. Rarely in her final months did she emerge from her muddy silence; even then, however, only let a child – the smaller the better – come into sight and the ghost of my mother's old flirtatious smile fluttered across her face.

One afternoon my mother and I were sitting before her incessant television. Suddenly, she turned to me.

'I wasn't a good mother to you, was I?'

A mind can stagger; mine did. In the whole of our time together, during all my youth and all my mother's maturity, I could not recollect one word from her of praise or pride. I still can't, except that sometimes she showed an arch concern.

'Irma, straighten your shoulders.'

'Don't let winning that little prize go to your head, Irma.'

'Irma, you will never be a writer.'

'Why, Irma, you've started to go grey.'

If my son and the other grandchildren knew what a hard time their amazing granny gave me – her scorn of my baby wit, her mockery and embellishment of my school essays, her suspicion of my determination to escape – they would not believe it; they would not believe me. My mother was meant to bear sons; it was impossible for her to take joy in raising a daughter, especially a daughter fortunate enough to have her as a mother. She envied me, first of all for having herself as a mother. Oh, what extraordinary attention she would have demanded, what applause, what triumph, if she'd only had my chances!

She shook her head and said once more: 'No, I wasn't a good mother to you.'

'You have always been a stunning woman, Mome,' I finally replied; and then at last: 'I love you.'

She turned away to the blurred and anonymous comfort of the screen. And it was then, as my mother was drifting back into her terminal position, that the perplexed child who was me crossed the frontier into her own old age.

'Your mother was so proud of you,' one of her acquaintances and regular correspondents told me years later. 'She always said glowing things about you. Behind your back.'

But one truth is universal about all grannies: we are not only older than the principals but are usually the oldest women in the story. Of course, in the West, 'old' has become an insulting adjective; wisdom and experience take second place to 'focus groups'; and 'who' is no longer as important as 'how many?' Elective cosmetic surgery is being confused with operations of the life-saving variety. 'Granny' is no longer a title that every newcomer to it welcomes, not in the way our own grandparents universally did. There are plenty of grannies now still working, still youngish, and quite a few on the prowl too, in heavy disguise.

'Believe you me! I have been there! Make the kid call you by your real name right from the start,' said one Botoxed, detoxed, foxy old lady to whom I announced my impending grannyhood. She formed a cross with two paint-tipped fingers, as if warding off the devil. 'None of that "granny" shit! Granny! Brrrr! It's so bloody ageing! And take it from me, honey, you make it clear from day one that you have your own life to lead, or else they'll have you babysitting every hour of the day.'

And yes, it is true, too, that here among the affluent, just as in areas of the third world that know hunger and premature death, if Granny is in the region, she is expected to be on tap. The difference is, here in the long-lived West it is a working mum she stands in for, not a mum dead or vanished or in labour with the next baby. When my son was little, his fellow toddlers at our local drop-in club and nursery were only ever accompanied by mother or, once in a while, by a hired au pair. On my recent grannying rounds of pre-school-age clubs, among the dozen or so mothers I always meet four or five grannies like me, and a father or two sometimes, as I never used to see at nurseries and 'one o'clock clubs' back in the 1970s. I have not yet encountered a grandad among the attendant 'carers', although I have been told there are a few who serve occasionally, if reluctantly. Old men do not play easily as new men; as a rule they feel themselves essentially miscast in the role.

Grannies today have a hard time when just one third of women in their late twenties are officially married, compared to 85 per cent three decades ago. These statistics do not mean all single women live alone; many are in friendly and stable sexual relationships with the fathers of their children. However, it is a fact that an increasing percentage of single women are mothering darling little bastards, as I myself did, by the way, ahead of my time. And my son's. There is also our phenomenal divorce rate, adding to the numbers of puzzled and mildly disapproving grandparents around, born into a more conventional and long-suffering culture.

Furthermore, the traditional role of *über*-matriarch grannies used to assume by right has been overtaken by racks of how-to books and rows of DVDs on child-rearing that make an old woman's experience passé, irrelevant, and totally wrong. Modern daughters and daughters-in-law impose dietary strictures in the nursery that would be practically religious if they did not change so often. New mums scorn any but the very latest versions of childcare; intuition and common sense are judged less reliable than the affected spouting of TV gurus. When we old-timers volunteer or are drafted in to babysit, never mind how many offspring of our own we have raised, it is now the young mums who instruct us on the minutiae of feeds and foods, on bottle-lore, potty-lore, and nursery etiquette. Racy little sports prams with brakes and gear shifts should require a licence to drive them, while baby bottles of unlikely shape and enriched contents must be sterilised in microwave ovens. Velour sleeping bags, colour-coded nappies with Velcro fastenings, and countless other newfangled gadgets and gimcracks baffle Granny in the nursery nowadays. That is, if the modern grandparents are around in the first place. On every flight home from America, Australia, Canada – practically anywhere, in fact, outside war zones - can be found sighing grannies and silent grandpas, returning from visits to their overseas families, collecting air miles that attest to their frustrated devotion.

To make a granny's lot harder still, horrors! There is another granny in the wings. The bitch! Naturally enough, grandparents have always arrived in duplicate. However, not that long ago they had offspring of both sexes and to spare unto the next generation. Nowadays, as often as not, two ardent old women are both crazy about one little body. Grandparenting is a final passion for most of us and grannies especially generate a ferocious amount of competitive love for today's small, fractured families to contain safely. In days of yore they used to say that whenever a wedding took place the groom's side did not lose a son, it gained a daughter. However, time has turned yet another truism on its head and it is now the maternal progenitors who have an edge in grandparental sweepstakes. Mothers of sons today can be heard everywhere complaining bitterly to each other that pregnant and nursing daughters-in-law turn to even the most troublesome family of their own for support; rarely, if ever, do they rely on their troublesome in-laws. The tension between husbands and mothers-in-law has been fodder for centuries of jokes. But in spite of there being so many gifted modern female comics, the relationship between a man's wife and his mother remains too hot to handle humorously. Two women who love the same man? It is just not funny.

And every time that commonplace, divorce, happens, as it will for one in three modern marriages, with custody assigned to the mother as is customary, the paternal grandparents find themselves 'exed' too, stranded out on the shakiest limb of the family tree.

'I have one child, a son, and two adorable little granddaughters from his first marriage,' said a widowed Londoner in her late sixties. She was wistfully watching other people's kiddies at play in our local park, many with a granny in attendance. 'They live with their mum in Dorset and her new husband. I'm lucky to see them every few months. And never, not once in five years, have they spent a Christmas with me.'

Her tone was angry but her eyes blurred with tears.

An English university survey of two African villages concludes that children lucky enough to have a maternal granny who is herself unencumbered by young offspring have marked advantages of health and survival. They cite their findings as evidence to support an evolutionary theory that the menopause evolved as nature's method of contraception: specifically to keep older females baby-free themselves, thus enabling them to help out their own daughters still involved in serial pregnancies. Only maternal grannies count; only the maternal granny can be absolutely sure the babies born to her own daughters carry her genes. Mothers of sons, certainly before DNA tests evolved, had no real evidence, nothing more than hope and hearsay, that the new baby of his bedfellow had the slightest genetic connection to themselves, which, logically, ought to make us on the paternal side less attached. But then, logically, those of us who have had only a son or sons should not undergo the menopause at all, not until we finally give birth to a daughter who needs us to help out in her nursery. Is it not unjust and illogical of nature, and sexist too, that we who have borne only sons must nevertheless flush just as hotly as maternal grannies? But, in truth, who cares? I would happily sacrifice lubricious sport for the delight of a grandchild's smile; coins saved on tampons and Nurofen come in handy, too, to buy treats behind the backs of disapproving daughters-in-law.

We writing women, who are the products as well as the perpetrators of latter-day feminism, document every step of our passage in a way unique in the history of journalism and popular writing. From menarche to menopause and beyond, we examine and analyse the distaff phenomena as they happen to us, and then we lay down the law to our sisters with the fervour of born-again solipsists. Fake orgasms or demand them as a right? Ditch an imperfect or unfaithful mate or put up with the jerk? Choose kids or a career? Adore kids, should you decide at last to have them? Or declare noisily and proudly they bore the hell out of you?

Now we of the original scribbling sisterhood are growing old – some older than others – readers encounter us protesting in print the sheer delight of reaching forty, fifty, sixty. Yippee! Sixty at last: free of time-wasting passions; done with uncertainties. Come and get me, life, I'm sixty! And don't I look great for my age? This delirious twittering fills me with the wry amusement a twenty-year-old would feel, hearing a precocious ten-year-old hold forth on the joys of adolescence. For those of us who have started to do our sums on the morning paper's obituaries, one year makes a world of difference. In age and senescence, as in childhood and adolescence, a single twelve-month carries more than its own weight when set against eternity. For the budding young, of course, the long year holds surprises and changes, heartbreak, ecstasy, and hope. Among the withering generations, on the other hand, a year's importance lies not in its length; on the contrary, a year is a matter of urgency and awe because of the speed with which its days pass faster and ever faster, as if life were on a downhill run. Samey days and identical nights slip away with barely a pause between. Is it really Friday? Is it Friday again? How can it be Friday? What happened to Monday, to Tuesday, and all the other days? It cannot be October; March was only yesterday.

'Have you seen the Christmas crackers already on sale in supermarkets? Time is being packaged and pushed and gobbled like salted crisps,' I complained to my friend Janie, twenty-odd years younger than me.

'You are such a cynic,' she replied.

'I'm a realist, dear heart, not a cynic. I take no joy in what I see as true and, God knows, I make no profit from it. The fact is I'd be a lot better off if I endorsed disgraceful shenanigans for wrinklies and made our descent from prime time sound like a geriatric joy-ride, purple scarves flying. Youth is no longer a passage to wisdom; youth has become a transcendent ideal central to a cult: the youth cult – the only cult I know, by the way, that does not envision any kind of afterlife. Somewhere in the 1960s the brats did away with middle age, inveigled by consumer interests, I suspect. A lot of businesses grew fat on getting the young to spend and they still do. Now the young and the not so young are attacking the very notion of old age too, and being old, honestly old, has never been more problematical.'

'You're only as old as you feel,' said Janie.

'Oh yeah? Tell that to the roots of my hair. Apropos of which, a dear friend of mine, Jeff Bernard, RIP, used to say we can only know for sure we are certifiably old when our pubic hair goes white.'

'Look here, listen to me: being old can be fun. It has got to be fun. You simply must make it sound fun and sexy. Otherwise nobody will want to read what you have to say. Getting old has got to be sexy, otherwise people won't want to do it.'

'Would they prefer the alternative?'

'See what I mean? You are so damn doomy.'

'You think I'm damn doomy, honey. Just you try Simone de Beauvoir.'

In Simone de Beauvoir's book *La Troisième Age*, she wrote: 'the sadness of old people is not caused by any particular event or set of circumstances: it merges with their consuming boredom, with their bitter and humiliating sense of uselessness, and with their loneliness in the midst of a world that has nothing but indifference for them.'

When the book appeared in 1970, de Beauvoir was in her early sixties, yippee! There comes a point in every long life when existence must cease to be what we make of it and become what we made of it. The erudite philosopher and surviving soulmate of Jean-Paul Sartre did not anticipate a high old time in the years left to her. It has been argued, and of course de Beauvoir agreed, that intellectuals are interpreters who belong to a specific time in history and thus, like great beauties and athletes, they have more to lose than most people to the erosion of years. They lose it fast, too, as their moments of triumph pass, relegating them to the terminal depression de Beauvoir was evidently feeling.

'Of course, Janie,' I said, 'de Beauvoir was childless. She had no claim or attachment to life beyond her own existence and her perishable paper trail.'

'I hope,' she snapped, 'you are not suggesting in this day and age that a woman can't be fulfilled unless she has spawned? Gerry, you know, my partner Gerry? He and I don't want a kid.'

Janie, a solicitor, lives with Gerry. He too is a solicitor and whenever she refers to him fashionably as her 'partner', it puts me in mind of a law firm.

'Fulfilment has always seemed to me a tragic ambition for human beings,' I said. 'Fulfilment is over and done with as soon as it starts. I mean, come on, Janie, do you fill a bath in order to pull the plug? But can you call your bath fulfilled until you've pulled the plug? Female plumbing is installed by nature for a purpose: atavistic, animal, a whole lot deeper than free will, believe me, Janie. Turn on those sexy taps and the purpose agitates to be undertaken and accomplished now, right away, at once. Yes, a woman can decide not to give birth, and I agree wholeheartedly that in modern life she must be able to control how and when she gives birth. But why do we now deny the savage, primordial ache, the febrile curiosity, the haunting of our wombs? I have noticed, by the by, women who choose never to fill that nursery generally move into it themselves. Report me to the political correctness cops if you must, but I have to say that childless women of a certain age often end up as their own pampered brats. Yes, yes, I know the "maternal urge" is derided in modern society; it is the newest love that dares no longer speak its name. But the fact remains babies are an existential triumph over time; they are our masterpieces.'

'You had really better watch out,' grumbled Janie. She topped up her drink with sugar-free tonic. 'You'll never work again. You really are starting to sound like a silly old granny.'

'PC is getting me down,' I grumbled. 'I think I'll have to write a book called *Lip Service: Sucking off Success.*'

Last spring I was coming back to London from a few days in my studio flat on the Channel coast of France. A young man sat opposite me on the train from Dover to London. About halfway home he unplugged himself from his hissing, strumming iPod and took a mobile phone from his pocket. He punched in a number.

'Hello, Mum?' he said and my heart sang in chorus: 'Hello, Mum?'

My boy used to say, 'Hello, Mum?' on precisely the same eager rising note, as if to ask: 'Are you still there? Still with me? Good! Oh, great! You're still there!'

I dreamed of having his 'Hello, Mum?' set in gold to wear on a necklace so I could lift it to my ear when I needed cheer or when we were far apart: 'Hello, Mum?'

These days when I phone him, or on the rare occasions he phones me, his 'Hello, Mum' has a downward intonation as in: 'Hello, Mum, you see I really do call once in a while whatever you think.' His current 'Hello, Mum' makes me immediately fearful of being importunate and demanding; I hear myself rambling apologetically in response to it. But of course some of us need no passport for the state of apology; we were born there.

The boy across the aisle was on his way back from a week in Paris. He delivered what had to be a heavily edited version of the trip, punctuated with 'All right, Mum,' in the rhythm of 'Now, now' or 'There, there' every time she asked a question.

'All right, Mum,' he said ten times in as many minutes before finally saying: 'All right, Mum. See you soon, Mum. Goodbye, Mum.'

Immediately he punched in another number.

'Hey!' he said. 'Is that you, man?'

Whereupon he launched into a rollicking version of his trip, not once using the friend's given name, just occasionally saying: 'man' – man to man.

Meanwhile, London was gathering itself together outside the window, and suddenly ancient memory grabbed me and pushed me into one of those senescent reveries that can make an old lady miss her stop on the journey across places haunted by her younger self.

A dozen of us lay in the neonatal ward like collapsing balloons in an acre of long-stemmed roses. Most of us were dozing; a few smiled vacantly over the heads of guzzling sprogs. I had been shaken awake from the anaesthetic, my baby having been finally delivered by Caesarean section, as many had started to be in the early 1970s.

'It's a boy,' a woman's voice said close to my ear. 'A fine, healthy boy.'

Someone put the newcomer into my arms. He opened his eyes. His eyes were as deep as space; his eyes held everything, everything known and everything forgotten, everything called to an awakening over and over again and each time for the first time: called to life – the only miracle. I raised the warm bundle against my shoulder where his breath feathered my neck. My baby's head was not yet hard; gently I kissed the velvet over that blessed ark of testimony and the great leaning tower of love soared high in my heart: the love of my life and the love of life.

Thirty-four years later, a March morning; I had not slept the night before, worried and distracted. Up at six, I compelled myself not to make the call, not to interfere. Only just before midday did the phone ring at last; I raced to answer it.

'Hello, Mum?' said my son in the golden old upbeat rhythm. 'Carolyn has had the baby. It's a boy.'

And so a new clock starts to tick and time begins again.

My grandson's picture is framed on the desk before me now; he is smiling, his funny little ears on either side of wide and merry eyes. This feeling when I look at him is not the savage love that claimed my fidelity and could have claimed my very life when first I looked into my own son's eyes. Yes, I would die for my grandson willingly, should he need a vital part of me to make him well or whole. But this feeling, this deep feeling, is goo-goo too, madly sweet, brand new and at the same time familiar: beautiful new shoes made for dancing again. Young women who reject motherhood never imagine they are rejecting grandmotherhood too: a renaissance of fun and purpose in a life that is losing both to time. When her own child is born, a woman steps from the centre of her stage to give the newcomer that place; when her grandchild is born she is beckoned back to a new role.

'Dibby-dibby-doo!'

Did I burble those inane syllables as I swept the spoon into my grandson's eager mouth?'

'Dibby-dibby-doodle-doo!'

Who said that?

'Dibby-dibby-dibby-doodle!'

Did I say that? Yes, I admit it; I did. I heard myself say that. My daughter-in-law read somewhere that psychologists have decreed babies should always be addressed in real, polysyllabic words. Nonsense sounds do them no perceptible good and teach them nothing, which in pedagogic circles is tantamount to doing harm.

'Dibby-dibby doo!' I've said it before, and I'll say it again: 'Dibby-dibby-doo!'

What sensible words can ever so perfectly express love that surpasses vanity, reason, and self-control?

'Dibby-dibby-doodly-doo!'

Granny knows what she is talking about. And, believe you me, Baby does too.

Falling in love again, what am I to do? Never wanted to, can't help it. Who would have expected it at my age? I hum the old songs; I kiss the photo of him until the glass is blurry. And I gaze into passing prams too with an intensity parents find alarming until, as recommended to me by another goofy granny, I ask the baby's age. A simple question that, mysteriously, rarely fails to ease parental qualms about the old weirdo leering under the hood at Junior. I coo at other people's baby pictures, too, without side or envy, with a pure love vast enough to encompass the whole of babydom. I have known even glamour grannies, who abjure the title attached to their new role, go worshipful and besotted on the sly. Grandpas don't get it. Grandpas almost to a man say they prefer the kids when they are old enough to talk and to listen, not yet so old they turn away in boredom. But we old women, we who will never again come first in any heart, and some of us who never have, we feel adoring thanks for new arrivals to precede us once more in our own hearts.

'Hello, Janie? Do you remember when I was going on a while ago about babies and de Beauvoir and all that stuff? Well, I'm calling to say you were absolutely right.'

'Of course I was. I knew you'd come round. A woman can find fulfilment in this life without procreating. I told you so.'

'Oh, no, no, it's not that. I'm not calling about that. To hell with fulfilment, Janie. Fulfilment is a dead end. I'm calling to let you know you were right. Oh yes, you were right and how! I really am a silly old granny. Yippee!'

A Good Granny's Voice: Jane Fearnley-Whittingstall

Safe to say, there is not and has never been a little girl anywhere who wants more than anything to be a granny when she grows up. Grannying is one ambition and one supreme joy that belong to later life.

Jane Fearnley-Whittingstall is a granny par excellence, author of The Good Granny Guide, *a wise and best-selling compendium for the perpetual brigade of new and old grannies. However, even Jane was not planning to be a granny in her youth. Professionally, she is a garden designer, having studied landscape architecture, albeit only when she was in her late thirties and her two children were at school full time. The qualities that make Jane a good granny to her four natural grandsons and one fostered granddaughter also make her a delightful companion for adults: she has a roving mind, a quick laugh, and that irresistible spark of irreverence children adore in grown-ups, and grown-ups with any sense rejoice to find in each other.*

Help the Aged asked me to look at a post-tsunami restoration project in India and talk to the little old grannies they had been helping. And I saw these gnarled little old women and I thought they must be ninety if a day and they turned out to be younger than me. Such is the harshness of their life. I am a mere sixty-eight, you know. And upstaged by my son (*she laughs*). My son is famous. Sometimes I am asked to do interviews on television and they don't want to hear about me at all, they want me to come on and talk about Hugh, my son, the celebrity chef! Ah well, we all need a good recipe for humble pie in our cookery books!

The idea for *The Good Granny Guide* just popped into my head. And I asked my husband and the children about it, and they all said it was such a good idea, I had to do it. I found that in America there are umpteen guides to grandparenting, but nothing here at all. So I thought: Hurray! Here's a gap I can jump into. A lot of inspiration came from reminiscing about my two grannies, who were chalk and cheese: one a rich lady from the English countryside, and the other a tough, leathery, ex-Indian Army wife with a tiny flat in London. My own mother never saw much of her children when they were little; she and my father were living abroad. She was sad not to have the chance to be a proper granny as she loved children. Of course the role has changed; grannies can be very, very busy women nowadays. I feel a little guilt from time to time when I cannot follow my own good advice. It is an irony that I am too busy writing about being a good granny to get in there and do the good granny stuff.

I think about getting old a lot; I dread infirmity. I find all the trivial aches and pains very tiresome, the twinges of arthritis; I haven't had any new joints but no doubt there will come a time when I need them; my mother was practically bionic. Towards the end of her life she lived with us and I watched her becoming infirm. So I think a lot about ageing and about dying; I wonder how much longer I've got. Ten more years would not be unreasonable and, as the average age is going up and up, perhaps another five or ten after that. Discounting, of course, falling under a bus. When my husband and I are not going to seventieth birthday parties, or eightieth, or even the odd ninetieth, we're going to funerals. I'm not being gloomy. I love a funeral, I really do; they are the best kind of party, better than a wedding any day! There's something about going to the church or wherever the funeral takes place – it can be anywhere nowadays, like weddings – and you feel sad. You weep, and then you go and have a few drinks. You probably know more people at the funeral than at a wedding because there isn't that 'other lot' where you don't know any of them; you also probably see people you haven't seen for years and you're really, really pleased to see them, once. And then you wait a few years until the next funeral. Also, there is usually good music and often good speeches in celebration of someone whose life has joined you all together. Only the funerals of the young are utterly tragic. I've often thought that if I were down and out and couldn't afford to eat, I would look up in a daily paper where a good funeral would be, shuffle along to it, and then shuffle along to the reception afterwards. And if anyone said to me, 'How do you know the deceased?' I might say, 'I was at school with his sister.' Or perhaps I would just say (*in a tone of outrage*): 'You mean you don't know who I am?'

I was thinking about the wearing of purple and scarves flying in old age. And it seems to me that however old you get, there will always be someone you don't want to embarrass; I know my grandchildren wouldn't give a damn if I turned up wearing purple and pink dreadlocks and whatever wildness. But my children! They would say to each other: 'Oh my, look at Mum! She's losing it, poor old Mum!' So old ladies are never going to have fun with the purple unless they are the so-called glamour grannies who have worn purple all their lives and embarrassed their own children with it, too. It is surprising how many women I found while researching the book who said, of their own mothers, that they were terrible at mothering but wonderful grannies.

Grandchildren allow us to reinvent ourselves: you can boast to them and tell them what a helluva girl you were; your children would know that was a fiction but the little ones are happy to listen. Sometimes I stand in front of the mirror and pull back the floppy bits and think: Oh yes, that would look a little better . . . And then I think how much it would cost, how uncomfortable it would be, and the bruises! As for contact lenses, I couldn't bear to stick my fingers in my eyes every morning before breakfast. And most of all, the damage to my principles: it is against my principles to try to look younger. Laughter lines are honourable; plenty of laughter lines are good. So why not call them all laughter lines?

The mother's mother is number-one granny and always will be. Even if you don't get on with your daughter, unless you live in another country you are the one she will come to. I get letter from young women sometimes, complaining that their mothers-in-law always want to be with the grandchildren. 'Why doesn't she get a life?' they ask. Where, I wonder, do they expect a woman of Granny's age to get one? My parents divorced when they were in their late sixties. That was fine for my father who had another wife lined up. But my mother couldn't start a new life aged sixty-seven. Whenever I think about being old, I think I do not want to be a nuisance to my children. I don't want them ever to say: 'What are we going to do about Mum?' If Robert, my husband, died, I would be very lonely. Even a couple of days on my own, when I come down to London from where we live in the country, are never as much fun as I expect them to be. I could not go out looking for another man at this stage in my life, I'm not interested. You get so used to someone, to the one who becomes a habit that you don't want to fix. I would miss the little jokes and routine. I know I would not eat properly; I would have Marmite sandwiches all the time and doughnuts. And by the by, have I mentioned I am working now on *The Good Granny's Cookbook*?

Pessimism about the world is a symptom of old age. The aged always think the younger generation is more depressing and worse behaved than their own generation or even their children's. And yes, I am appalled by the general yobbishness of young people, teenagers (*laughs*), in fact, anyone under forty! Everyone complains about their bad manners and how they don't get out of the way on the pavement. Well, I don't get out of their way any more; I stand right there and wait for them to go around me. Ageism makes us invisible; it is depressing. And their reliance on technology leading to non-communication is the new thing connected to another disappointment: the children's books and stories I loved and thought I would enjoy reading to my grandchildren. One of the pleasures of life, reading to grandchildren! But they are so bombarded these days by flashy images, their attention span has shrunk. They are so bored by the books we loved! I haven't even dared try them on *The Secret Garden*, one of my all-time favourites, in case they turn away, yawning. I think it is because of telly that they only like things in bright, strident colours now; anything low-key they will not sit still for.

The upsides to growing old? Well, there is time to learn something new; it's not easy when you're old, yet it is fun to try. Painting, for example, is something I like to do and have to learn. Robert and I have got to a stage where we both like to travel to new places, too, not radical travelling, just hopping on a plane for Bruges or Milan. But now that we are never going to get to South America, and Australia is too far, we probably won't bother. We are making a list of priority places we really, really must go to before we run out of time. Istanbul is top of the list right now. Otherwise, there's not much good about old age that springs to mind.

Nothing is better than this wonderful new love affair with your grandchildren, even multiple love affairs; just when you were expecting not to have another love ever in your life, you get the same sort of butterflies fluttering when you are going to see a grandchild as you used to get when going to see a lover. It is just wonderful! Say that to any man of my age and he will think you are barmy. And obviously there must be a few women who are not natural grandmothers and don't get this feeling. But most of us do. And, oh, the sheer delight of it!

8

Old Friends

W E ARE BORN without words but not without dreams and questions. Even before the foetus emerges to take its first breath, whenever the pregnant woman feels it fall asleep within her she feels its dreams too, throbbing and wondering under her ribcage. The newborn's first friend on earth is a soft toy or even just the chewy end of a blanket, which has nothing to say for itself either. To this inanimate proto-friend are entrusted emotions that arrive long before words.

When I was growing up we girls were more than just allowed the impulses of our difference from the boys; we were encouraged and even commanded to elaborate on them in aid of matrimony and procreation. Watch children in a playground now and you will see not much has changed: girls play with girls, boys with boys, their intersexual exchanges teasing and mildly aggressive on both sides. To this day a little girl soon singles out one special friend: her best friend, the successor to her teddy bear. It is to this chosen one she spills secrets and compares notes on the other girls, on teachers, parents, and in due course on sex and boys. To lack confidantes is to be a lone outsider for a girl; to have friends with no best one among them is to be a lone insider. And this is true right to the end, just as it is that boys need companions-in-arms as well as at play.

Recently a body of psycho-researchers in America went around draping microphones on hundreds of young people in order to listen in to their chat. It beats me why a seat at the rear of any urban bus would not have served as well. The expert conclusion was that, word for word, young women nowadays talk no more, even a little less, than young men; or, at least, that girls talk less when wearing mikes. Precisely what the kids talked about was not part of the brief.

However, yet another bunch of professional eavesdroppers later researched topics discussed by anglophone adolescents; they deduced that the enduring feminine propensity to discuss with friends our woes and inner workings serves only to exacerbate depression. Presumably the busybodies would prescribe mood-changing drugs and recourse to professionals such as themselves, as if to feel bad periodically were not absolutely essential to feeling better in the long run. And did they consider, I wonder, why the suicide rate remains higher among young men? And the murder rate?

To talk about our troubles with friends, and to gossip about the behaviour of others, is one way we women learned to keep our eyes open to the world around us and to resist the total domination of our hearts and minds; it has helped us compile the dos and don'ts that kept caves and campsites, homes, children, and the eternal mundane shooting match in running order. Besides, a life fully lived is a drama, too, and dramas need an audience lest they descend into delusion and illness. The tragedienne, while she expresses her unhappiness, feels a little better if only by being in a dramatically worse predicament than her listeners and arousing their sympathy, possibly their envy. Boys, meanwhile, continue to build teams and put team-mates before friendship, and to keep secrets en masse, team from team, business from business, nation from nation.

Both systems of intimacy, male and female, encourage well-being, yet both invite treachery, too, especially in youth when we are bursting with the hopes and secrets so susceptible to betrayal. Come extreme age and we move beyond fame or defamation, so our darkest secrets are no longer of general interest and, anyhow, we maundering old gits are always spilling our own beans without any help; or, if we have achieved the slightest renown, some vulturine biographer will do it for us after we have joined the skeletons in our closets.

My first best friend was Dujy Renbern, so called by everyone thanks to a game, 'name-agrams', invented by my mother. Mercifully, 'Turkz Armi' did not stick to me except in my memory. Both dark-eyed and skinny, Dujy and I were sisters by choice from the moment we tangled on a climbing-frame in kindergarten. We remained best friends for the next six years, forming the axis of a circle of girls who took lunch together every school day, exchanged homework, and giggled about boys. Then one Monday morning, Miss Carnes, our teacher, announces out of the blue I am to represent the school in a national oratorical contest, a terrifying prospect that makes me tremble. The lunch-hour arrives at last; I enter the big cafeteria and pass along the counter, collecting the usual sandwich and container of milk. Dujy is already installed with our group at the usual table and as usual I make straight for them, eager for their company and encouragement. Dujy, seeing me, shouts into the room: 'Don't you dare sit here! Teacher's pet! We don't like you any more!'

I see now the milk slopping onto my green metal tray and feel again shock, then confusion, as she turns to whisper to Evelyn Lipton and they laugh together. On the spot I know that Evelyn is Dujy's best friend now. And I have my first best enemy.

'The little fool is jealous,' my mother said when she found me sobbing in my room that night.

'But why? Why?'

'She envies you,' Mother said.

'But why? Why envy me?'

Mother gave me her tilted little smile. Of course! Dujy envied me my mother. Dujy was jealous because I had a mother who ran a weekly 'Story Hour' at our local community centre, a mother who made up games like 'name-agrams', and told us really scary M.R. James ghost stories. What had I done to deserve such a mother?

Envy is childish. And it hurts; as it roars into full-blown jealousy it is no more agonising to its object than to the one who feels it within her, blazing around what she fears is her own failure. Envy is thick as a brick. The stupefied girl can persuade herself the other has stolen the honour, the high marks, the approbation, wit, or curls and curves that are rightly her own. Once she has first deluded herself the other is guilty of this impossible crime, she can then bitch about her to others and despise her publicly as she would a common thief. Alas, envy is the sisterly vice. It is a delusion of the harem that thrives in small places with restricted aims. I think — I hope — it is not as widespread or as virulent now among young women as it still can be among friends of my generation, born to ideals of feminine perfection a lot more numerous and constraining than today's coveted size zero.

Nearly sixty years after my last lunch with Dujy, Mother and I sat beside the swimming pool at her retirement community. She was never athletic or physically energetic, and now in the lethargy of her eighth decade, it was a job to persuade my mother to join me on a gentle stroll to the pool. She sat in a deckchair and watched her coevals paddle dutifully back and forth, their combined age rivalling that of a nation. Conversations between Mother and me in her final widowed years were composed mainly of brief questions and even briefer answers about old friends and neighbours.

'So tell me, Mome, how is Marcia?'

Marcia, still a supple figure well into her seventies, worked out every day and could be admired on warm mornings as she swam laps of the community pool.

'Oh yes, Mar-see-ya.' Mother mocked her friendly neighbour's preferred pronunciation.

'What an extraordinary person,' I said. 'Still so trim and fit. I haven't seen her this visit. I guess she'll be turning up at the pool any minute now.'

'Now that would be a miracle,' said Mother.

Her snort and chuckle told of a lifetime bereft of its youthful promise.

'Mar-see-ya died last month. That's where swimming got your 'extra-ordinary' Mar-see-ya.'

And thus do envy and jealousy snarl and shrivel into senescent *schadenfreude*.

Thirty or so years ago two old friends and I crossed the cusp of menopause together, all of us single in a mostly married or remarried crowd of coevals. I alone had a child, a son who was bound as sons still are to take care of a younger woman some day, not his old Mum. Our trio had weathered the ups and downs of youth, survived our smug disapproval of one another's choices, and emerged from the long periods of cold silence that followed disagreements. One day in conversation we decided that, rather than ever go alone into care, as soon as we felt age leaning hard on us we would pool our assets and make a jolly shelter together, each with rooms and preferably an entrance, too, of her own. It was a good idea. In principle. Communal ideas are always good. In principle. I have seen a number of old women friends follow a similar plan, especially in small seaside retirement communities. And it ends in tears. The bossiness, ingrained opinions, and habits that make old women useful grannies in the nursery, and competent carers for ailing older husbands, do not suit us to live with each other. Deprived of family and purpose, of hugs and smiles, with nobody on hand to blame for our unhappiness, we all too easily blame one another. Would it have worked with me and my two old friends? I cannot know. They died within a decade of each other, long before we could try to beat the odds.

My family was not endowed for friendship. There were never guests at our table, except my paternal uncles who brought their wives and children for the occasional summer Sunday at our house in the country. My father was born in an elective ghetto of downtown New York just as the twentieth century began; big brother to seven siblings, he had neither leisure time nor a facility for games; least of all had he trust to spare for other tribes. In general, the first generation of immigrant families are not gregarious or relaxed outside their own home and streets.

Mother on the other hand, a second-generation American, grew up a solitary and fatherless child in the deepest Diaspora of the American Midwest. Before the Great Depression and the Second World War, the Ku Klux Klan had power in the American heartland, with elected officials in many towns and an appointed judge in the Supreme Court; they were the bogeymen of Mother's childhood. Being Jews in such a place was a dark secret best kept within her aloof little family. One day, standing on tiptoes, Mother peeked out from behind the shutters to watch a parade of local Klansmen through town. She never forgot the terror and grief she felt upon recognising the brand-new, patent-leather shoes of her best friend from school, skipping alongside the marching feet of the giants, and swathed like the others in a white sheet. After that, my mother cared little for friends; she trusted only admirers.

My brother, the doctor, has always been well liked by his coterie of companions at school and at play, and later at work, though I recollect no best friend, not by my exacting feminine standards. Medicine is not a notably convivial profession; wary and independent colleagues must engage with patients from whom distance must be maintained. From the early days it was I, the tail-wagger of our litter, who was born to solicit friends promiscuously, as I do to this day, although no longer at such great risk now of being savaged by the occasional envious bitch. Who envies a woman in her seventies? Except just possibly a woman in her eighties.

Half a century or so ago when the earth was mysterious and practically boundless to a youngster, overseas travel was no ordinary holiday. Even if the voyage had to be undertaken in fear or hunger, to cross water was always an adventure and a hopeful odyssey. For me and my classmates at university in 1950s America, a summer tour abroad between college semesters also constituted a bargain-basement dollop of posh. Two months travelling around Paris, London, Venice, Rome, and Switzerland was considered edifying for an American girl, civilising even, and it moved her up a notch in a marriage market overstocked with females barely a decade after the Second World War. When I was eighteen and had finally saved enough money, I booked a summer jaunt to Europe with a group called Study Abroad. My best friend, Marjie, had already been on the tour and I was able to assure my worried father that she recommended it as very educational. I did not tell him Marjie also said the tour leader, an Englishman called Tony, was gorgeous; nor did I mention her warning that Italian men pinched. And, oh yes, Marjie said to pack plenty of tampons as Europeans had not yet invented them.

Crossing water must bring risks; once in a while there will be a footloose fluke like me who returns home from abroad with no desire except to sail away again and again, if not for ever. A few months after I came back starry-eyed and emboldened from Study Abroad, I sat alone in thin sunlight on a bench in the green around my college; I was dreaming of the boulevards of Paris that in my new geography led straight to art and every earthly joy. Marjie passed with a group of classmates. She nodded towards me.

'Everything she has,' Marjie said, pointing at me and loud enough for me to hear, 'she got from me.'

What had I? I had nothing. I could not play the piano as she could; my cheques, had I possessed a chequebook, would not be written on Daddy's bank as hers were. I had no big sisters, no Kandinsky on my wall; I did not see myself as being as pretty as she, either. Nevertheless, not long after my return from the same European tour Marjie had taken the previous summer, she flounced out of the digs we shared and never again spoke another word to me. I had no idea why. Surely her rancour was due to something more important than the snap-shot of tour guide Tony in front of Notre Dame de Paris with his arm around my shoulders? Had she not noticed that the Englishman was homosexual, for goodness sakes? What had I done? What did she imagine I had stolen from her? I never learned why I lost her as a friend. However, what I did learn then, painfully, is that friendships belong to their seasons and places. Flying the coop, as I was bound to do, entails leaving old friends behind. Even now with emails and instantaneous imaging that can span great distances, moving in space and in time, too, attenuates friendly ties and often gently breaks them.

'You could write your life story in friends,' said my friend Janie. 'Use a friend for each chapter. And when you get to me, make the chapter sexy.'

'Why not dentists? I've had plenty of them, too. Good and bad. And sexy . . .'

Memory slapped frivolity down; I felt my father's white coat stiff against my cheek, heard the racket of his dental drill, unstop-pable as time, making it impossible either to speak to him or to listen.

'How about hairdressers?' said Janie, who is not yet sixty and blonde. Again. 'My best hairdressers have all been men.'

'My best dentists, too. But not my best friends.'

Sex is fun; if it weren't fun why would anyone undertake such ungainly manoeuvres more than once a year or so and only to make another baby? Sex can be comforting, it can be profitable, it can be safe or dangerous, passionate or dutiful, and heterosexual intercourse continues at least for a while to be necessary to procreation. But friendly? Sex ain't friendly. Not the way we do it and we do it the best way we can. For lads, the deed will hold elements of triumph until they feel the weaknesses of old age, after which they rise from each encounter relieved at having got away with it one more time. Triumph and later relief: are these not emotions that pertain to armed combat rather than to what my generation called 'making love'?

Sexually liberated young women still crave exclusivity and devotion, though rarely nowadays referring to it as 'marriage' and never 'wedlock'; in the chilled sweet-talk now current, it is 'a partnership' they hanker for. An increasing number of girls write in to agony aunts to say they have had sex with no strings attached, just for comfort, with a man they still call 'my best friend'; so why, why, they want to know, does it hurt so much to learn that the 'best friend' is having sex with others, or, worse yet, with one other? Why not? I ask them. Nothing we have, whether it is sex or a slice of cake, can last longer than the having of it. We can always hope, however, and be seen to hope, that whatever we make, especially love, will last. Girls, when they find themselves falling for a long-time man friend, ask agony aunts whether having sex with him will destroy the friendship. What can I say to them except, yes, having sex together could well start something else, but it will certainly destroy what my correspondents still call being 'just' friends.

A declaration of love – known as 'commitment' in the fashionable obfuscation of the 'L' word – is one deal in which possession counts for more than nine-tenths of the law. In love, possession counts for keeps. I realised that about four decades ago while working on a story in an American city where I bumped into a man I had known in London. After a drink or two, both of us being fancy-free at the time, we went to bed together, something that young women had recently started to do just for comfort, even out of charity.

'You know,' I told him in the smoky afterglow, 'I see a lot of Tessa back in London. We're good friends.'

He and Tessa had separated in bitterness and boredom many years earlier.

'Oh?' he said and nodded towards the bedside phone. 'I could change that with one call.'

He was right. It had been my rule never to sleep with the husbands and lovers of friends; and I knew on the spot I must never sleep with their exes either. Was that why the liberated sisters of the 1970s tried to poach one another's boyfriends? So it was reported to me in high amusement by more than one of my lovers back then. Did the sisterhood want to demolish all the old restrictive rules, including those of fidelity and friendship? Or was it no more than the competitive urge of the seraglio?

'So you think friendship is not possible between a man and a woman?' said Janie in here-we-go-again mode, bordering on low dudgeon.

'Possible? Sure. More possible now than ever before. The sexes are starting now to make friendly alliances at last in the boardroom, in the surgery, and at the front of the shop, because both sexes are paid equally – well, almost equally – to work for the same goals. But friendship remains problematical in the bedroom where goals are not clear and certainly not always mutual.'

Janie, who sees it her concerned duty to keep me skipping rope, said: 'Don't be old-fashioned.'

Am I old-fashioned? Does it matter? Anyone who has been around as long as I have must have noticed old fashions circulating again as regularly as skirt lengths. In my youth pop music and movies used to spread thickly the message there is one man on earth for one woman, and by definition vice versa.

It is an idea that continues, if a tad diluted, in lyrics and fiction nowadays. Our movies were less sexually explicit back then, ending in the first, closed-mouth and tongueless kiss with the heroine's one and only hero, her rescuer, who was always handsome, but never younger or shorter than she. What else is new? What else is old? Some of us have always been too bright, too romantic even, to fall for that corny myth. We dreamed of creative and powerful soulmates who would support us in every way – superb lovers, poets, philosophers, and artists – who would be older, of course, and taller than we. Each of us tried to make of herself the one and only heroine her one and only hero would love on sight and for all eternity. On the faces of other renegade women of my generation who never paired off, or not for long, I glimpse sometimes the wan smile of disappointment and anger that I felt in my late fifties when I woke up alone one morning and knew I was going to be alone thereafter. Prince Charming had not found me nor would he in time for the last act. The gallivanting idiot! The self-centred jerk! Had he imagined we would live for ever?

Divorce was uncommon in my childhood. If any of my classmates came from broken homes, they did not mention it. There had just been a world war; missing daddies were a tragic commonplace. The fact that more marriages lasted in the old days does not mean they were happy, not by a long shot. Nobody knows how many unions then endured in hostility, even abuse, which modern Western women need no longer tolerate, morally or financially.

Friendships are built around imperfections, shared or accepted; 'love affairs', even when called 'relationships', depend on high hopes and hot desire; marriage requires respect, balance, and compromise. When a marriage survives the cooling of ardour and carries on over ups and downs, it is called, in demotic market-speech, 'making the marriage work', something that happens often enough to suggest we really are nesting critters at heart. Our males especially may find marital fidelity a chore; however, it is one that the greater number manage to fulfil. Most husbands stay faithful out of concern and courtesy, or in obedience to their religion. A working marriage is an admirable accomplishment that remains a superior retirement plan for both sexes. There is undeniable romance, too, about old couples who finally have become close friends, so perfectly mutual in experience and outlook the survivor will be mortally diminished by the death of the other.

'Friendship between the sexes seems to be possible only after the sex is kaput or when it is switched on like a low-wattage night light to aid fading eyesight; ideally without blowing a fuse.'

'Watch out! Gerry is my best friend,' Janie said defensively.

'Really? Your best friend? And tell me, if you came home and found him in bed with your neighbour, what would you do?'

'I'd kill him!'

Shared gigling is a raucous delight of women's friendships.

'Anyhow,' Janie said and giggled again, 'our neighbour's a bloke. I guess you'd agree that gay men are the only ones young women can have as just friends?'

I shook my head.

A novel on the imagined shelf of my imaginary collected works is entitled *Fag Hags: A Tale of Will and Grace Under Stress*. Back in the 1950s when intellectual curiosity was not respected as a feminine virtue outside the sexually segregated lecture halls and classrooms of our university, we closet-swots had to wear camouflage if we hoped to be asked out by boys or invited to fraternity parties at Harvard, Yale, Princeton, West Point, and similar all-male enclaves of the highest education. A few girls who, like me, were hiding their eccentric wit and irregular ambitions, stumbled upon men in hiding back then too, and befriended them. Don-Don and I came from the same small city across the river from Manhattan; we had known each other in childhood, though only slightly as he was two crucial years older. When we met again at Columbia University, Don-Don was already established as a scholar and poet, and, more discreetly, as a homosexual. We became steadfast friends and for a brief time I was obsessively in love with him. To fall in love with a friendly homosexual is to this day an error made by clever girls who will ignore the evidence and continue to hope that their brains can be sexual attributes as desirable to Mr Right as their tits.

In his last year Don-Don won a fellowship to Cambridge University where, awestruck and breathless, I visited him once. By the time I came to live in London in the late 1960s, he had been employed there for several years, gainfully and cynically, as a copywriter in an ad agency. To spend the occasional evening with my old friend was ever a delight; conversations soared, boosted by drinks or a joint and once or twice a tab of early LSD. Meanwhile, I made many new friends, too, among the Brits; I fell in and out of love, travelled, wrote a book or two, bought a house, and finally gave birth to my son. Not long afterwards, Don-Don returned to America to care for his ailing mother who had retired long before to a backwater community of the Deep South. After she died he stayed on in her anonymous little house. This was pre-email, so we wrote letters or telephoned; I visited twice. After a while, his replies to my calls became infrequent, then chilly, and suddenly they ceased. Between us lay a bleak neglect, mysteriously hostile. I erased his name from my passport as the one to notify in case of trouble. Decades passed.

And then a year ago I was home alone one evening when Prokofiev's *Lieutenant Kijé* suite came marching out of the radio. I had heard it first sitting with Don-Don on the floor of my student flat in Manhattan. Its wry and frisky cadences delivered the memory of my old friend as only music can. He was there. We were there. Don–Don, I asked him, is art dead? Don–Don, must every success now attach to fame in order to be true? Don–Don, you used to say God did not exist, not yet; mankind, you said, was in the process of making Him. But all we care to make these days is money. Don–Don, do we adore gold now instead of the sun? Are we so proud of the vehicle we drive we take no more pride in the journey? Don–Don, you used to say drugs are what we take them for. Too many aspirins, you said, bring on a headache. Does that mean flight and futility are the common destiny? What do you think, Don–Don? Tell me, my dear, my first, my oldest friend.

Without hesitation or thought, I riffled through the Rolodex; there in fading ink was his number in Florida.

'Hello?' came the familiar querulous greeting.

'Hello, Don–Don.'

'Who's that?'

'It's me. It's Irma . . .'

No shot has ever resounded more sharply than the click of his receiver; there is no silence as suffocating as the one that ensued. It is the silence of two graves.

I am not a scientist, nor even a galloping pollster, merely an old woman on a tight schedule. Retrospect is central to wisdom; to remember is as close as a human can come to seeing in the round. Long-term observation in pursuit of general truths will always find exceptions, too. And yes, by being exceptional, they do help prove the rule. From experience and observation, I conclude that friendship between a heterosexual woman and a gay man does not stand more of a chance than friendship with a straight man, not while we are young or youngish. Rejected as an object of desire, not equipped to be his playmate in nocturnal games, too disparate for the healing exchange of secrets and opinions that defines friendship for women, a woman must find herself cast in one of the roles that his history has designed for the female. Willy-nilly, she will play for him the part of a spoiled sister who pulled the blokes and had it easy. Or she will be the glamorous, promiscuous auntie whom he worships, and worship will ever be the furthest cry from friendship, further even than envy. Or she will be kept in the wings, as I have been often, to understudy the mother he was born to disappoint. Unless connected by a mutual passion for art or business beyond their mere selves, she will be dumped by the gay man, or she will dump him. It still does happen that a homosexual man and a heterosexual woman – both immensely world-weary and one of them, probably the woman, immensely rich or celebrated and a good deal older – marry each other, their eyes wide open, to travel along together, discreet, respectful, and tolerant to the end. That classic if rare bohemian route to friendship between the sexes seems in the process of being overtaken in liberal societies by gay marriages. A good thing? A bad thing? Just another small lost thing.

Some aged do cling for dear life to the things that remain; however, by and large we also become much less acquisitive for new things, even those of us who can afford them. These days I shop for the old girl I am, no longer for a hopeful fiction that includes scintillating dinner guests and invitations to the ball, and never again for the vamp whose silks, bought and paid for on impulse, hang unworn in every younger woman's wardrobe until Oxfam receives them. Most of the objects around us and in our cupboards carry the memory of a friend and a time that is dead or has drifted away. The cup I washed a minute ago is emblazoned with the words: 'Norman! London's Rudest Landlord.' That dear curmudgeon, now retired, gave them to his favourites at Christmas over the years. I have five; a sixth was broken when I moved flats. It was at the corner of his bar I made my best London friends: all gone now. This cardigan I wear? I bought it in Scotland almost thirty years ago when my son, his father, and

I took my parents on a trip to the Isle of Mull where the wind blew waterfalls in its path up over slopes and mountains. And my great-grandmother, 'Gay Gammaw', carried the vase at my elbow to America from her homeland, Transylvania, now probably Hungary; her father, she told me, used to carve the crucifixes placed at crossroads, a job for a Jew because, in the European hinterlands of the early nineteenth century, it was considered irreverent for a Gentile. We grow old in museums of ourselves. Take us from the memorabilia of a lifetime, put us into a new room bereft of our relics, furnished efficiently and impersonally by strangers, and we can fade – even die of homesickness.

Travellers between nations, jobs, or social classes, and we who are travelling deep in time, had better make new friends along the way. Otherwise, should the natives be hostile, we are sunk. This region of the aged is unpopular territory, despised by the young, and dreaded by those who begin to see its foggy flat-land on their own horizons. We need friends here and it will have to be new ones, for there is a steady solemn tolling under the riffle through Rolodex and Filofax and address books, flimsy indexes to our autobiographies that are being edited ruthlessly by time. Hark, the bell tolls for Rhoda, my last American friend abroad and a sporadic enemy from college days; and for Jill, brave and tormented; for dear Midge, doomed to outlive her damaged child, waving her hat and her rings to ward off immi-nent tragedies; for Liliane, her courage as big as her heart, who loved only women, but not herself; for Jeffrey, the unwise charmer, who went wisely in the end; for life-loving Sandy, and for so many other names in fading ink, gone for ever. It must have been a dozen years or so ago I picked up an English paper discarded by a previous traveller aboard a train, and there, between the business pages and the sport pages, was the obit-uary of a man I had once upon a time been in love with. The train entered a tunnel and in the sudden darkness old age chor-tled in my ear: 'Going, going, gone!'

Thanks to the gallery of old friends collected in a gregarious lifetime, there arises a phenomenon of old age similar to that of proliferating coincidences. I've heard it called 'recognitis' and 'spitting imagery'. Do you see over there, across the park, that tall man with white hair and blue eyes, and a sailor in his heart? He is the spitting image of both the first and the last of my important lovers: bookends on a shelf of romantic paperbacks. Occasionally, and increasingly with age, we come across days and places where we can find ourselves starting towards one old friend after another until they come close enough to reveal themselves as merely spitting images. Recognitis extends to family members, too, if they are long gone or far away. On a visit to Jerusalem recently, at every corner I saw my uncles Max, Abe, and Aaron, as well as my father Isidore, too: handsome and wary, all spitting images of my family that used to be. And, by the by, to a man, they turned out to be Palestinians.

Perhaps it is true as one old friend, a scientist, offers in explanation: there are only so many human physical types on earth and thus after decades of encounters we old folks are bound to arrive at the limit of them, whereupon they start to repeat themselves. But of course faces are also in part our own creations, built from within on inherited frameworks. In the Frick Collection of Manhattan, I came upon a portrait of a French countess by Jacques-Louis David; I gasped and looked again to see the spitting image of an Irish woman, a new arrival in the small community where I once had a flat in France. I would not be at all surprised to learn that David's sloe-eyed old countess fomented discontent within a walled city, too, and a festering mistrust among its inhabitants that helped persuade some, like me, to move closer to the sea.

It seems that an unconventional investment in youth can pay off in old age after all. In the conventional frame of things, by now I should be one of the legion of old ladies shuffling along the supermarket aisles, using my trolley as a Zimmer frame, while I take, replace, and take again the smallest possible amounts of what I can afford: not really shopping, not really caring, just killing time before it turns on me. All of us who grow old wake sometimes in mourning for that friend we loved, our younger self. I am sometimes lonely for the woman I used to know, the one I used to be. But I am not lonely for company. My new friends are mostly a lot younger than I. Well, they would have to be, wouldn't they? With each day that passes more people are younger than me and fewer are older. One good friend now was my son's babysitter when she was eighteen. Some new friends I seduced into conversations on the street, in a gallery, or in a bookshop. The workplace is also a good source of friendships with young and younger people, giving us old-timers who cannot or will not retire an insurance policy more effective against loneliness than against inflation. No man would fancy me now – certainly not one who was himself the least bit fanciable – and thus I count more men among my easygoing companions today than there ever were in my sexy past. In the main my young and youngish friends of both sexes now are left-footers, mostly unmarried, arty, or loners, but then my best friends always have been. And so have I.

Envy, that nasty despoiler of friendship, is kaput at last. Nobody envies an old woman except for a few of her coevals, stuck in time and still fishing for compliments. As for retrospective envy of what an old lady used to be and the adventurous life she led, is that not one definition of admiration? Admiration is not friendship; it is, however, an opening in which friendship can sprout, as long as an old-timer is not too proud to risk a few weeds in the garden. Listening to old voices and seeing what is happening around me in this new country of old age, I have been amazed how frequently it can happen that, even though our families may be few or far away, and our old friends dead, a young man or woman can attach themselves freely to a much older person, whether man or woman. It is usually someone who retains wisdom, a special knowledge, perhaps a love of music, and sometimes an indomitable ambition. One example is the veteran of Monte Cassino, far into his eighties, organising his memoirs at last with the help of a young enthusiast not half his age; another is a centenarian, nearly blind, dictating her bimonthly column for a local paper to a devoted amanuensis who loves her sizzling wit and idealism; yet another is a retired doctor in his eighties, childless, and a widower, sharing his small flat, meals, and evenings at the opera with a beautiful young musician who enjoys his company. These relationships are what the French call 'in all simplicity': platonic and respectful. Often the younger person is the child of a long-gone old friend. Sometimes these unorthodox young 'carers' receive a salary. Why not? Nevertheless, such intergenerational unions, albeit rare, are an emergent kind of friendship, one that bridges the decades with mutual interests, affection, and respect.

Every so often I catch a glint of anxiety in the eyes of a young friend watching me – have I repeated myself? Are my shoulders slumping? Has my back begun to hump? Have I lost the thread? Run out of steam? Have I crossed wonky old wires? But I am not yet a burden to my friends; I walk, I pay my way, I take note of what is, not simply recollect how it used to be. When that all ceases to be true and I grow decrepit, younger friends will fall away, I know, and finally I will be left, as we all are eventually: in big communities, with the occasional visit from my busy offspring, strangers, and a friend or two.

I have a new view now from a new window. The vista is high and wide over this splendid city with its ancient neighbourhoods, old flavours, street markets, greens, cemeteries and church spires. And yes, on its horizon I see a thousand tall and spindly cranes poised to make a meal of it. My possessions are out of storage at last; however, I have not quite taken possession of this, my new place. I am not entirely at home yet. When I went back for a look at the old place, barely a mile away, where I lived for two decades and which I left barely six months ago, I strolled around, already invisible and estranged. I am not yet here or there.

The caretaker of the building where I have my new studio-flat comes from the Côte d'Ivoire; his sparkling wisdom is the brighter aspect of a grim national inheritance.

'And how long did you live in your last place?' he asked me while courteously holding open the heavy lift door.

'Twenty years,' I told him.

'Ah,' he said as the metal grating closed, its antique clatter dating, like the building, and like me, from the 1930s. 'You are between lives.'

Between lives: the words induce that bitter-sweet, senescent melancholy so similar to nostalgia – nostalgic for a future, for all the time in the world. Never before have I taken the keys to a place of my own without a mother in my life. Nor have I ever before furnished my room with one single bed; sensible old ladies travel free of a hope-chest. Never again will I have rooms to spare; never again will I cook for friends; never again tend a garden into maturity, never will I close my own door behind me and climb my own stairs to my own rooms under my own roof. So what will I do in this new life and new space? I will remember. I will repeat myself, saying old things in a new way, saying new things drawn from aged perception. I will read and reread books; I will hear music again as for the first time; I will meet strangers and make new friends among them. I will watch my new view and mark how it, too, changes with the seasons.

Between lives: yes, I am between my last life and what will be my last life.

I am a last-time buyer.

A Grumpy Old Voice: Norman Balon

I call Norman Balon my old friend in spite of knowing he would not like the description; he would not want to be called friendly. Simply growing old does not make us lovable. Norman certainly would not want his many discreet acts of kindness catalogued or mentioned. Norman is eighty years old; his generation of males were raised to guard their emotions and many of them, like him, developed spikes, sharp and bristling. For more than sixty years he was landlord of the Coach and Horses pub in central London: 'London's rudest landlord' as the sign outside warned passers-by. His keynote phrase, 'You're barred, you bastard,' was often heard, delivered in an ineffable growl.

In grumpiness Norman was early on in rehearsal for one classic permutation of old age: he was set to be a curmudgeon. After Norman inherited the pub, it soon became a legendary watering hole for bohemians, artists, and actors, the setting for Jeffrey Bernard's 'Low Life' columns and the subsequent West End play by Keith Waterhouse, Jeffrey Bernard is Unwell. *Until Norman's mother died in her nineties, she used to sit at the bar, counting and stacking coins from the nightly take. Retired voluntarily and only recently, Norman cannot tear himself away from Soho and its hang-outs. He can be found most days playing obscure continental card games with cronies and keeping a beady eye on the new managers of the Coach and Horses, renamed Norman's, presumably to cash in on its erstwhile bohemian fame.*

Old is not a dirty word. Getting old is coming to terms with the fact that you're going to die soon. I had a fantastic life; I don't object to dying. Why should I? I get respect from everybody here in Soho. Everybody calls me Norman; most people call me Mr Norman. I accept it. I don't suppose I deserve it. I was always a lazy bastard. Sixty years ago I was working for my father and Soho was run by gangs. Underground drug-taking has increased enormously, which I frown on, but I believe where there is a demand there will always be a supply. That makes me cynical. I have always been a cynical bastard.

Nothing gets better. Everything has always been the same. No. No. No. A few things get better. Years ago people used to bring their children to Soho and make them stand outside the pub while they came in to have a drink. I would serve those bastards only one drink. But you don't see children outside pubs any more. And people are better dressed than they used to be. And despite the government scares, people are a lot healthier than they used to be. They complain that people are obese, and drunk, and one thing or another, but when you went to a cemetery in 1960 and looked around, everyone died about the age of fifty. Now everybody dies at seventy or eighty. I'm eighty and I'm not dead yet. Dying would be a relief; you don't have to get up in the morning; you don't have aches and pains; and you don't know anything about it. To an extent I'm fed up with life. You shouldn't get old. You should die young.

I realised I was old the day I decided to sell the pub. I couldn't run it any more in a satisfactory manner. Everyone said, 'It's a shame you're going. It will never be the same.' Well, things don't regenerate themselves. They wither and die. And my public house was going downhill under my management. And so about a year ago when I decided to sell it, that was the moment I thought I was old. You suddenly realise: Christ, I am old!

I never bowed to anybody in authority; I never had to. I am completely spoiled. And I'm totally selfish. I could always insult people and get away with it. I still can. In that way I am not old. But I find it difficult to find things to do. Despite what they say, people who have retired find it difficult to find things to do. They look forward to retirement and then they die of boredom. I haven't died. But I'm bored.

The benefits of old age? When I cross the road cars stop for me. Your children ask you to babysit. And you have to pretend you want to. I have four grandchildren, two boys and two girls. The respect I get from them is amazing. And from my two sons-in-law too, whom I have put in their place once or twice. I have gradually bonded with my grandchildren. But I don't think men look on grandchildren the way women do. No. No. I'm proud when they do well. But . . . I don't know. Maybe I'm peculiar. The lady I live with was thrilled when her daughter had a . . . a . . . a . . . Oh, I don't know, a girl or a boy, it was a baby. I can say babies are a complete waste of time. I can be politically incorrect and that's another benefit of getting old.

I know I'm old when the lady I've lived with for twenty years screams that the television is too loud. In the privacy of my own home I wear a hearing aid. Normal conversation I can hear; television sound was the first thing that went. I like television. I don't know why people run it down. People like to run down everything that's popular. I'm much more tolerant than I used to be. That's getting old. I don't let anything upset me now. But some things haven't changed. I still want instant solutions. I get annoyed when people don't jump to my beck and call. How you get old depends on the kind of life you lived when you were young. I lived a full, interesting life. I used to go to a lot of first nights in the theatre because I knew lots of actors from the pub. But I don't want to go out at night any more. I sit at home watching television. Is that a waste of life? No. No. No. Why should anyone tell me what to do? Why should anyone tell me television is terrible and theatre is good? You get a lot of people saying, keep the old things going; you should not change old buildings; everything old is venerable. Well, I never believed that. Why keep anything just because it's old? Who knows? And who cares? We're all going to be dead in fifty years.

During the latter part of the war I slept once or twice down the tube station. It was very frightening. And I remember hearing Churchill's speeches. What a great feat of oratory! But as for memories in general? Forget 'em! Forget memories! You should never jog backwards. All memories are subjective. I had tremendous opportunities that I didn't bother with. But maybe I'm a one-off; I don't jog backwards. And old friends die. Everyone says, 'Don't you miss Jeffrey Bernard? Don't you miss John le Mesurier? Don't you miss all the people who were your friends?' But I do not look back. Is that wisdom? No. No. No. That's just cussedness. The difference between wisdom and cussedness is a night in jail.

My grandparents had two tobacconist's shops in East Ham. In those days tobacco was sold loose and they used to spray it with water to make it weigh more. I remember a man who came to sell my grandfather a National Cash Register when they first came over to England. In those days we had a little box under the till and it was hard to keep staff honest. Money is the great temptation in every business, big or small. And the man said this machine would cure dishonesty immediately. Why? Because the clerk comes to the till and rings up tuppence and then he has got to put tuppence in the till! And this machine costs twenty quid or something. So my grandfather said: 'And what happens if he just doesn't ring the sale up?'

And my grandfather never bought a cash register. I did without one for years and years in the pub.

I remember a time when a woman never paid for drinks. If the man couldn't afford it, the woman used to slip him the money surreptitiously. Now the woman comes up to the counter and buys the drinks. Women now have no shame. I can't get used to that. I've never let a woman pay in my life. See, I could never have been a judge. Or a liar. I'm too biased in my opinions. I have preconceived notions about what's right and what's wrong. If I had it to do again I'd have a hundred pubs. Not for the money. No. No. No. For the power.

I was bought a computer as my leaving present. I've only recently become computer literate. I'm teaching myself how to use it. If there was anything I couldn't master in the first three minutes, I just lost interest. I still make a lot of mistakes. Email? No. No. No. I never believed in writing letters either. I believe in getting on the telephone and screaming down it. Screaming down a phone gets results.

You know your trouble, Irma? You live in the past, that's your trouble. I see you as a bitter old woman, shrunken and shapeless. No. Not shapeless. Yes, a dried-up woman. Hearing me say that most likely hurt you. Disagree with me if you want to. I like disagreement. I don't agree often. No. No. No. If you agree, there's no conversation. The best thing for conversation is to take the opposite view and it doesn't matter how untenable it is.

Those who complain the most live the longest.

9

Mint Sauce

BEING BEAUTIFUL IS a full-time job. Beauty is employed just to be beautiful and nothing else; before long the brightest young beauty expects no more of herself than to be beautiful, rousing in men the desire for possession and, in plainer women, envy of her gilded cage. Like a gruesome scar, beauty blinds its beholders to everything hidden behind it, and distracts them from anything other than their own reaction to what is before their eyes, especially if they are seeing it in the mirror. Beautiful women want nothing more than to captivate; their looks can bring them fame, lovers, and rich husbands, including a few of their own.

On my imaginary shelf of unwritten books is a compendium titled *Sweeping Generalisations: Notes from Under My Carpet*, in which I would dare say that most great beauties, after they have divorced money a couple of times, attach themselves to younger men as if they were jaunty accessories. They generally make problem mummies, too, demanding and self-centred, terrified to move out of centre stage into an alien and empty darkness. Famous beauties, once they are too old to pursue the education they sacrificed to the crippling demands of their good looks, turn to cultish faiths or causes. Rescuing abandoned animals was a favourite in my day, a last-ditch attempt to give their existence a meaning deeper than that shown them in a tarnished looking-glass. These days, thanks to elective surgery, market-driven fashion, industrial-strength cosmetics, and contact lenses, pretty people of both sexes now are a dime a dozen, too similar to tell apart by those of us outside their own age-group. Poor pretty dears, currently in decline, resort to drink and other addictive painkillers to dull the agonies of time's inexorable disfigurement.

Time takes from us all whatever we possess of sexual attraction, the only physical power women were designed to exercise, for a long time the only one allowed us, and to this day the one any average girl would kill for. Every old woman can remember the turning point on a Saturday night long ago when she showered, dressed, and painted herself as usual, then set out for a party, contriving to arrive neither early nor late. At the threshold she straightened her shoulders, fluffed her hair, her smile, and her mind, inhaled deeply, and entered the crowded room. Everyone in it turned to look at the newcomer in the doorway, then turned back to their noisy companions, and for the first time not a single man, not one, looked back again in lingering appraisal. Unless she arrived with a boyfriend or a husband, she will leave the party on her own, possibly for the first time and pretty much every time thereafter. In a flash it seemed she had lost her allure; overnight she had become a failure.

But not much happens to us overnight, after all. If the young could read the signs ahead as we who are old discern those behind, they would be able to mark the paths to most of what they call their luck. Success and failure, love and heartbreak, inspiration and monotony, too, are part of a life's landscape arranged methodically by nature and the nature of its inhabit-ant. Under the artifice, maybe even in spite of surgical intervention, fading hair, a squishy inch or two, a hint of a crease beside the mouth, and the dimming of a woman's allure accumulates, as does the loss of sexual prowess among men, gathering like symptoms of flu before the first sneeze.

Even the most eminent, strong-minded, and strong-boned of

us old people must become plain and struggle for visibility among the opportunistic young and middle-aged. Uncharacteristically I like to indulge in the modern taste for being positive and remind myself on the crowded pavements how much more I see when I am unseen, notice while unnoticed. And how much easier it is to watch out when travelling unwatched. The only other vantage point as instructive as invisibility must be disguise. Disguise: the essence of spying, it spells adventure and always danger, for it can boldly go where its hidden substance is despised, or worse. The idea of sashaying around for a day or two in disguise has always been tempting.

Forty years or so ago, before the good sisters mostly wore mufti, I asked my favourite editor to commission me to walk the streets of London dressed in a full nun's habit and report on the reaction of people around me. A Roman Catholic, he refused, suspecting shrewdly I intended to end up in a pub for a smoke and a drink to gauge the effect of my masquerade on the boys at the bar. Nor would he allow me to hire designer clothes and jewels and a chauffeur-driven limo, then swan around discovering how it feels to be very, very rich in central London. He said the budget would not stretch to such extravagant make-believe. Did he guess that I planned to find out whether Harrods would agree to close its now-defunct pet department to the general public so my diamond-encrusted self could browse its lapdogs at my leisure? And that later I meant to pull up in my rented Rolls, have the hired chauffeur tell the guard at Number Ten I was expected, and so discover for myself just how near a passing Yankee millionairess might come to chatting with a prime minister?

Of course, nobody beats time, not for a moment longer than it takes to play the piece. But why not try stealing a march on time just once and for the hell of it? To see how it feels? How it feels to be seen as young again, if only by the astigmatic? I have no great dignity, no large audience; I live on my own; no hawks watch me for signs of dementia; if I prance around disguised as a juicy, nubile woman what have I to lose? Only a little time. And I have never been good at keeping time: ask any boy who drew me as a partner at compulsory dance classes when we were teenagers, or, if as usual there were not enough boys to go around, one of the sulky girl-on-girl partners.

Be grey-haired and wrinkly, evidently on a pension, wear baggy old tracksuit-bottoms, trainers, and a weather-beaten coat and hey presto! No Houdini could as easily escape attention as an old frump browsing the racks of Knightsbridge's fashion boutiques. The chi-chi salespeople ignore me and that is understandable, for their livelihood depends upon the better- and higher-heeled. But where is a library anywhere in the world as well stocked with cautionary volumes for the young as an experienced old memory?

Once upon a time, when not long out of school, I worked in the PR department of a high-fashion shop in New York where the staff used to seek me out with tales to tell for the in-house magazine. The naughtiest stories came from the lingerie and fur departments. We are back in the days, you see, when to wear a fur coat was not merely politically correct; it was coded evidence of arrival and prosperity. Mink meant new money; sable meant established money; ermine meant Broadway showbiz money. If you saw a young woman on Fifth Avenue wearing outmoded Persian lamb, you knew her mother had recently died.

The three saleswomen in our store's phenomenally expensive fur department did well enough, working mostly on commission. Business was slow that early autumn day; they gossiped over cups of coffee brewed to order by the new girl at the bottom of their chain of command. When the lift was heard approaching at last, the women brightened, but only until they saw the crone emerging. She was dressed in unmatched layers none too clean, and the bulging old shopping bag on her arm was emblazoned with the logo of a downmarket, down-town chain.

'You take her,' the senior saleswoman commanded the new girl with a wave of her hand.

'Can I help you,' said the new girl; she sighed and added, 'madame?'

The old woman pointed to a Russian sable on a display mannequin.

'I'll have that, dearie,' she said. 'And get us a hat to match.'

Whereupon she started pulling hundred-dollar bills by the handful out of her carrier bag.

'The new girl's commission on that one sale doubled her annual income.'

'I wish . . .' sighed the young salesgirl to whom I had just recounted the story. She looked up from wrapping my new jeans and glanced at the Tesco carrier bag on my arm. 'Oh, I don't mean . . .'

Not able to afford high-maintenance chic these days, nor ever guiltlessly comfortable wearing it, I had ended up in a girlie high street chain-store with a cute name. Luckily for my planned espionage, jeans are in fashion, though in an absurdly skimpy form.

'Some old ladies get fat,' my mother said to me not long before she died. 'Other old ladies get thin. You're thin.'

Her words echo as a twisted compliment only because modern taste no longer equates skeletal thinness with extreme poverty; on the contrary, these days starvation is the rich and sophisticated diet for women and increasingly men, too. Not that my modest camouflage was going to be cheap. The skinny jeans on sale were six times the price we used to pay for Levi's when I was a girl; in those days neither Levi's nor anyone else manufactured jeans for girls so we renegades had to wear the smallest men's sizes to prove we were not enslaved to 1950s full-skirted, ballerina fashion. And did any of us babes in jeans note the double-take at thighs and bums as we walked past lounging men?

'D'oh!' as derision puts it now.

A lot of the girls used to don their new jeans, jump into a hot bath, and then wear the denim wet until it dried tight against their skin. But even in youth I was not much good at strutting whatever there was of my stuff. As Mother liked to say, I was 'pretty enough for all normal purposes'. It needed a nose job, something done about my bookish posture, my stubby toes surgically lengthened, my straight hair permanently waved, and, most of all, a look in my eyes less curious and seeking, more haughty and self-contained: it needed all that and a glossy wardrobe, too, to make me a stunner. In preparing my disguise now I must eschew pink dreadlocks and purple turbans, long skirts and the flying scarves favoured by senescent flirts who are determined to continue turning heads and seem neither to care nor notice whether those turning them are sniggering or stunned. It takes a lot more chutzpah than I have ever had to pull off bag-lady bling.

'And what about boots?' asked the young salesgirl. 'You'll need boots.'

She was being very helpful. I had a lot to learn; I needed help. Her courtesy had already taught me that a woman of my age and aspect is smart to go out early before the crowds, and preferably on Saturday morning when young saleswomen are likely to be university students working part-time, as she was, free of market preconceptions and attentive to shuffling old shoppers.

'High heels?' I asked.

She must have heard the quaver in my question: any woman over seventy traipsing around in high heels needs professional attention more rigorous than podiatry. Or she soon will.

'Flats are OK,' she assured me, 'as long as they're clingy and fit, like, up to your knees.'

'Thank heavens!'

So these legs, which jeering boys at my high school called 'pipe cleaners', have finally come into their own; as long as I show contour and hide texture, they can help me pass as a hungry young thing of today. On top I will wear a short black jacket hanging in my cupboard and still attached to its price tag, bought a decade ago for the young woman even then I had ceased to be. I came across an old belt, too, in the bottom of a suitcase where I must have stowed it back when my waist became no longer worth the nipping. Fortunately, I never burned my bra. As long as I hide my upper arms in a long-sleeved T-shirt, I can pass undercover to the neck. Everything above the collar, however, is a problem area. I bought a bottle of non-permanent hair dye that seemed to be more or less as I remember my original colour. The mass of instructions, with their references to 'skin sensitivity' and 'professional hoods', and the command to put on gloves before I touched anything at all, made my blood run cold. When a friend who had tried a similar product warned me that it took weeks to wash all trace of it out of her grey mop, I threw the stuff away and opting for a Kalashnikov over chemical weaponry: I went to find a wig.

The small, secluded wig department is discreetly set off to one side of the ground floor in the Oxford Street store. The young salesgirl seemed non-judgemental when I asked to see false hairpieces. But was she serious when she told me her mother wore a duplicate of the first, frizzled, waist-length mop she showed me? Or was she making a joke to share with her lurking colleague later? My embarrassment embarrassed me all the more, stemming as it did from residual vanity pathetic in a woman of my age.

'I need a wig for, well, call it research,' I told her defensively, 'to find out how it feels to be young in this day and age.'

'Really?' she said.

Did I imagine a subliminal 'Fat chance'?

'For a book,' I told her. 'I'm a sort of, like, a writer, journalist sort of thing . . .'

'Then why don't you go all out? Like, why not go for blonde?' she said.

Her image in the mirror before me was serious now. She believed me; she was on my side. Good. Out in the field I was going to be strictly on my own; but a spy without a network at home is a spy without a cause.

'Yeah, I thought about going blonde,' I said, trying to sound cool. 'But I've never been a blonde. And it's myself, young again, I want to discover on this mission, not a total stranger. Like, the best lie always sticks close to the truth. See what I mean?'

'Like, totally,' she said.

The wig she chose for me was well coiffed, not long and shaggy as I used to wear my hair until I was nearly forty, and its fake brown was mellower than my real colour had ever been. The trouble was not the wig – the wig was fine – but the face looking out from under it in the mirror set me back. Who on earth was that old trout under my new locks? She pouted her crumpling lips at me and raised her eyebrows to hoist up her drooping lids.

'Botox?' the young saleswoman suggested. 'It doesn't last long. That's what they say . . .'

The stranger in the glass shook her head so emphatically, her youthful bob flew back to reveal incipient jowls and white hair roots at her temples.

I had earlier browsed through a pamphlet called *Cosmetic Surgery* in a second-hand bookstore; among the list of 'minor complications' that could follow a facelift were depression, hair loss, and 'early recurrence of deformity', which has to mean recurrence of time's invincible trail, and that must mean yet more surgery. Furthermore, the former reader had left a receipt for £250 from a Harley Street plastic surgeon tucked between the pages. And that was merely his consultation fee. No Botox, thank you, no collagen, and sure as hell no plastic surgery. Any disguise that necessitates breaking the bank or breaking the skin, this agent 0072 will undertake only to save her nation from tyranny, nothing less. False nails were the single chemical artifice I dared in aid of subterfuge; even so, it was dodgy and emotionally draining to superglue the bitty things on my right hand with my left. Nor is it done, I soon found, to use a keyboard or wash dishes while wearing talons. I have read that men are increasingly opting for facelifts and liposuction; I wonder how long it will be before they, too, glue on false nails to suggest pampered ineptitude, which is the only point of painted, pointed nails even for today's liberated generation.

The day of deception dawned cool and clear. Shrouding myself and my tight jeans in a long black coat, and carrying the wig in its box for fear of meeting a neighbour or a local friend, I skulked off to the department store where a young make-up artist was dragooned into my back-up team. Skilled though she was, her applications looked to me about as effect-ive as Band-Aids on a mortal wound, until the moment when she attached false eyelashes like a pair of spiders to my lids where they spun an arachnid spell: the eyes beneath them appeared big and clear, the face around them not so wilted. I stowed my long coat in a posh carrier bag borrowed from my daughter-in-law for the day, took a deep breath, counted to ten in four languages to quiet my jumpy nerves, and stepped out onto the bustling pavement. For an instant I stood still with the remains and the embellishments of my youth on display. And nobody paid the least attention. Even when I strode along, tits first, bewigged head high, past a bunch of workmen in phosphorescent jackets, only one of them turned and then turned away again to make kissing noises at an oncoming young blonde in high heels. OK, let the bitch upstage me in a public thoroughfare; a pseudo-girl like me was made for more discerning and intellectual attention. In the museums of London and especially the fashion-conscious V&A, I had enjoyed a few flirtatious encounters in my distant past; that is where I would go now. I started across the street for the bus to Kensington, hesitated on the other side, and stopped in my tracks. I recalled an old friend, once a moderately well-known actor, who refuses to apply for the freedom pass he has been entitled to for several years.

'But why?' I asked him. 'It goes beep like an Oyster pass. Nobody needs to see it. Nobody needs to know.'

In public and dressed now for my one-woman show, I understood for the first time what he meant when he replied: 'I will; I will know.'

My long-nailed hand flashing Mother's diamond ring, too big for me and secured for the occasion with string wound around its hidden side, rose as of its own accord to flag down a passing taxi.

Meandering through the nearly empty corridors of the museum, I saw things, wonderful things, but not one of the few people around showed any interest in seeing me. Only a bored museum guard looked my way when he heard me gasp aloud in front of a 'character head' by the Austrian sculptor and paranoiac, Franz Xaver Messerschmidt; its grimace as if at a bad smell was telling me more than I wanted to know about scarlet lip-gloss on a dame over seventy. I deserted the wondrous halls of history for the day outside. And it was there on the steps of the museum the first essential fact attaching to my masquerade came home to me when I found myself wanting a cigarette, gasping for one as I have not done in more than twenty years. Youth is animated by cravings; any successful disguise, if it wants to be more than skin-deep, is bound to mimic them.

'What can I get you?' said the barman.

I have been exclusively a sundown drinker for decades now; nevertheless, when I entered the oaken corner pub I intended to order a glass of pre-lunch red wine to boost my courage. I thought: Why not? Then I thought again. Whatever message my long eyelashes tried to transmit to the five or six early boozers in the place, when it comes to matters of digestion only the genuinely young dare ask themselves: Why not?

'A mineral water, please.'

'Still or sparkling?'

'Still.'

So here I am, all dressed up and nowhere to go, with nothing to do but wander the busy streets of my adoptive city. After growing up in Manhattan's line-drawn grid, then living for a while in Paris, a singular gemstone of a city reflecting no light generated from outside itself, finally more than a young-ster's lifetime ago I found myself in London, the most pris-matic capital on earth. Memories are anti-cosmetic; their weight mists the eye, tugs even a painted mouth downwards, and wrin-kles the brow. I shake my bewigged head to clear it of the London memories that swarmed even here on a posh street unlikely for the likes of me, yet, I must remember, around the corner from my little boy's first school. So what would bring an unemployed woman twenty years my junior – maybe thirty in a dim light – to an overpriced area like this? Shopping, of course. What else?

'I wear glasses as you see; don't you think long earrings as well make too much jingle-jangle around my face?'

'Oh no,' says the saleswoman who is stocky and in her fifties. 'You can carry off both,' she assures me with a glance at my skinny legs, then up to Mother's diamond ring. 'Glasses are "in" these days, you know. A lot of girls . . . women, I mean . . . are wearing glasses, plain glass too, no prescription.'

In fact, I had noticed how many more young women are bespectacled than in my day. *Pace* Dorothy Parker: the new fashion – if not exactly for girls in glasses – at least in their frames spared me from putting in contact lenses as part of my disguise, and the still greater trauma of taking them out later while wearing permaglued false fingernails.

The saleswoman shakes the earrings a little impatiently to make them glitter in the light. It is ages since I have gone shopping imaginatively and unspecifically, in the way young women shop before every party, every job interview, and every occasion, even the first day of spring. I have lost the knack of disengaging from importunate salespeople.

'How late are you open?' I ask.

I want to leave her in hope and not reveal myself as too old and too poor for her glitzy trinkets.

'I'm going to think about those earrings.'

Back in the street I am dismayed to find myself doing just that: thinking about those earrings. Whoa! What is happening? There is no place and no time I will ever or ever again wear dangling earrings; there is no way they can bring romance or excitement into this old life, let alone brake its descent into decrepitude. Why do I feel myself enticed by the passing windows? Why does that four-letter word, SALE, flutter my heart? Has the make-up permeated my brain cells? I quicken my pace to put the siren-shops behind me.

Old people amble; a brisk pace invites pursuit. Several young and quite young men look mechanically into my fringed eyes as I hurry past, but not one old man turns his head; every last ageing or old woman, however, seeing me, sees through me, and with palpable disapproval, too. They are not amused: who do I think I am fooling? I stop to catch my breath in front of a small art gallery; according to a sign in the window it will not open until evening. The curator looks up from a crossword puzzle; seeing me at the window he rises from his desk and walks over to unlock the door. His dark eyes look me over and take me in, and I am shocked to recognise in them a calculation long gone from my everyday arithmetic. He is figuring ways that he and I together might once or twice make one. He glances down at my legs, then up again. He is tall, in his forties, and not bad at all. Little moribund parts within me quiver and stir, struggling to come up with the answer he wants.

Then I imagine myself telling him: 'This brown hair comes off, you see. And these nails? They're sharper than nature intended. There's a frame under that bra you're ogling. And I think we'd better have all the lights out.'

He asks whether I would like to come in and have a look around his gallery.

'I would have loved to,' I say. 'But I'm afraid . . .' And I make a show of looking at my watch before I walk away.

And I am afraid too: afraid I have the wrong idea. Or he has.

I slow my pace through the luxurious urban green of Hyde Park. A young man runs towards me along the path; he is wearing a dark suit and polished shoes, and carrying a briefcase under his arm. I stop to watch him pass, his young male body compact and armed, hard and beautiful in the heat of chase. I cannot recollect ever noticing before with what easy grace a young man in his prime runs towards something he wants or needs to do. Must a woman grow old to appreciate his elegance? And does my disguise help me to see male beauty with detachment? And, by the way, it is time to check my make-up: my fake-up? A public lavatory is just ahead; rummaging there in my bag under the beady eye of what's her name in the mirror, I cannot for the life of me find the most important tool of my undercover trade. Would you believe I have forgotten my bloody lipstick? And to make matters worse, how long has it been since the pinkie on my left hand reverted to its scrubby old self, minus its virtual nail? When did that happen? God help me, I am falling apart.

Expensive new lipstick is applied in the mirror of a Mayfair chemist; the deprived pinkie is hidden in a glove where the sight of it can no longer chide me with the memory of how I laughed once upon a time to see my pretty older cousin weeping real tears over her broken red nail. What now? It is almost two; I'm hungry. I pretend to be reading the menus outside restaurants; they are all crowded inside with groups and couples. At last I come across a little corner café with a few tables, all empty except for one solitary woman, young, seated alone, and texting assiduously on her mobile phone to show the world she has lots of friends, really. The Polish waitress who brings my sandwich probably took a degree in Chemical Engineering. No such luck with the chef; judging by the French fries, his was in Geology. Pushing the oily shards to one side, I allow myself one of those satisfying internal snarls that rumble increasingly in droopy old breasts. Suddenly, alarmingly, my own mobile phone resounds. I have a mobile for when I take my little grandson out on my own; otherwise I would never carry one except, of course, as an imperative accessory of today's youthful disguise.

'Hello, Mum?'

My son is in town for a meeting, and only a few blocks away. Would I like to meet him in an hour or so and then go back for tea or a drink with his wife and the baby?

'Would I? Oh, darling . . .'

I glance over to check whether the waitress and the other customer have heard my endearment. See? I may be all on my own in furry eyelashes and knee-high boots. But someone loves me, too.

'Yes, my love, oh my, yes.'

The problem of how to spend the rest of the day lifts from my lightly padded shoulders.

My son was about to turn three years old; we had crossed the Atlantic to visit my parents for a week or so. I left him alone with them in the country one day while I went to Manhattan on the bus to touch base with contacts – it is customary in general to have contacts rather than friends in New York City – and I was also going to have my hair cut. Since girlhood I had worn my tresses long and shaggy, a coiffure that as I approached my fortieth birthday started to suggest the greying, hirsute drapery favoured by old pop stars and the ever so arty beldams of olden days. The nice Manhattan crimper said the short cut took years off me: a new compliment, in my experience, and worrying. My family came to meet me at the bus stop. My young son ran towards me, calling out, 'It's my mum! It's my mum!' I knelt and opened my arms to him. More than thirty years later, I enter the café where he is waiting; he sees me, knows me, and then his eyes fill with precisely the same accusation and scorn when as a child he stopped cold at the sight of my new hair and cried: 'You're not my mum!'

Amused and bolstered to have a handsome young man as my companion, I use my freedom pass ostentatiously to board the underground train. My son, however, seems to me a little embarrassed at our appearance together. No need for him to worry; the underground is an unnatural and nerve-racking location for humankind; subterranean travellers tend to be wary of each other and mind their own business. If anyone around us even notices when this maternal travesty leans her painted face for a moment against his shoulder, they do not show it. My daughter-in-law is waiting to pick us up for the short drive to their home.

'Oh my,' she says with her ineffable smile, 'doesn't the girl scrub up well!'

The baby, not yet two, is in the back seat beside me in his carrier. A chip off the old paternal block, for sure, his mouth arches, his eyes narrow, his darling ears fairly flap suspiciously: who is this oddball climbing in next to him? I hear him think what he has not yet words to say: 'You're not my granny!'

'Hello, darling boy. Give me a hug.'

Hearing my familiar old voice, his eyes widen and his jaw drops; then he stretches out his arms and the little silver bells of his laughter make precious every day and every last moment it took to get me to this age and place.

'That young man over there is flirting with you,' my friend said.

We were having dinner in an offbeat Italian restaurant. Janie had ended her critique of my disguise by pointing out my broken nail with exaggerated tact as a flaw I needed to know about for my own good.

'He's not flirting, sweetie. He's looking. They've been looking a lot more since nightfall. But he won't look back.'

'Because you're not giving him a come-on.'

'I'm not sure. Maybe the animal in men can sniff out a body that's past it, no matter how much paint and plastic it's wearing.'

'I've been told,' said Janie in her best solicitor's voice, 'by someone who teaches at uni that young men these days are seriously into older women. Fewer demands,' she said. Half turning, she gave my would-be admirer the glad eye, presumably seeking evidence for her contention; although half my age, he was not even two-thirds her own.

'What are you going to eat?' she said, returning chastened to the menu.

'I find myself favouring the leg of lamb.'

'But you never eat meat.'

'I know,' I said. 'I haven't eaten meat in ages. But a carnivorous appetite seems to come with this territory.'

'And what can I get you ladies?' the Italian waiter asked, with a Latinate glimmer that made the question sound suggestive.

'I'll have a vegetable lasagne.'

'I thought you wanted lamb,' Janie said.

'I used to. I used to like lamb. But it, I don't know, it sort of gave me up. It's not so hard to stop wanting, not if you make the most of it when it is there.'

The wig was making my scalp itchy. I could not wait to take the damn thing off and donate it to charity.

'Once it was wonderful,' I said. 'And once was enough.'

A Glamorous Old Voice: Jocasta Innes

The young believe, as they always have, that they invented sex. Furthermore, no fashion is ever considered to have had any edge at all before whatever the current one happens to be. But some glamour really does go deeper than fashion and outlast passing fads.

Jocasta Innes was born in Nanking, China, back in the days of empire, to a peripatetic family; her father was employed by Shell. She read Modern Languages at Cambridge, then translated books, worked as a journalist, and wrote Paint Magic. *That book was more than just a huge-selling blockbuster; like her subsequent books, it was also evidence of her idiosyncratic and delightful taste in decor. The way that Jocasta thinks, lives, and sees things continues to be 'maximalist'. Twice married and the long-time partner of the architect Sir Richard MacCormac, she is mother, granny, writer, journalist, working woman – for a while with her own business – aesthete, thinker, and energetic hostess in a home she loves. Jocasta is fun, too, by the way. Age cannot wither her.*

'I had a bit of a reputation as a Zuleika Dobson at Cambridge but nobody immolated himself for me. I was chased around for a year or two by a rather sad young man who had a fantasy about me. He had written a novel that he insisted I read, in which I was 'Lady Jocasta', a sort of sadist with a whip. Do I look like somebody who would take a whip to my boyfriend? But I'll bet you don't see me as the domestic drudge either, do you? Well, let me tell you what I've been doing today. The biggest thing I did was iron eight shirts for Richard. Ironing is one of those ritualistic things; I have to do it on a Monday and when I've done it I feel good: better. In fact, I don't find what's called housework drudgery. Sometimes, yes, I do get bored wondering what to cook for dinner, but that's when I excel myself, and do something really wonderful. Not that I am often assailed by gloom. I think my best characteristic is that I am a merry soul (*laughs*) and Richard agrees. My daughter Tabitha is merry. And my son, Jason, is merry. The other two are more volatile.

Oh, sure, I have been depressed. If depression means not wanting to get out of bed in the morning, then ten years or so ago when my business collapsed I was really depressed for several months, even longer. And before that, I did almost go mad once when my father died. I used to make poor old Joe, my then husband, walk and walk and walk with me, the idea being to walk so far and so hard that I would be bound to sleep. But then night would fall and I'd sit up in a state of panic. I don't have the energy for that kind of depression any more. That is the depression of youth.

I'm not quite seventy-five but creeping up to it. I genuinely forget my age. I think I'm seventy-three but I must be seventy-four. I'm old. But I am not elderly. I hate that word. And isn't it odd the way people creep around the subject? 'Forgive me for asking your age . . .' And if the question is asked in public everyone cocks an ear. Or at least you fear they do! Why should we feel that way? We should wear a look of pride at achieving great age. But we don't. I've been interviewed by lots of journalists. The last one was from *Saga* and I knew she would come to the subject. Of course towards the end of the interview, after lots of chat about clothes and decorating, a coy look came over her face and she sort of simpered: 'How old are you, Jocasta?' I retaliated equally coyly: 'Well, I won't see sixty again.' I was not lying, it is perfectly true I won't see sixty, but I wasn't going to say, 'I won't see seventy again either,' was I? She bloody well checked it out and printed my age. I got my comeuppance then because I was deluged afterwards with correspondence about making my will, leaving money to my old university, and other terminal priorities.

I have nine grandchildren. Lucky? Am I? It hasn't much to

do with me. And it's by no means over; I wouldn't be surprised if a few more pop up. Grandchildren make you feel cannibalistic. It's all I can do not to take little bites out of them. If somebody had told me in my twenties I'd be a doting granny, I'd have thought: Oh yeah, sure. But not for ages! Not for so long I can't even imagine it.

Truthfully, I don't like old people as a crowd. Yes, I like individuals very much; they're my friends from way back. But I get a slight rage when I see old people piling out of charabancs and being herded around, grey-haired tourists, agape. I find cooking for young people for a birthday party, say, rewarding. They laugh and scoff, and the roar of enjoyment that rises from the table makes it all worth doing. When we have our more select contemporaries it's a bit stiffish.

Some women grow old like Marianne Faithfull, looking ravaged and dressed up at the same time. It's a look gay men find attractive. I get dressed up a little; I use eyeliner and a bit of make-up. But how to dress and present yourself as you age is a problem. Designers every year think of things that only a certain age group can get away with and when it catches fire all the older people complain: 'Bloody hell! No, I don't think I can wear a miniskirt now or a plunging neckline down to my navel.'

Fashion can be misogynistic and ageist. It rules out anybody over the age of about thirty for bare midriff and miniskirts, too. True, I do know rather beautiful old and oldish women who wear short skirts but always with opaque black tights to take away from that 'Look at my legs!'

A lot of things in the 1960s were cutting-edge fashion: we were cutting edge – we were cool chicks. Somebody once asked me which period of fashion I liked best and I remembered my sack dress. I was so pleased with it; I thought it was just the best. I do not know why but I felt really elegant in the sack! (*She laughs.*) My clothes sense has always been eccentric, not to say erratic, and increasingly so. But you cannot wear just anything when you grow old. If I were to write a guide for old dressing, I'd say, for example, never wear beige; it makes old skin drab. I wear a lot of black and I like the way Swedish women wear bright red. One great thing about being blonde is when you go grey it looks more blonde than ever. My favourite coat now is one with a badge that says 'Welfare' stitched on the shoulder. My mother used to have it in her dressing-up cupboard, not for children, but for people who acted in the plays she wrote for the WI. The thing I miss now in clothes is humour. I don't mean funny-funny; I mean witty. I have a coat made entirely of red and black feathers; I got it from a local shop called Frock Brokers. There it was, not very expensive, and I love it. It is witty and very warm, too, so you suddenly realise what it's like to be a bird.

When the menopause is over, a woman doesn't look or feel too different in herself. But men do pick up on it; not consciously, it's animal, it's pheromones: you are suddenly this invisible woman. I suppose movie stars must constantly inspect themselves for signs of deterioration. I don't even have a mirror these days that goes below my waist. I couldn't check myself out even if I wanted to. Every now and then I catch sight of my upper arm and I think: What? That isn't my arm! It looks like old washing on the line! (*She laughs.*) What is the point of getting depressed about it? I have a mantra, from a book I translated from the Spanish: 'It is not sad, for it is true.' A bit hard-hearted, perhaps, but spot on. I know women who have had their eyes done and they ask me: 'Notice any difference?' And when I say, 'No, not really,' they are frightfully dejected, having spent £3,000 or so. But, of course, they feel they look different and it's the feeling they pay for. I know some old gentlemen who have had their eyes done too and their excuse is that their eyes got so many folds around them they could no longer read very easily.

Men also lose to age. I don't think Richard would mind my

saying that Joe Potts was the love of my life. When he first stripped off (*she gasps*), I thought: It's Michelangelo's *David*. I was staggered by his beauty. He wasn't naked when I first clapped eyes on him, by the way. It was at a party and I knew everyone there, but not this guy who was giving me hard looks across the room. Then he came up and said: 'Come on, let's dance.' He had written a book; I helped him get it published and by publication day I had seen him naked. Then I ran away, left my rich home, my husband, and the father of my first two children. All I have had cause to regret was not having those two with me; their father made jolly sure I didn't. So I have had two husbands and I'm not divorced from the last one, out of sheer laziness and ineffectualness. I don't even know where my marriage lines are. It's going to be a nightmare trying to find all the documentation, now that my daughters have started saying they really think I should make a will.

Occasionally I still see a young man and think: Yum! But it's rare now. I was in the underground not long ago and there was a young man of spectacular beauty; everyone's eyes were burning covetously at him. He looked like a Roman coin, dark-eyed and exceptionally beautiful. I admired him as beautiful. But I felt no lust after him at all, just pure admiration at the texture and effect of his looks. You see, my days as a paint lady come out in me sometimes. How sexy are the young now? I think they lack passion. Not that long ago we had parties upstairs for waifs and Goths, friends of our children, all public-school boys and girls really. I used to rush upstairs from time to time to see what was going on. And they were not snogging away or sloping off into bedrooms; they were all a bit hugger-mugger, like puppies in a basket: it wasn't erotic, more like super-friendship. I suppose that has a good side; they respond at once to any misfortune of their friends, even if they are not so tender and helpful to their parents' generation.

I used to think I was in for the long haul and that meant

always taking the hard way out. I'd walk rather than drive; I didn't learn to drive until I was in my fifties. I used to carry my kids on my back, and they had towelling nappies that I washed myself; I didn't have a washing machine. I used to put the nasties down the loo, then trample the nappies in the bath. I rode all around London on a bike, too. I bought a new bike recently and heavy-duty padlocks, but little books of instructions came with all of them and I cannot read those awful little books, can't even get them open. Fortunately our Hungarian au pair boy can read them and tell me in real words. I do the gym thing twice a week now, the kinesis thing. I feel my endorphins running around again. If I didn't do it I'd become a sludge. Sure, if I had the money and was really, really hating my appearance, I might think about plastic surgery, but when that day comes I'll be too old to care that much. And I would not trust the surgeon; I could not be sure he would understand how I think I look. It could be very depressing. And what is it for? You're not going to have sex more often, if at all, just because you've had your face done. It's a bad moment in a woman's life when she thinks – if I may be so rude – I'll never get another fuck. And the chances are she's right.

10

Old Bones

'GETTING OLD . . .' MY father used to say regularly after his sixtieth birthday. 'Getting old . . .' he said often and to nobody, to the kitchen clock, to the towering catalpa tree he had planted as a seedling in our garden, and finally to the lunch-tray delivered to his bed in the nursing home.

'Getting old . . .' he'd say once more and shake his whitening head. 'This getting old is murder.'

'Oh, Dad'n,' I replied when I was near, 'if that were so, if it really were murder, there would have to be a perpetrator. Know what I mean? You can't have a murder without a murderer.'

He looked at me – who was I? – his puzzlement giving way after a second or two to a memory, sometimes of me or just as often of his youngest sister, Sylvia; whichever of us it was he saw beside him, he smiled sweetly, shook his head again and sighed. 'Getting old,' he said, 'is murder.'

If getting old is murder, then doctors must be detectives looking for the villains and traitors who are hiding time-bombs in our systems. While in my thirties, actively gathering evidence for what would become a lifetime's hoard of gener-alisations, I decided finally that these cops of our bodies often choose areas of specialisation where they have fears or prob-lems of their own, presumably in hope of curing themselves and those they love. My 'heal thyself' theory had begun to take root a couple of decades earlier when I was a teenager employed in a summer camp to help look after affluent children, many of them, it so happened, offspring of the medical profession.

'My daddy gave me these,' screamed one little drama-queen, the daughter of a shrink, as I struggled to take away the box of white pills she had been swallowing by the handful. 'He says to take them when I feel sad. You can't have them! Nobody can have them! These are my "happy pills".'

I tasted one. It was a mint. And as it was melting on my tongue, I began to wonder how many psychiatrists tended to be bonkers. Subsequently I found increasing evidence that, if it could not precisely prove my theory of medical specialisation, it certainly established it as a provocative generalisation. For example, are male gynaecologists, by and large, validating misogyny? Are females of that discipline seeking the source of their own deepest trouble and a cure for what ails them? Do obstetricians feel themselves to be priests at heart, even godly megalomaniacs, bringing forth life several times a week? And doing it increasingly by scheduled Caesarean section, too, so never on a Sunday. Does surgery attract the bent docs: the killers manqués and the antisocial control freaks? I must ask my brother whether he remembers how as a teenager he thought for a while he had a gastric ulcer. I'll bet he doesn't remember any such thing. Why worry about it again after he had qualified as a gastroenterologist? The most cerebral woman I know, a grand and distracted kind of genius, is an oncologist.

'As long as nothing else gets you first,' she says, 'it will be cancer.'

How could someone with her investigative gifts and towering intellect go after anything less than the kingpin villain and godfather of all mortal ills?

'I got into the field of gerontology by default to some extent, a bit like an arranged marriage; the love came afterwards,' said Raymond Tallis, Professor of Geriatric Medicine at the University of Manchester.

Professor Tallis appeared dubious about my theory of elective medical specialities, though not quite disproving it, as he himself is a published philosopher as well as a medico who also writes poetry and fiction. Is any chapter in life as thought-provoking and enticing to an abstract thinker as the one that ends this earthbound plot?

'Essentially,' he said quickly, before I could wax fanciful, 'my main interest is neurology, neurological rehabilitation, and people with chronic disabling conditions. In 1981 I did some locum work in geriatric medicine and absolutely loved it because it is a combination of rehabilitation and also acute medicine.'

Furthermore, it seems to me that old age is a chronic disabling condition. But I did not like to say so. We were meeting in the café at the Royal Medical Society headquarters and being outnumbered by healers made me a little bashful.

'I liked geriatric medicine more and more; finally, I liked the product so much I bought the company. My patients in the 1980s were largely in their sixties and seventies. By the time I hung up my stethoscope in 2006 most of them were in their eighties and quite a few in their nineties. And there you have a very small and unreliable marker of the postponement of decrepitude, as it were, to a much later age.'

Dr Tallis is in his sixties; could I take his age as further evidence for my theory of physicians choosing a specialty attaching to their own personal concerns? No, I guess not. Otherwise they would all end up as geriatricians.

'Ageing is a biological phenomenon and it clearly occurs at different rates in different people. Ageing also gets confused with the pathology that comes with age: as you get older, you have more of a chance of something going wrong.'

'But I assume that is not to say that ageing itself is a malady,' I said, remembering how we expectant mothers on a prenatal ward in the 1970s felt we were being treated for the disease of pregnancy.

'Exactly. Ageing is a biological thing that gets confused with pathological things. But ageing is a social construct as well, isn't it? How old you are depends on who's looking at you. Or what audience you feel is looking at you.'

'And on how old you say you are, too.'

I had that very morning been ticked off by an old friend and fellow journalist for giving my true age to run next to a byline over a short newspaper piece. She thought I was nuts; she always lied about her own age, she told me, as a defence against being consigned to the dust-heap wherein lay countless discarded wits of our generation.

'Yes,' Professor Tallis agreed, 'and it depends on how old you say you are, too. Which indicates that there is an amount of disregard for older people among us.'

True enough. More than half a century ago when I was young, we sheltered our old people at home and showed them conventional respect, too, whether we liked them or not. Nevertheless, some of us seemed to have kept no respect in reserve for our own aged selves to be. But of course in our youth we neither expected nor intended to reach the age we are now; the young never do.

'To be much more than halfway through life seems to the young, and always has, to be barely half alive,' I said.

'Yes,' said the professor, 'there is a chronological apartheid, in which old people live apart in elder villages or institutions, or simply lose contact with their children who are scattered all over the place. Someone once told me I was going to find practising geriatric medicine rough because the low status of old people rubs off on those who look after them. Geriatric medicine is definitely the bottom of the heap. I have no problem with that. I don't mind being at the bottom of the heap. It's the most interesting part of the heap; everything weighty goes to the bottom.'

'Try telling that bit about the bottom,' I said, 'to the fashion-conscious readers of my agony column.'

The professor laughed, which he does well and youthfully.

'And likewise,' he said, 'what is being young? That, too, depends upon who's looking at you. It used to be policemen; now retired chiefs of police look young to me. I suppose we are all worried about ageing. Why does ageing worry me? Because there are more and more chances of something going wrong. And because there is simply less time left. Simone de Beauvoir summarises it brilliantly when she says that as you get older you define yourself – you did this rather than that – and the range of possibilities grows narrower and narrower. But of course she felt that once over the age of forty a woman becomes immediately unattractive; Sartre made sure she felt that by pulling in one chick after another.'

Here at last was someone old enough and knowledgeable enough, too, to appreciate my experience with a name that is hardly worth dropping these days among the young. Should I tell the professor how, when I was new in Paris back in the late 1950s, I almost met Jean-Paul Sartre? He happened to be seated at a table next to me in the café, La Coupole. And how I blushed that the grand-daddy of existentialists was flirting with me until my companion pointed out that it was his wall-eye fixed on me; his seeing eye was directed at a buxom blonde across the room. I restrained myself from retelling this anecdote to Professor Tallis, however, and tried to stay firmly in interviewing mode, tape recorder running and mike on.

'Think of the standard narrative of life,' he was saying: 'education, then child-rearing and career; and, hitherto, decrepitude as part three. But now we have a part three that is no longer decrepitude. The children may not be off the payroll, of course, but the critical interval between their calls for help is no longer every ten seconds, so you do have time to relish things. Of course, the things you relish are also the things you have had more often so they've lost their novelty. Yes, that means there is a waning of appetite. This is not the same as a waning of desire: desire and appetite are different things.' The professor frowned a little at the common confusion of body and soul. 'If you look at any period of life, such as surveys of teenagers in *Heat* magazine or whatever, and, when asked, 90 per cent of people believe themselves to be miserable. We're eaten away by desire and when desire goes we're eaten away by the desire for desire, I guess. Boredom is the hunger for hunger.'

I simply had to interrupt to tell him about the friend whose husband, several years into his retirement, cannot be unglued from the television screen, especially when sporting events are on, which they are all the time.

'Studies have shown that older people are among the most avid telly viewers,' Professor Tallis said. 'There are two reasons: one is that the quality of the screen has got better. And, of course, TV viewing is an easy default position to take in age; you can be serious about sport – for women it's soap operas – but at the same time you know it's not serious. It is a voluntary seriousness, even a distracting one, but it's not compulsory like worrying about your finances or your health. Do things get better? There are periods not of peace, because peace is a bit dull in a way, but there can be periods of freedom.'

'Can old age really be a period of freedom?'

I heard the doubt in my tone later while transcribing the tape. Everyone spends most of their lifetime saddled with a burdensome characteristic or an inconvenient emotion or an unwanted responsibility. For example, from what has senescence, if not quite senility, freed me finally and for ever? Is old age bringing me freedom from feeling always on trial, always awaiting judgement; will old age at last let me rest my case? And when I have rested my case, what then will I do without it?

'Freedom or loss?' I asked. 'Are they not related?'

'Perhaps freedom is what happens in age,' Professor Tallis said. 'As long as you're financially OK and your health is all right.

And you're not in a state of grief or bereavement. And as long as you don't feel threatened or humiliated by others, then there is a chance of old age being a glade in which you can enjoy things,' he said.

But did I not note his frown deepen? He was taking into account, perhaps, that what could be a glade in life might also be a sunless, narrow valley.

'There is the joy of enjoying something just for this moment, for this day, enjoying that thing in front of one. You lose the alibi of the future with age. To lose the future tense as an alibi for postponing something can perhaps be positive. Enjoy today for there is no point saying that next year you will go some- where else. Life itself is a condition with 100 per cent mortality. Do we learn with age? We learn not to make the mistakes that we weren't going to make anyway, a bit like the lessons of history.'

'What about those who hang onto youth like an umbrella in a windstorm? Those once-famed beauties, for instance?'

'They suffer from that enormous free gift of admiration from childhood onwards. Who would want that? You wouldn't want that! A world-famous neurosurgeon goes into a crowded room next to someone like Joan Collins and the world-famous neurol- ogist ceases to exist. Admiration that has barely been earned is a massive free gift and it is very difficult to give up.'

'Or have snatched from you . . .'

'Exactly. Who would want that? The appetites of youth come home to roost in some sort of sense. The things you do when driven by appetites, for example, you can subsequently rue, or other people can rue. The way you can wreck other people's lives through the pursuit of an appetite; the way you wreck your own body. There can be positive enjoyment when passion is spent. There can. Yes. I think most passion is anguish in any case, rather than joy. Anguish lingers; joy passes fast.'

'I have a friend,' I said, 'whose mother has Alzheimer's disease.

We took her for a walk in the park and it was wonderful to see her joy, profound joy, in watching children at play.'

'Yes, you see, even Alzheimer's disease targets a particular sort of memory, episodic memory, the biographical facts of here and now. But you can retain an awful lot of knowing and of knowing how; it can take a long time before that is eroded. So the patient may not be able to tell me what she had for breakfast, but she can remember distant memories, procedural memories, a whole raft of memories. I have a colleague, a senior lecturer in English, who is doing work with old people who have dementia; she is reading poetry with them. You might think that would be a lost cause as poetry is so complex. Interestingly, it is the more complex poems they like best and which some remember from the past.'

In his eloquent and angry book, *Hippocratic Oaths: Medicine and its Discontents*, Professor Tallis brilliantly lays out a sorry fact. We the aged must all come to suspect it, but mostly we dare not say so, or do not know to whom we should say it. There is subliminal euthanasia at work among us. Why, for example, when it is known that the incidence of breast cancer increases in women after the age of seventy, is that precisely when local health authorities cease to summon us automatically for regular mammograms? They leave it to us instead, with our new and unfamiliar calendars of old age, to remember when check-ups are due. And why have I received a flyer offering a free home-testing kit for bowel cancer for those 'between fifty and sixty-nine'? Presumably bowels over seventy are retired from business. There is no profit in them. The truth is that treatment of cancer among the very old is considered to be worth less than it will cost in the long run, which is inevitably going to be relatively short.

'There is evidence,' Professor Tallis writes in *Hippocratic Oaths*, 'that older people are sometimes denied treatments – supposedly on the grounds that they cannot benefit from them or that the benefits are outweighed by the risks – simply on the basis of age' (p. 231).

'So it does appear, Professor, that there can come a point where old bones, no matter how great the continuing joy or the quality of the lives that they support, are not considered worth the upkeep in this pragmatic and materialistic Western society.'

'You say "Western society" as if you imagine it could be better somewhere else. I am suspicious of stark contrasts: looking after elders and traditional respect on the one hand; nuclear society and not looking after elders on the other. I am not sure it is so easy,' said Professor Tallis.

'Do they not do it better elsewhere?'

'National differences in terms of attitudes towards ageing, you mean? I wonder whether we don't romanticise them.'

He had a point. We like to assume that oriental communities especially cherish their ancients in a fashion we have forgotten or never knew. But in Los Angeles recently I stayed at a hotel in Chinatown: a part of the city where the atmosphere and the population are so absolutely oriental that it hardly seemed as if America really was all around me.

'Was it naive of me to be shocked, horrified in fact, when I came across a poster in the local market, giving a hotline number to "stop elder abuse" and illustrated by the photograph of a Chinese great-granny?' I asked the professor.

'When I worked in Liverpool,' he replied, 'I saw a lot of people in the Chinese area, which was part of our catchment area, and actually, no: they were not attended to with any special concern. Often it was the contrary. The mythology about how other cultures treat their aged has not been tested in places where people do not live long after, say, they've had a stroke, but die pretty promptly. If you have an elderly mother who has been living for twenty years with a severe disability, then that is much more of a test than listening to the wise elder who does not require hands-on care. Hands-on care has no real status. I see this in nursing. The one bit of scandal that I do really believe pertains to the NHS and other places, too, is that hands-on care is very poor.'

Nothing is had for nothing. Our new longevity, despite the great improvements to geriatric health in general, brings new problems with it, for both young and old. Can we solve them with imagination and honour? Of course, to raise a sensitive and intelligent child who decides to become a gerontologist is one good start for an ageing mum.

'I always tease my mother when I see her and say, "Let's have our one-woman ward round now, shall we?" And then we work our way around all the aches and pains. She is in her nineties now and I see her nearly every day. We have brought her to live just around the corner from us.'

'When my mother needed home care in America,' I told Professor Tallis, 'the private agency I found to supply it was called Rent a Daughter.'

'Yes,' he said, shaking his head with a sigh. 'It seems to me that the forced altruism of women – an abuse of women in a way – is gone. And we have nothing to replace it. One trouble is that women were used and now they are not going to be used; nobody is willing to be used, apart from low-paid foreign labour on the first rung of our local ladder. Of course you can get some very good and caring people that way. But very caring people are often also very deferential, so I could do a ward round with a nurse who never questioned what I said. And that is dangerous, virtually like flying blind. The tradition of caring for the aged coexists with a tradition of deference that is both bad and good. Certainly women who were raised to be deferential traditionally were stoic; they provided the care and the men received it, partly because men started falling apart sooner than women. The male used to be generally the older partner, and life expectancy for males in most Western cultures has been five years less than for females. These days, both sexes are gaining years but the men faster. Women can't get rid of their men so easily because, for instance, they've stopped smoking themselves off the scene. This is an anecdote and thus very poor-quality data,' said Professor Tallis, which I took as a gentle warning against my freelance style of thinking, 'but forty or so years ago when I was a student I used to work in a pub. The men came in every day of the week and then with their wives on Saturdays. And the men seemed to be reasonably well preserved. But when the women came in with them, I was shocked; they looked so ragged and haggard. I remember thinking that their wives looked like their mothers. Now that has changed; nowadays on the whole women look younger than the men they are with, and they cannot all be trophy wives the second time around. Women seem to be ageing in terms of appearance less fast than men.'

Was I to take this as a chivalrous compliment? Could I? No. The professor was not looking at me, but signalling the young blonde waitress for a refill.

'Well, the cosmetic industry is massive,' I said, 'and it advertises widely in magazines like *Saga*, too, for ageing and old women.'

'True,' he said, 'and also women are less destroyed by intense physical labour. And nowadays obstetric hazards are fewer too. I am amazed by how much it has turned around.'

'Will humans some day live for ever, Professor?'

'There is a man with whom I had a passage of arms at a science festival. He says at this moment there is living a sixty-year-old who will be the first person to live to be a thousand. He argues that with all sorts of stem-cell treatments and so on, we should be able to postpone mortality. And if you postpone it for twenty years, then you have another twenty years' worth of science to enable you to postpone it a bit more, and so on and so on. He argues way out from gerontological thought.

It is a dream he fosters. He has absolutely no grounds for saying it, of course. But he has an amazing beard.'

Indeed he has, as I saw when I Googled him later. And a glorious moniker, too: Dr Aubrey David Nicholas Jasper de Grey, chairman and 'chief science officer' of the Methuselah Foundation, a non-profit organisation devoted to research into and methods of life extension. Dr de Grey, London born and based at Cambridge University, is not very far into his forties, and therefore at the point in middle age when youth feels the tentative pinch of mortality in its knees or lower back; his horizon must be darkening slightly, too. Extreme longevity, if not immortality, could be starting to seem preferable to Dr de Grey than the fact of his matter.

'What would a body do with a thousand years if we could have them?' I asked Professor Tallis.

'Exactly. How many performances of *Don Giovanni* could you enjoy? A hundred? A thousand? A hundred thousand? Life consists of projects, unfinished projects. With a thousand years ahead, at no point would you have unfinished projects. However, there is no good time to die. You don't want to die while your children are alive; you don't want to die while your grandchildren are alive. Are you happy, I wonder, if you see great-grandchildren on the dole? Is that it? Can you then say farewell?'

'Perhaps a thousand years wouldn't be so bad if we were assured of happiness?'

'Suicide sticks out more when young people do it. But in fact there is a considerable rise in suicide with great age; it seems to correlate with health. But depression too can occur in older people.'

'And how!' I said and bethought myself that according to national statistics the suicide rate has been increasing steadily among the aged, particularly in women over seventy-four.

'Insurance', my mother called the poison pills that, she liked to tell me with affected nonchalance, she had stowed in the top drawer of her desk.

Once her depression had settled in and become clinical, she never again referred to suicide. Perhaps the prescribed 'happy pills' mitigated her flair for melodrama. And I found no poison when going through her effects, only a few aspirins that I swallowed on the spot. Depression's dark wings beat around me too nowadays with a sound more sombre than the bluesy bass notes of my youth. Many mornings I wake up early, wondering: Why? Why bother? It passes. That faith in answers, that stubborn curiosity, continues to triumph. One of the few survivors of the Jonestown Massacre in 1978 – did you know? – was a woman aged seventy-six who hid under her bed while nearly one thousand other cult-followers were taking their own lives and the recalcitrant having them taken by order of the boss.

'Bad health can bring depression,' said Professor Tallis, and I had a hunch he knew first-hand what he was talking about when he continued: 'Yes, also a sense of constraint and nothing to look forward to. Not having long-term planning is a benefit of old age in one way because it allows you to enjoy the here and now, but it also takes away a dimension of meaning. You can no longer say, "This is where I am going to be," because you know where you are going to be: food for worms. Or ashes: green ashes – I want to be recycled when I grow up. When you are very old you commit yourself to being rather than becoming. You could say that old age is characterised, not by a monotonous and predictable progression line, but by increased variants. I used to tell my medical students: "All old people are different, that's why they're interesting. All young people like you are the same, that's why you're all so boring."'

Lean, alert, with his high-domed forehead and neat, greying beard, the professor is a man open to thoughts and possibilities. The impertinent old gremlin stirred within me: is he, after all, in pursuit of a cure for his own approaching old age? Or is he trying hard to welcome it instead of minding it awfully, as who does not? Poets, perhaps, mind it more than most.

'First of all, people have had different life courses,' he said, 'and so they have diverged; second, the age of rot varies enormously, both within old age – between sixty and ninety, say – and within a stratum of old age. Yes, there is residual ageing, systemic and non-focal: call it harmonious decline. Most studies of the ageing of organs are flawed because they have not separated the impact of disease from wear and tear. When you do cross-sectional studies – say, comparing a thirty-year-old with a seventy-year-old – the differences are not due to ageing alone but are also due to the fact that the younger person has had a totally different life experience. The seventy-year-old has been through a war, may have had poorer nutrition, has not had the same educational opportunities, etcetera, so the studies may be flawed.'

Resonating around us was a note of thinking more wishful than scientific. Professor Tallis heard it, too. He smiled and shrugged slightly.

'We all of us have been young or are actually young. Nobody has been old,' he said. 'Not until you reach it. So in that sense, when you're old, you are a sort of alien in a way. Furthermore, alienation is increased by a marked resentment that still exists of the authority of older people. I know there is little respect left for the aged but there is an historical memory still of when authority was earned simply through seniority: the "gerontocrat" who could order you around simply because he'd been there longer.'

There was a small tussle for the bill for our coffees. I lost. Or do I mean I won? The professor paid.

'A lot of things that seem paradoxical and unsatisfactory about the way we grow old,' said Professor Tallis as we were parting, 'are actually paradoxical and unsatisfactory about life.

My wife and I have a place in Cornwall and every year we find it more difficult to arrive. We say: "When did we arrive in Cornwall? Was it when the car drew up outside the door? When we were barefoot on the beach?" The postcards of the mind refuse to turn into animated experiences.'

We shook hands at the door.

'Now in old age, when you lack distractions,' said the professor, 'you're forced to say: "I am going to experience today . . ."'

Walking home, I found myself on the street where I had lived before my recent move. A wave of nostalgia took me over again in its geriatric form, free of the desire to return. My remembering was so absolute that, for a moment there where I used to live, I felt life as it was, knew it again in my very bones before it became what it now is. I rose again to a sense of promise in the morning post, to the sharp taste of black grapes, to the twinge of hangovers from uproars the night before.

At last, I thought, I am old enough to experience yesterday.

'Long in the tooth?' said my dentist.

It was my own fault for opening my big mouth; now I was prevented from closing it again for most of our allotted half an hour.

'Well, it was assumed that as you got older, inevitably you would get gum disease. The gums receded so that when older people smiled the teeth looked longer. That's a misnomer today because gum disease, if it is treated as we can now, won't cause that recession any more or maybe just slightly. Flossing, for example, really took off in the sixties.'

Flossing was not the first thing that came to my non-orthodontic mind as a high point of the swinging sixties. My dentist was now reaching for a sophisticated tool against dental decrepitude that my father, who started his dental practice back in the 1930s, would not have believed possible. He could no more have imagined doing without the darkroom where he used to develop patients' X-rays and our holiday snaps, too, taken with an old box camera. Now, the image of my teeth and jaw rose up before me in alarming detail on a TV screen in the surgery.

'Until then,' said my dentist, barely audible over the noisy drill, 'being long in the tooth was inevitable. And then generally they had dentures and the dentures became more and more worn, so the whole jaw shrank and you'd get a chin-to-nose appearance as people pushed their jaws forward. Teeth become worn, too, from grinding, so old people lost the vertical dimension; the lower third of your face goes like this . . .' I could not see, only imagine, the face he was making over my gaping head. 'The bite is not locked in any more so old people naturally push the jaw forward. But we have much better restorative dentistry today and far fewer people lose all their teeth. When I started practising twenty-five years ago, I would do two to three full dentures a day. Now? I cannot remember the last time I did a full lower denture. But that's a socio-economic thing too. I started off in a lower socio-economic area. Now, have a good rinse . . .'

I took the opportunity to say how dentistry seemed to be turning into a cosmetic industry; leaning back again in the chair, I started to tell him of my surprise that his two younger colleagues in the practice advertise injections of what it was too late to pronounce. His experienced ear got my drift: Botox.

'It doesn't matter what the age, people want to improve their appearance; it is this quest for youth. I have people in their sixties and seventies wanting better smiles. Why not? It's giving back what they had. That's the whole revolution with implants. Dentistry always used to be taking something away. For once we are not taking it away; we are putting something back. Yes, it does cost. But it is getting cheaper. Relatively. You Americans are more attuned to going to the dentist and, dare I say it?

Paying for it, too. The Health Service started in 1948 and dentistry was heavily subsidised until, I think it was, the mid to late 1970s. And when that came to an end people were not prepared to pay for it themselves and dentistry became an expensive commodity.'

He could have said that again! The bill for implanting a fractious crown was going to be £600. And my private insurance would not cover even half that sum. Meanwhile the provider had raised my swingeing monthly payment by 25 per cent, due to my advanced age, don't you know? For the first time I might soon need to claim for more than the occasional scan or dental work on an insurance policy I have been paying dutifully for thirty years or so.

'I think I could actually have survived with the space between those back teeth,' I said, returned to speech and preparing to leave the surgery.

'You could, but it wouldn't be nice. You would miss it. And you would feel . . . Well, it's a trauma, something is going. You'd be losing part of your being; a tooth is part of yourself, your power, your vigour.'

As I walked homeward from the dental surgery, down the busy street, I was thinking of my father and of how painless dentistry has become, except in the region of the wallet. A young man in a doorway started forward to hand me a leaflet; his companion in whatever trade they were plying grabbed his arm and said: 'Not her. She's past it . . .'

And what precisely is 'past it', you young idiots? Past caring? No. Not past caring. Let my grandson smile as he reaches out for a hug and I care with all my heart. When we hear doomsayers declaring that the resources of this planet will be exhausted in a decade or two, do we old folks not care because, what the blazes, we won't be around to share what's left? You bet we care; we love this place no less because we're due to leave it sooner than you. Of course, I know you two ugly boys mean past caring or being cared for sexually. So what? Old-timers play golf instead; is there really that much difference between the two games? Once procreation is taken out of the equation, both are a bumpy race to the thrill of a hole.

'Excuse me asking,' said the anonymous woman from the bank, quizzing me over the phone to verify my identification, 'but what is your birth date?'

Excuse her for asking? Why? Should I be ashamed of my age? Ashamed of being a Jew? Being born American? Being a woman? Ashamed of being 'past it'? Past it?

Can someone tell me precisely what 'it' is? Taste buds become dull, true enough, and put us past gourmandising, even should our finances still stretch to feasting; sexual desire, if it remains at all, is no longer a lush and verdant oasis, merely a canteen of water to share with a beloved old fellow traveller in the desert; vision dims or doubles, requiring smart little windows before our eyes; and if we do not hear as well as once we did? In urban life a degree of deafness could be a blessing. Granted, there does come a point in a very long life where one is no longer able to take good care of oneself; but does that mean no longer caring about oneself? No. That is not what I have been hearing voices older even than my own telling me. They care about themselves and their memories, their opinions, their remaining pleasures.

Health and illness make news these days; obesity, anorexia, DNA, Alzheimer's, HIV all appear in the headlines of an average week. One in this morning's paper announces that, according to yet another university group of researchers, 'Today's young men will live to ninety-one'. Statistics make for bemusing quibbles. Why not ninety-two? Nevertheless, we the pioneering generation of the well-kept aged had better not allow ourselves to be pushed 'past it'; otherwise how will all those predicted nonagenarians, our beloved grandchildren, have anything interesting left to do with their numerous decades beyond the youthful pale: their own 'past it'?

Yes, I thought, standing before the still-unfamiliar view out of my window: it was time to dust off my passport again; time for a journey. I needed to make some more memories for shelter and sustenance on the road ahead. Viva Peter Pan! Whatever contempt comes our way, and impatience, and scorn, whatever we relinquish to time and nature, we old-timers owe it to ourselves and to the future, too, not to lose our bite.

An Old Pillar of the Community: Dr John Madden

In these forty-plus years since my transplantation from the US to Great Britain, not much has changed in the Western world as much as the role of the local GP. Remember your local GP? Unless you are a good bit over fifty, the chances are you do not. But for anyone in old age, a doctor is part of their childhood memories: 'the family doctor' – practically a relative.

John Madden, who is now in his lean and fit mid-eighties, qualified at Oxford after the war and spent two years in the Radcliffe Infirmary as a house physician before moving to a practice in Hounslow – 'On the Piccadilly Line', he says with a grin – where he was a local doctor for most of four decades. Is it merely coincidence that, as with all the GPs I knew in my youth on both sides of the Atlantic, John is devoted to classical music and theatre? And he is ever so slightly and charmingly eccentric.

As a GP I was doing everything – delivering babies, psychiatry, skin diseases – everything a GP used to do. After forty years you found yourself delivering the baby of somebody you delivered. People ask me now, 'Don't you miss it?' I miss the colleagues and nurses; I miss the patients; I do not miss the work. Bank managers, dancers, musicians, they haven't changed much, have they? But doctoring has changed both for better and for worse. That's what change always is, isn't it? For better and for worse. The vocational aspect was stronger in my early days. Now there is big money to be made fairly easily, at least by medical management. And the GP spends more time now in front of his computer than at patients' bedsides. GPs today hardly ever pay house visits. And they have these things called quotas: funny almost, even a bit obscene. Mind you, I did not always want to be a doctor. For me as a child medicine was death, vomit, smells, diarrhoea, blood, pus, and I did not fancy it. But nature intervened. I found botany and zoology were the only subjects I took to. I was a scientist, a natural scientist, not physics; and of course there is an increasing amount of science in medicine.

I know a few young doctors now. The chap who took over from me was young; now he's middle-aged. They are always complaining, but when you earn £120,000 a year for less than a five-day week and are finished by six in the evening, with two afternoons off, and no weekends or night calls – why complain? We had a twenty-four-hour day, seven days a week. Now when I visit my old practice, the GPs are all stuck at their computers. My brother and his wife are both doctors in Chicago; it's even worse there – there is an almost total lack of diagnostic skills. Most people there have a scan before they are even seen by a doctor. It's started happening here, too. Ask a medical student to examine a knee and they waffle, waffle, never having been taught how. And the knee is simple: if you rotate the thing and it hurts, that's probably cartilage; if you bend it and it hurts, that's probably the ligaments. The knee is one of the first things that goes in age. And hips.

A few years ago when I was eighty-one, I ran three miles or so at the end of a marathon. My mother died fairly early, of breast cancer when she was about sixty; my father lived to be about eighty-nine, not quite as spry as I am, but pretty good. I remember to everyone's horror that he used to climb the tree in our back garden to get the apples. He was eighty at the time. The genetic thing keeps me spry.

And then there is curiosity. I am curious about everything. If I were on the way to my own execution and we passed a cobweb with the light striking it a certain way, I'd say: 'Oh, look at that! See how the light strikes it. I've never seen a cobweb like that one before!' I am curious in science still, about all the things I vaguely know about but not enough: quantum theorem in physics, and quarks, that's the kind of thing I enjoy trying to understand. I read about it on and off. But my curiosity moves quickly to something else. Maybe that helps keep me spry too?

In just this year I've been to Prague, Athens, and Chicago. I know I must be getting old because my vision isn't as good as it was. There is still someone inside me who feels like a teenager. But you cannot any longer do what you used to do, not only the athletic things, but learning things too. I taught myself Modern Greek but after all the effort I put into it over the past few years I should speak it better than I do.

And in age one finds oneself thinking of all the things that did not happen, and all the things that happened that you cannot do anything about. My mother shouldn't have . . . Oh, I mean to say, her cancer was so far advanced before she even went to her GP. People didn't go to their doctors then as readily as they do now, and that is a step for the better. But, remember my saying that change is always for better and for worse? In my day – the 1920s, 1930s, and 1940s – when we got mumps or chickenpox we never called the doctor. Our mothers gave us whatever they gave back then and probably their mothers before them; but no doctor. Now a lot of mothers have lost all confidence in their own judgement and opinion; if the child is even slightly feverish they take it to A&E, cluttering the place up with what could have been dealt with just by a calm mother, or a phone call to the GP. Or even a call to Granny. Yes, the possibilities of medicine have increased fantastically, though sometimes common sense is the best medicine.

In the 1920s and 1940s everything started to happen: penicillin, vaccinations against this, immunisations against that, antibiotics; in 1946 when I qualified we felt that in a few years cancer would be curable and everyone would be healthy. Also of course after the war we thought everyone had learned their lesson and we would all be brothers. But people kept on dying of cancer and wars started again. Until the end of the nineteenth century there were not many drugs or procedures that you could not have had in ancient Greece. Supposing I was transplanted to ancient Greece, the only useful thing I could tell them would be: 'Boil water before you drink it,' and 'Hold your instrument in a flame before you operate.' If they wanted to know why, I guess I'd have to say the demons of fire are more powerful than the demons of disease. These days, you know, patients needing surgery feel cheated if the surgeon uses a scalpel; they feel cheated if it's not a laser. And so many scans are done unnecessarily. And at the same time there is a growing scorn, a mistrust almost, for medicine and science in general, probably connected to the general current impression that if doctors did their job properly we would all live for ever. Look at the rapidity with which people sue these days! My brother tells me that in Chicago a neurosurgeon's insurance can equal half his income.

I don't think respect for the aged should be automatic. But yes, I feel the scorn of the young. I try not to resent it; I try to understand it. But I do find it curious when young people say: 'What do you know? You lived in a different world.' Do they think we don't see the world? I see the world. I see its unpleasantness and its good bits, too. And I can look back at what the world was like; the young cannot do that. It wasn't so hot then either; there was brutality and poverty. But there were good things then, too. I sometimes feel sorry for young people today. They have computers and Nike shoes and designer this and designer that. But they seem a troubled lot, many of them; there is a loss of confidence in the future, a loss of the enthusiasm and genuine optimism that we used to feel.

Sometimes I regret that my art master didn't tell my family to get me into Birmingham repertory to be an assistant stage manager and go around with the props. I would have loved that! I am stage-struck. And music-struck. And ballet-struck. And I regret the relationships that didn't work out. That's the

Doctor Faustus thing: I would not sell my soul to be young again, whatever a soul is, but sometimes I think: Oh, wouldn't it be wonderful to find somebody new who loves you, not just an old friend, wonderful though they are. Yes, at a certain stage you regret the fact that you can never really fall in love again. I have no children. My wife had bipolar, manic-depressive disease. This was before lithium, and she was afraid she would not be able to cope. At times I wonder what our children would be like if we had had them. But we did not spend our years together bemoaning the fact we had no children. (*John reaches for a pack of cigarettes on the sideboard in his living room.*)

Yes, yes, I smoke; I have since I was a tiny little boy. My father didn't smoke, but his friends would often leave a cigarette end and even at five or six I would play with it. Again, I am genetically lucky. I wish tobacco were not there. But even more I wish there had been a beneficent god who would not have given man a lovely little pleasure with a sting in its tail. Tobacco, booze, sex: they all have a sting in their tail. But I am not a believer. God is a simple way of expressing all the beautiful and wonderful things mankind can do and be, all the love and beauty and art and music.

When my wife died, the following year and a half were lonely; most of the week I was on my own. And then three years ago the daughter of an old friend, someone I had known for sixty-odd years, decided to move from France, where she had been living, to work in London. Fortunately I had a spare room. And it has transformed my life: the fun, the intellectual chat, the companionship; we have a shared love of music and take meals together as often as not. And yes, I know too that if I have a stroke or a heart attack, there is somebody there to care for me when I come out of hospital. Oh, she is a young and beautiful woman who will go her way eventually. But when that happens, it happens; who knows when? We are friends; it is an unlikely friendship but on the whole I think the love of friendship can be stronger and more durable than being in love. And as long as you have curiosity and vitality, and you do not grow distant or grumpy, you will continue to make friends, probably younger than you. And so this doctor prescribes for the condition of old age.

I I

Going North

NORTH, SOUTH, EAST, and west: where would we be without them? Where on earth? These opposites, each distinct, all define a planet of our own that we can camp on for a while, cultivate, and plunder. The points of our compass carry myths and music; they are freighted with history and weighted with metaphor. East for the Americans of my day was the way to our roots and the source of our transcendent faiths; eastwards lay the inspiration of the early Yankees. West tickled ambition; to be westbound for our forefathers was first to sail hopefully and then to gallop into derring-do, and conquest, and the kind of boyish adventures later exported by Hollywood as 'westerns', an outmoded genre that was eventually overtaken by war movies and space odysseys. South is the holiday direction, the way of time off and retirement. South is lush and sensual for the young; for the old it eases aches in bones and brains. South is unreal life and someone else's problem. And north? North, the autocrat of our compass, holds the other three in check. The polar regions do not entice, they compel; explorers choosing the north are driven men, more solitary and less protected than astronauts. North is stiff and ponderous, up and down. From where I stand, here across the frontier of old age, north is the last great gasp of curiosity; it remains to be seen.

As we grow old we draw in and trim our sails; we hoard what we have left and ration it to last, while life outside our encampment becomes increasingly hostile and full of new threats to body and soul. The long summer days of the north hold too many hours to fill to any purpose and their endless brightness defeats our dreams. Then its winter nights arrive, growing longer and longer until one of them must last for ever. I saw how my father's life shrank into a winter of enduring night, his joints locking, each breath an ethereal fog, his reason unhinged, and his memories offering the only warmth in his chilly solitude; beyond his door lay darkness and hungry animals. Later, I watched Mother withdraw into her own Arctic, where spoken words were little more than a buzzing in her ears, while her purblind eyes remained fixed on the TV's heatless glow. To grow old is to enter the polar regions, and, in the hemisphere where I live, that means going north. I am now entering the north of my life.

'But why, why?' everyone cried when I said I planned a trip to Alaska. 'Isn't it cold enough for you here? Why go there?'

'To see the Northern Lights.'

'You can see them in Scotland,' volunteered my hairstylist, a Scot.

'We see them best in my country' said the Finnish girl behind the counter of the shop where I buy brown rice and honey, mainstays of my latter-day diet.

'It's symmetry,' I tried to explain. 'Symmetry becomes irresistible with age. It is our last chance to make sense of things, or try to. I have never seen the aurora borealis. How many more new things will I see in this life? I like the idea of seeing this one back where I saw everything for the first time.'

'But Alaska! You're having me on. You cannot mean it!'

Just like the idea of being seventy-two, eighty-one, or ninety-three years old, Alaska is a destination inconceivable to the young.

Disbelief in my fabled destination continued after I landed in New York. From my hotel, I rang Amtrak for information about trains to the outpost of the continent.

'Hello! Thank you for calling Amtrak. This is Julie,' the damned thing enunciated, every bit as if it were a christened human being. 'Where do you want to go?'

'Alaska.'

'Greensboro?'

'Alaska,' I corrected it sharply.

'Got it! Orlando!'

'Al-ask-uh, Al-ask-uh, Al-ask-uh!'

'Sorry. I did not understand.'

'A-bloody-lask-uh!'

'Are you calling about our auto-train service in which you take your car between New York City and Orlando, Florida?'

I slammed the phone into its cradle, took a deep breath and dialled again. This time I applied the teachings of a committed Luddite friend and punched in a zero before I could be launched on another robotic misadventure.

'Thank you for calling Amtrak,' a girlish voice replied.

'Are you real?'

'Yes, I am real,' came her reply: weary, fed-up, no joke.

'Please can you tell me about trains from New York to Alaska?'

'This is Amtrak,' she said. 'We do not concern ourselves with Alaska.'

'But I don't understand. It hasn't seceded from the Union, has it?'

'Amtrak does not concern itself with Alaska.'

'But it is part of your land mass.'

'Alaska is not Amtrak's concern,' she said, and clicked me into oblivion.

Poor old Alaska: no concern of Amtrak; unmentioned in continental American weather forecasts. Alaska is like a super-annuated remittance man, returned home at last to be sheltered within the family, though barely, and only so distant relatives can mine his remaining wealth.

'Nobody reads Jack London these days,' said Michael on the phone when I complained of a general failure of concern or interest in the forty-ninth state.

That my brother happened also to be in New York when I arrived there en route to Alaska was a happy surprise. His home in California and mine in London are half a world apart; it is always a treat to meet again, and especially where we were born and grew up, in the middle.

'Hey, Irm, I was reading a fascinating new book about Lincoln's assassination.'

Let it be months, even years between our meetings, and Michael's opening words are bound to be: 'Irm, I was reading a fascinating book the other day . . .' My brother is a dyed-in-the-wool bibliophile; shelves are his first furniture, the rustle of pages his favourite music; the mere smell of books en masse intoxicates him. His wife says he buys books as other men gamble or drink. It is unlikely that many more of us will grow old with my brother's addiction to the printed page. A few years ago on a visit to New York, Michael discovered that his all-time favourite bookstore, the Coliseum, had closed its doors for ever. His distress at the loss was heartbreaking to see; he grieved as would a pilgrim deprived of St Peter's and so of heaven, too. It was a joy for me to be able to tell my brother that I had learned that the Coliseum was reincarnated downtown from its old address. Naturally, we arranged to meet outside his blessed bookstore within the hour.

I saw Michael from afar. He stood four-square and stockstill across the street from the bookstore. Since he had arrived early, I knew he must be itching to browse. Only when I drew closer was I struck by my brother's momentary resemblance to our father, his face clouded by morose bemusement. Michael's rueful gaze was fixed on a pair of workmen high up on ladders either side of what hours earlier must have been 'The Coliseum Bookstore' and was now 'oliseum Boo'. Nor would it be that for long: it was clear the re-incarnation had failed. Each workman was in the very process of removing an 'O' from either side of the overhanging sign. Below their ladders the shop front was boarded up, and this time for ever. I took my brother's arm and led him gently away from paradise lost.

'Maybe I should have asked if I could buy an "O",' he said after a while. 'I'd like something to remember it by.'

He sighed. We walked half a block east in silence.

'You know what I saw today, Mook? They've turned the Plaza Hotel into condominiums. The Plaza Hotel! Remember *Eloise at the Plaza*? Maybe boys didn't read that book. We little girls sure did when I was a kid. The Plaza Hotel! I used to work there back in the 1950s, remember? The Palm Court. The Oak Room. I went down in the elevator once with Cary Grant. The Plaza! Gone, all but its shell, gone.'

We sighed and walked another silent block.

'You know, Irm,' he said, 'I'm set to retire in a couple of months.'

We waited on the corner of Fifth Avenue for the light to change, then started in silence across the street.

'So you're really going to Alaska? You're heading for sub-zero temperatures, you know. I'm going to get you a ski mask,' he said on the other side.

I was going to find out in Alaska that ski masks fuddle old codgers by forcing steamy breath to ascend and fog our spectacles. Nevertheless, I cherished the ski mask as a token of love and concern from my first companion, and the last remaining since practically the outset of this long trek north.

At five o'clock next morning Manhattan's streets, still ablaze with coloured lights, were as empty as a funfair before its gates are open to the public. My compulsion to turn up early at ports and stations of departure has a source sweeter than Freudian travel angst, or so I choose to believe. It is while waiting among strangers for the call to a destination – watching them, listening, and talking to a few of them – I feel the journey start to turn into an adventure. As my fellow passengers accumulated in Pennsylvania Station, the stealthy romance of the open road started to take me over so that by the time the classic call, 'All aboard,' came at last, it sounded like an invitation into the first reel of a *film noir*.

'Canada?' asked the ticket man at the gate.

'Toronto,' I said.

'That's still in Canada.'

'Glad to hear it,' I replied and we exchanged flutters of a smile.

The most interesting way for me to get to Alaska had turned out to be first across Canada from Toronto to Vancouver by train, then to wing it north to Fairbanks. I have always preferred steerage on the road welcoming the long, hard trail as a link to the hobo-poets of my youth. Nevertheless, in a stiffer, prosaic old body these days, I was not sorry to find that seats on the Toronto-bound train had plenty of legroom and even a panel that could be lifted to allow a passenger to recline at almost full stretch during the twelve-hour journey.

'You guys should move forward,' I overheard the conductor say behind me.

He was checking the tickets of an aged English couple; the woman had told me in a brief waiting-room chat that they were on their way to visit a married daughter and new grand-child in Canada.

'You guys have got first-class tickets,' the conductor told them.

'You mean this isn't first class? You mean it gets better than this?' said the woman.

'Excuse me.' Having heard her accent, an American boy leaned across the aisle to ask: 'What are Yurpin trains like? Like, I'm going to Yurp for the first time next year.'

'Some of them are fast,' said the woman, rising for her trek forward to first class. 'But I've never seen one, not one, anywhere near as comfortable as this . . .'

'I'll take, like, speed over comfort any day,' the young man replied.

'Not when you're our age, you won't,' said the snowy matron, and looked at me: 'Am I right?'

A title on my imagined shelf is *Working Beauty*: a big coffee-table book of full-page vistas of industrial architecture as it can be seen from road and rail all over the world. Our train was following the steely Hudson north out of town where factories and foundries, most of them retired from use, lined the tracks. They are not as solemn and elegiac as industrial architecture in the North of Britain, although the pipes of aluminium, the strutting derricks and chimneys, a few still smoking, achieve a silvery abstract jumble that glamorises American pragmatism into practically an art form: a practical art from. Not long past the George Washington Bridge, the rhythm of American railway tracks went into its old bluesy syncopation with my heart.

'What does the train whistle remind you of?' Mother used to ask when I was still too young to be reminded of anything. Now, I remembered my first long journey alone; I was sixteen and travelling by rail to a poetry-reading competition in Chicago where I was booked to recite Tennyson's *The Lady of Shalott* for the judges. It was then, as we rolled into the great American flatlands, I felt a train whistle wanderlust into my virginal soul for the first time. My young heart beat fast and hot: 'The mirror crack'd from side to side . . .'

Barely an hour out of Penn Station, the porches of passing houses were jagged with foot-long icicles. As a child I used to wake and see icicles, sharp and hard as steel, suspended over my bedroom window. It had occurred to me then, years before I ever read a thriller, that an icicle would melt without trace in the warmth of the body it penetrated, giving it a rare homicidal potential.

'And phallic, too, I guess, old girl,' I told myself. 'Oops!'

If I had indeed spoken carelessly aloud as I thought, nobody was bothered. The car was not crowded; the seat next to me was empty. Outside, the day was clear and cold; no smoke rose from the chimneys of the houses; the parking lots were jammed with cars; everything was waiting for its life force to return on the 6 p.m. express from Manhattan. Window-shopping life as usual from within my passing bus or train, I reckoned it too late – far, far too late – to fit myself into a clapboard house on the Hudson as I could have done, and probably would have done long ago, if I'd stayed where I belonged and become a dedicated car driver within commuting distance of the city. Or married one. My long, sweet freedom on the road has paradoxically been thanks to never having owned a car. Or married one.

Our compartment was overheated. I kicked off my snow boots and fanned myself with my hands as younger, menopausal woman do. The bald old chap seated alone in front of me had gone forward to the buffet car; he now returned with two bottles of chilled water, one of them for me.

'I could see you were suffering from the heat. It is too warm in here,' he said in a middle-American accent.

His rare kindness was appreciated all the more for being the prelude to merely a brief exchange.

'I've never been outside the US before,' he said, turning back to his window and its moving view.

I was surprised. He certainly did not have the prickly air of a bumpkin on the road. Was he perhaps a cleric? Yes, of course, a priest in mufti, always at the command of others and alone least of all in his own company. But his interest in the passing scenery was earthy, critical, even a little calculating. So maybe he was a working man recently retired; a hard-working man, too, going by his build, still solid and stocky in age. Evidently not long ago he became a widower, whence the coffee stains on his tie and his pensive concentration, as if seeing trees and houses for the first time all by himself. He placed his left hand on the window as if to touch a passing tractor and I saw that he wore no wedding ring, nor was there an indentation on his finger; husbands of our generation, however, his and mine, did not customarily exchange rings at the altar. On our approach to Albany, someone had scrawled 'Abolish homos' in big red letters along a siding. Yes. Of course, that must be it. The bald old loner was gay and had been made reticent in a time when his dangerous secret needed keeping.

We drew near the Canadian border and the public announcements had begun to sound downright churlish.

'We have to close the refreshment car now,' said the disembodied male voice. 'The Canadians take over at the border. But this train belongs to Amtrak. The Canadians will restock at the border and open up again when they feel like it. But this is an Amtrak train . . .'

All but six passengers in the coach had already disembarked by the time we crossed a bridge and stopped so Canadian customs officials could board and take away our passports. After a long wait at the border station a uniformed guard, not much more than a teenager, finally entered our carriage to return the documents to us. He stopped and perched on the arm of the aisle seat next to the bald man.

'Who are you going to see in Toronto?' he asked in a carrying voice.

The reply was spoken softly; I could not hear it.

'I'll need their names and addresses,' the kid said.

The answer was audible only as a long, low mutter.

'So, like, tell me exactly what were you in prison for?' asked the boy, sharp and clear in the silent carriage. 'And how long for? Wow! That's long. Did your divorce happen then?'

As soon as we were under way again I went forward for a coffee and brought one back, milk and sugar on the side, for the bald man. He was crumpled in his seat.

'Thank you,' he said without raising his head to meet my eye.

Whatever his crime, the sentence was for life.

The wintry chill at the northern frontier does not strike suddenly but gathers slowly like the ache in an ageing knee. As I strolled in Toronto's silvery morning sunlight, a van passed carrying pensioners to lunch or bingo; otherwise everyone in sight appeared to be young and moving briskly.

'I saw Margaret Atwood walking on this very street once,' said the driver-guide later to me and a Japanese couple, the only passengers on his tour bus. 'Margaret Atwood,' he said again, sighing like a lovesick boy.

On first impression, and there was barely time for more between trains, it would require a rare and powerful imagination to transcend a city as cool, handsome, and self-contained as Toronto. Immigrants from all over the world, quick to become new Canadians, blended their colours in the tidy streets. I bought Kleenex tissues from an Estonian chemist; a Brazilian poured my coffee; a Chinese woman gave me directions to the post office. On a subway grate in the central shopping street sat an old lady surrounded by carrier bags and draped in a blanket that billowed in an uprush of warm air. When I offered her a dollar bill she summoned a beautiful smile.

'Oh no, thank you,' she said in the accent of the Russian steppes. 'I am so warm, so fine now, thank you!'

When I was young my best journeys were less premeditated than my dreams. Whether on Greyhound buses all over America, hitch-hiking to Istanbul, travelling on public transport around India and Mexico, or sailing before Mediterranean winds: except while my child needed me at home, I used to take my old miles as they came, my ticket always an open return. So why had I booked Canada's VIA transcontinental train in advance of its departure instead of taking potluck with the plebs? Why reserve a hotel room in Fairbanks rather than ask around as usual on arrival? Why this conventional forethought? What was I afraid of? Old ladies with no bed for the night are not left to freeze in the far North, are we? For whatever reason, the trip north had seemed to demand unusual planning and fore-thought; indeed, so does growing old if it is to be in comfort. Have I finally been strait-laced by age? Is it this nervous, para-noid era in which I am travelling north? And remember, too, that there is a new love in my life, and so my soul is once again not free of anchor.

'His name is Jasper,' I told the Canadian dowager next to me in the station where we awaited the station announcements.

'No!' she cried. 'Never! Would you believe that! I do not believe that! Jasper is my grandson's name, too!'

Out came the photos. Would you believe that? Never! And there in the northern hinterlands we two grannies danced the old coincidental jig before scampering for our trains.

I had expected to cross Canada in an ordinary working train with ordinary folks. But that is not how it turned out. The front coaches of our VIA Canada Railway train to Vancouver were carrying the young and youngish, bound for where they had to be, where they were expected, and where they were needed. They duly made themselves comfortable, most of them on upright seats for the three-day journey to Vancouver or a stop along the way. But a canny agent in New York had not so much as mentioned that alternative; she took one look at me and booked me straight into the pricier rear coaches where I found old folks, not needed or needing to be anywhere, land-cruising Canada because: why not? We had a bar, and a dining-car, and our own lounge, surmounted by an observa-tion compartment called 'the Dome'. Luxury has of course more strata than steerage; upon hearing me refer vaguely to my budget, the agent issued me a ticket for the cheapest of six berths on either side of the central corridor running through the posh area. When the seats were opened into bunks at night,

I saw that mine was going to be an upper, putting me directly above another lone traveller, a moustachioed Yorkshireman in his late sixties. Immediately after exchanging names and basic information – provenance, nationality, and, oh yes, he referred to his 'lady friend' back home, too, lest I get any funny ideas – a congenial silence was established between Victor and me: we knew all we ever needed to know about each other. When we chugged out of Toronto and the other four berths in our area remained unclaimed, I switched my gear to a lower one that put us in a less compromising head-to-toe position, with a partition between, to boot.

The train passed through a sprawl of suburbs, neat graffiti ran so low on the walls it must have been done by a gifted child or a crouching artist. Soon we entered a region of lakes and holiday homes where clumps of slim silver birches stood leafless, their trunks fashionably mottled black and white. My brother and I used to peel off the bark from the birches around our lakeside house and scratch messages to each other with twigs on the glossy inner side as we'd been told local Indians once did. The Indians bent saplings, too, to mark directions on their trails. By the time we took over aboriginal territory, the trails were paved roads and any surviving young trees had grown into crooked old arrows pointing to an unwritten history.

Gradually the seats behind me in the Dome were filling. Evidently my age on board was that rare and ambiguous comfort of senescence: average. The combined age of the twenty or thirty of us gathering there must have totalled a couple of millennia; if memories had corporeal weight, ours would bring the train to a halt. I opened my book. Long ago, travelling on Greyhound buses, I learned that to be seen reading makes North Americans think twice about taking the neighbouring empty seat, almost as effectively as to be heard coughing. But for all Katherine Mansfield's brilliance, or perhaps because of it, she was not a good companion on the road. She was the kind who would claim the window seat as her right and regale her neighbour with memories of betrayal and abuse, never in so many words though sometimes in too many. At least a book can be shut up.

'May I sit here?' the old man asked.

He was one of the four male loners I had counted aboard; I was the only lone woman.

'I'm eighty-seven,' he said, settling his big frame into place. 'I sold my house last year and moved to a retirement community. But I find myself doing things, helping others less fit. My doctor says only 15 per cent of my age group are as healthy as I am. When I told my neighbours in Toronto I was bound for Vancouver Island, they said: "But why? An earthquake is forecast there!" What do I care? At eighty-seven why would a little thing like an earthquake stop me? The worst thing that ever happened in my lifetime was the Second World War. No earthquake could be worse than that. Physical work gets you tired, you know, especially in winter.'

He then launched into a long and footnoted dissertation on Canadian timber yards.

'When you retire it gets boring,' he said at last.

I agreed.

'Have you any children?' I asked the retired timber merchant.

'I have three great-great-grandkids.'

'Gosh! What do your great-great-grandkids call you?'

'Old. Very, very old,' he said. 'You know what I think now when I wake up? Oho! I think, what do you know? One more day!'

The train pulled in for a brief stop and the old Canadian – as he was going to do at every stop, no matter the weather or the hour – was up and out to walk the platform briskly back and forth as if his life depended on it. And so it did, I guess.

'Will your husband be joining you?' asked the waiter.

'Oh, I'm not . . .'

Victor appeared at the entrance to the dining-car just then and the waiter bounded away to bring him back and seat him across from me, where he was to take every meal on board thereafter. Victor never visited the Dome or mixed in company on board; we saw each other only at meals and bedtime. We ordered and ate in our customary silence. The cuisine was rich and sugary; I was glad Victor did not order dessert. The man had just devoured a mountain of fried potatoes, for goodness' sake! Quite enough cholesterol for anyone his age. Unexpectedly expansive over coffee, he told me he was on his way to visit his brother's son who had married a Canadian. They lived outside Vancouver.

'A town called Chilliwack,' he said.

Chilliwack: rumbling syllables that could have been designed for his Yorkshire accent. For an untravelled uncle to visit a nephew so far from home probably meant Victor had no children of his own. We sipped our coffee in silence. A little girl in the back seat of a passing car waved at our train. Victor waved back and gave her a military salute. He was smiling. But in his greenish-brownish eyes I thought I saw the shadow of love denied.

And Victor snored. His snoring challenged the dulled roar of Canadian railway tracks; what was worse, he snored out of synch with them. I retreated to the Dome, quiet and empty before dawn. Outside, the snow-covered land lay brighter than the sky, both awaiting the late northern sunrise. For the first time I noted the spectrum contained within white: a full white moon silhouetted frosted trees; white bridges spanned whiter streams and cast faint shadows of white on white; waterfalls of molten, silvery white flowed from streaky-white mountain tops; snow bowed fir trees to the ground where here and there the weakest lay broken, bone-white on a white field. Beside our rails were deer tracks, mincing and neat; seeing them, I longed to be off the train, to lay my own trail in the snow as we used to do when we were kids, and then look back at our fancy footwork. The old canary fluttered and sang in my heart; day was dawning at last. Other people started arriving in pairs, exchanging fulsome 'Good morning's, as virtual strangers do when they are very old.

'Why do they all say good morning?' my father asked suspiciously when he and I went out for a walk and passed other aged folks from the retirement community. 'What do they want from me?'

I was too young then to know what I learned for the first time on the VIA train: they were sharing the pleasant surprise of waking to another day.

A translucent curtain of spindrift was hanging at our front windows. Spindrift: a beautiful word – another title, perhaps, for an anthology of overheard conversations? The women behind me in the Dome talked of their outrage that the showers on board had all frozen solid overnight. After barely two days in the deep northern winter, time had iced over, making it hard to remember 'before' or anticipate 'after'. Was it only yesterday I had disembarked for a walk during our brief stop in Winnipeg? The temperature was forty degrees below zero; tears and sniffles froze solid, as did my eyelashes and small nose-hairs; a surface numbness erased hangnails, eased the recurrent crick in my neck, and offered an inkling of why death by freezing is considered a merciful end to the journey north.

'We used to do this trip every year,' a man near by was saying, 'for my mother's birthday. Got stuck for two days once; snow-slides on the tracks. She was 105 last time. Didn't make it to 106.'

'Hello there,' said a woman on the aisle as I passed on my way to the lounge car for a cup of tea.

I had guessed her to be one of the oldest of our troupe, powdery and petite with the sexless, angelic beauty that sometimes attaches to extremely aged women.

'Do you ski?' she asked. 'Your husband, that quiet Englishman, does he ski?'

She meant Victor, of course, my first and only husband. Victor had to be descended from tillers of the soil, not a skier.

'No,' I said. 'We don't ski.'

'I am on my way to Jasper National Park. I go to Jasper every year to ski.'

'How perfectly wonderful!' I cried in delight at discovering that a national park was named not after, certainly before, my grandson, Jasper.

'Why, thank you,' she said. 'Thank you for not laughing. Most people laugh when I say I ski. I had a friend who skied into his nineties, too.'

That evening before joining Victor for dinner I rejected afternoon tea in favour of red wine. The small bar car had no windows. A young stewardess in attendance there explained that, 'Way, way back in the 1950s', when the train was built, it was illegal in Canada to be seen drinking in public.

'And our older lady passengers still prefer to drink where nobody sees them,' she said.

I lifted my glass to gentility on the northern journey and to the image of an old man gliding on skis into his nineties and eternity.

'A good run,' I whispered.

VIA trains give precedence to Rail Canada's freight trains, some of them miles long; I saw the incomprehensible warning 'Do Not Hump' written on their sides, too, as if anyone would dare. We were running very late for our arrival in Vancouver. Victor did not mind. On the contrary, I came upon him packing in our compartment and looking happy, almost animated. He told me our engineer had agreed to make an unscheduled stop in Chilliwack just so he could disembark there, a good few miles before Vancouver. What was more, Victor had at last found a signal on his mobile phone and so was able to call ahead to tell his nephew about the convenient change in plans that would spare him a drive to the station terminus.

'Oh, there's always another plane,' he said dismissively when I told him that I, on the other hand, was bound to miss my connecting flights to Fairbanks.

One car was parked at the small station of Chilliwack. As we were pulling in, a young couple emerged from it with a little boy who broke loose immediately and began to pack snowballs to throw at the carriages. I stood in the doorway and watched Victor's reunion with his family. He hugged his nephew, shook hands with the wife, then bent and scooped up soft snow to throw at the leaping, laughing child. But he did not turn around or so much as just look back to see me watching. He was not bothered to wave goodbye, and did not even cast a backward glance while the train was carrying me away and out of his life.

'Oh dear,' said one of the old ladies from the Dome, passing behind me on her way to the dining car, 'isn't your husband going with you to Vancouver?'

'He is not my husband,' I corrected her. 'We were only sleeping together.'

I was happy to change my plans and book a later flight; it made feel like the old young me, a liberated traveller again, not just another passenger. A short walk on the waterfront in Vancouver and I came upon a pretty hotel, checked into it, then went out for exploration of the unexpected city. Vancouver soon revealed itself to be one of those places good for raising children in: the sort of place that adventurous children cannot wait to grow up and leave. Although it was indisputably easy on the eye, its propriety felt downright Belgian. The monotone drone of local men in a café where I took a tea break hinted at why I meet so many jolly Canadians on the road, outside their native land. The kind of established order that appears to rule Vancouver's attractive streets can also inflame lunatic rebellion, producing serial killers and comics of tormented wit. I generalise, of course. There is no time to do more on the hoof.

A computer was available in the lobby for hotel guests and before dinner I duly went online to check my emails. There were a few messages about work, a few from friends, and the usual lot of junk. I scrolled down and stopped in alarm at 'The Worst Possible News'. It was a circular from an old friend and former neighbour on the street where I had raised my child. The elder of his own two sons, he told us, had that morning been found dead in bed, having apparently suffered a ruptured aneurysm in his sleep. 'No! No!' the childish logician within me cried out: 'That's not fair! It's not fair!'

My anger is unpractised and clumsy. When I banged my hand on the table, the impact knocked a vase of flowers to the floor; the girl behind the front desk glanced at me in alarm.

'It's not fair! It's not fair,' I said, softly now, shaking my head. 'Why? Why?'

I went out to stand looking at the misty waterfront. Only men mete out death as justice; time does not give a damn. And for those who say they believe in God, the supreme penalty – though it may be the worst men can do – merely transfers the responsibility for punishment to a higher power. There was no 'why'. There was no reason: time and its travelling companion are not open to reason. Death had snatched my own dear son's erstwhile playmate in the midst of his promising life and left me, twice his age, to shiver in the long northern night.

Two Loving Old Voices: Anne and Fred Black

To give love its leeway is not a lesson everyone learns; it is a gift of wisdom, and wisdom comes only to some and only with time. The young cannot know how to let love be; few of them ever will. The young want love to conform to their preconceptions and to obey the rules of romance they inherited or simply those in current fashion.

Anne Black is seventy-two and her husband, Fred, nearly seventy-five. They were on a short holiday across Canada for a sentimental return to places they had visited in their newly wedded youth half a century ago. Other passengers watched, the women especially a little wistfully, whenever Fred and Anne strolled along the platform as they did at each stop. Fred, tall and straight, adjusted himself to Anne's slight incapacity, and her slower, more halting pace. On board they often socialised separately; when they were together they were heard to share frequent laughter and there were almost visible links of warmth and love between them.

Anne: (*We are sitting side by side in the train compartment; Fred sits near by reading a book.*) Getting old is not so bad. A lot of growing old has to do with losing interest in the world; a lot of staying young has to do with staying interested and keeping active. I feel really lucky, but then I live in Canada, a lucky part of the world compared to some places. Canada is neglected but sometimes life here is easier than it was and more pleasant. I mean, it's difficult to be an American; there's so much responsibility attached to it. Europeans of our age know that America did so much for Europe and it is not appreciated there, not now, not any more. The young people do not know how much America did for Europe and if they do they think: Well, that's past, it's over and done . . . Over and done! It doesn't matter any more!

Fred and I have lived mostly in Canada. But we spent two

years in England when we first married, an extended honey-moon, I guess you could call it. We worked there and we made friends. We were lucky because it takes the English a while to make friends. We have been married for fifty years. We're very lucky. I have come to the conclusion a lot of it is luck; I mean who you marry and whether it is going to last. Fred is two and a half years older than I am. Our generation all married older men. It was perceived that the man took full responsibility to look after a wife and family, and how could he do it until he was a bit more established?

You know how we met? Both of us had parents who had been medical missionaries in Korea. My family returned to Canada at the beginning of the war. Fred's family left sooner. His mother used to say they were the last to leave with dignity. My family left with no dignity. We arrived in Japan with our steamship tickets ready to board for home, and we found that the Second World War had started in Europe and all the Canadian ships had been commandeered by the navy. There was not a ship in Kobe harbour. It was a wild scene; every-body standing on the docks with tickets in their hands. Finally an American ship, *The President Wilson*, agreed to take us but they pointed out they didn't have lifeboats sufficient for us, so as long as we were prepared to go down with the ship, we could board.

Of course, war was coming to the East, too. You know, we talk about how Pearl Harbor in 1941 was such a surprising betrayal. But in fact this was in 1940 and everybody knew, all the governments knew, that war was coming, and that's why they had ordered their nationals home from the Far East.

In the missionary community there were two schools of thought: those who thought their work was important, and those who felt the witness was important. Many chose to stay as witness. Medical people like our fathers, Fred's and mine, were more work than faith oriented and they felt that, if they could no longer get the supplies they needed to practise to a high enough standard, then they should leave.

Besides which, we were a hazard to our Korean friends. We were with the American Presbyterians and Fred's family was with the United Church of Canada, a union of Methodists, Presbyterians, and Congregationalists. Our families knew each other because they came together for annual meetings. Fred's family was across the Manchurian border but still working with the Korean community. Mine was in Seoul where my father was born in 1893. Fred's family were already settled in British Columbia when we finally left.

My father was not happy to come to Canada. He had given his life to Korea and now he had to accept whatever work was available. He went into public health and he travelled all over Canada. Eventually we got to British Columbia and we settled there, my father in public health and my mother a full-time person at home. In Korea she had taught at school; the American Church was very forward-looking, even a little Communist by today's standards. Each worked according to his ability and was paid according to his needs, which meant everyone was paid the same amount and wives were given a pay cheque equal to their husbands'. So back in 1920 my mother always had her own pay cheque. That was before people became very fearful of the idealistic Communist approach.

When the Great Depression hit us in 1930, the Canadian missions sent their newer people back home. The American missionaries voted on whether they would get their salaries halved or lose half their people. And they voted to have their salaries halved, so overnight my parents were earning half their previous income.

Fred and I are churchgoers; I wouldn't say we're traditional-minded people, nor were our parents. They may have been missionaries but they were medical missionaries, and very practical. I remember asking my mother whether she believed in a lot of the Church creeds and so on, and she said: 'Of course not!' And I said, 'Well then, why do you say the Apostles' Creed in church?' And she said: 'Because it's part of the service.' She felt it was a bonding thing among peoples, a coming together. She was very independent minded, so was Fred's family, if a little less so.

I am one of five girls; Fred is one of five too, four boys and a girl. Thus, in Korea his family was seen to have done well, his father particularly; my father was an object of pity with our Korean friends. He was quite happy with his girls but they used to ask: 'Who will visit your grave?' That was an important duty in Korea and when they married daughters were lost to their birth families. Fred and I have four children: one son and three daughters and eight grandchildren, four of each. We live in Toronto; we have three children in the Maritimes and one in Calgary. Our friends say it is a pity they live so far away, but we left home when we were married, our parents left home when they were married, my grandparents went to Korea in 1893, so it was all we expected.

What's the secret of a long, happy marriage? Well, first, as I said, there is luck. And for me it is partly at least that Fred can make me laugh. A sense of humour counts for a lot and I don't think I basically have much of a sense of humour, so it was wonderful to marry someone who did and who could make me see the fun in things. We had similar backgrounds, too, which made it easier, but we are not alike in many ways so it is not that, not just that. We both have missionary backgrounds, medical backgrounds, and our mothers were both teachers; nevertheless, our families behaved very, very differently. My older sister married one of Fred's older brothers and even though the marriage survived it was a difficult marriage for both of them. Maybe we are just easygoing people, I don't know, because our marriage has remained constant fun. And new things happen all the time. We respect each other's expertise in different fields and, more than that, we admire each other. Fred is an engineer, he is thoroughly practical. He said to me once that my head was stuffed with useless knowledge and I told him that was fine, as he had more than enough useful knowledge for both of us.

You have to give each other room to manoeuvre. Fred's a keen sailor and I'm sure it was a shattering disappointment to him that I was not. But he goes on doing what he loves to do, and I do what I love to do. We even took separate holidays sometimes; not long holidays. Even when we took holidays together, we would separate for some time and then meet, and it was so much fun to learn what the other one had done that day, and seen.

We never felt we knew everything about each other. I am arty and arts-minded, and I learned early that I had a real gift for teaching. The current belief is that you can teach anything as long as you focus on the student, on the child. That is not my feeling; I think the subject comes first. I loved my subject, English, and I liked my students. My pleasure was to communicate my enthusiasm to them. That is not a popular idea; it has gone from the theory of teaching. But it made me a good teacher and, I hope, an inspiring one. Does that sound old-fashioned? I taught senior grades – seventeen-, eighteen-, nineteen-year-olds – and then for a most gratifying time I taught adult education to people who had not been able previously to get their degrees. When our government decided to close down all-adult schools, such as the one where I had been teaching for some time, and go in for what was called the 'back to the basics' movement, I took early retirement.

Growing old? Well, we always assume our health is going to be pretty good as we approach old age, and we assume that if we have been healthy all our lives, it will go on. It is a bit of a shock to find we need new knees and new hips. In my case, I had a stroke eighteen months ago, which was totally unexpected. It has made me slow down and I rather resent it, especially as my speech gets clumsy sometimes. Fred has been very, very good but it is hard for him; he is someone who always has a lot of energy. I was paralysed down one side. I never lost my speech altogether and was able to communicate. I still have no trouble finding the words, only saying them: my mouth and tongue are numb. Nothing provoked the stroke. It came out of the blue. Well, except we were in the middle of making love at the time. Love can endure. Oh yes, it can. Oh my, yes. I have reason to be joyful; there is so much in life to enjoy.

(*Fred leaves off reading his book and crosses the train carriage to join us.*)

Fred: Deep concentration can be sustained for only so long! I remember when we called on my cousin after we were two years married, he said we looked as if we were still on honeymoon. That was our English sojourn and a fairly carefree time; not that I didn't catch the edge of her tongue a few times! The secret of a long marriage? Giving each other space has got something to do with it. When I found out what a lousy sailor she was, I stopped press-ganging her into coming aboard. But I continued to sail.

Anne: And I remember when you gave me a book on wild flowers. One of my passions is wild food and wild flowers. And in it you wrote: 'Good hunting, Anne.' The point being that it was a subject that did not interest him at all, something to please me alone.

Fred: Of course, there was the other time I gave you a wood-turning lathe . . .

Anne: I still hope to learn to use it some day.

Fred: She has a fascination for turned-wood items and she loves to spend my money on them.

Anne: Why, what do you mean 'your' money?

Fred: To take a piece of natural grain, every one of which

is different, and then shape it into a free-form object is a very high form of art. Well, to her anyway.

It wasn't precisely love at first sight. We'd known each other for ten years but there was a two and a half year difference between us in age and, besides, my younger brother was sweet on her. It wasn't until some years later, after her family had moved to British Columbia and I came calling once for Sunday tea, that I was surprised at how much she had changed in that time. A little later I was with an air force summer programme and they were going to hold a dance. Since I didn't know a soul in Vancouver, I started racking my brains and then I thought: Well, that was a very presentable young lady I'd just met, and maybe she'd come to the dance with me.

Anne: (*laughing*) I didn't know I was the only girl you knew in Vancouver! And there was I, so charmed to be invited out by this older man. Fred was eighteen; I was sixteen.

Fred: But there had never been anything like the magic of that night. (*He chuckles.*) It was lovely. It was . . .

Anne: You see, in many cases our generation married because it was expected of us. Also, if you lusted after each other, in those days there was only one thing to do!

Anne and Fred in chorus: (*laughing*) Get married!

Anne: And that happened to a lot of people who should not have married each other. You see? We were lucky. It's wonderful, isn't it, when people keep their minds alive? Who cares for what reason!

12

Aurora

THE CROWD WAITING to board the Air Alaska flight to Juneau and then to Fairbanks were mostly Alaskans, meaty and jovial. Everyone stood suddenly and burst into applause for our captain when he emerged waving from the departure gate while it was being announced over a loudspeaker that this was to be his last flight before retirement. One woman standing near me started to weep. Evidently I had entered a region where air travel is used for regular commuting; passengers know their stewards and pilots as once we knew conductors on our buses.

The man who sat next to me when we finally boarded and I claimed my window seat was someone I had already noticed among the waiting passengers. He was tall, a year or two older than I, bearded, and dressed in faded layers. A dirty white pony-tail stuck out from under his peaked cap and he was distinctly smelly. As we were taxiing to take off he started pulling hairs one by one out of his scraggly beard, then twisting each one in his fingers to examine it, I dared not think for what, before letting it fall into the aisle beside his seat. When he turned his glance momentarily my way, I saw one curtained grey eye and the other a very keen blue. On his worn ragged cap were the words: 'Kake Gold Mine Alaska.'

'The headsets are yours if you want to keep them,' came the announcement while the crew was handing out small portable screens. 'Otherwise when we come by with our trash bags you can give them to us as trash.'

'Don't have no TVs where I live; don't have no radio,' said the old gold-miner at my side, speaking a little to me, mostly to his anachronistic self.

Then he turned, unsmiling, to his onscreen comedy and I to the window.

Beneath us was an unfamiliar planet of snow-streaked, crumpled cliffs and jagged outcrops jutting into the sea. Just within sight lay a vast irregular island that had to be uninhabited; surely its terrain of frozen clouds could not support human life. It was only mid-afternoon and already the white land below was blushing in the early sunset of the late northern winter. Dusk had fallen by the time an announcement came to put our clocks back an hour. And then: 'If you don't think you can finish what you are watching before we land,' said a man on the intercom, his words made unintentionally significant as disembodied voices often are, 'you might want to fast-forward to see the ending.'

My first morning after landing in the far north of Alaska had begun at an outlandishly late hour for the fierce and assertive dawn that struck the tops of the encircling evergreens and turned them into blazing matches. The new sun illuminated a printed sign on the porch of my Fairbanks hotel it had been too dark to see when I checked in the previous afternoon: 'Be alert to the presence of bear and moose at all times. If you encounter a bear or moose DO NOT APPROACH! Walk slowly backwards.' Somewhere I read that the northernmost island of Japan, Hokkaido, is inhabited mostly by old folks, left behind in the far North when the young move south to seek a more congenial and profitable way of life. Local bears, said the article, getting wind of easy prey, have begun to prowl the island's settlements, picking off feeble, well-aged meat. Nevertheless walking backwards into the frozen landscape, as the sign recommended, would surely present as much danger for old bones as a moose, though possibly not a bear.

In the darkening early night I was waiting at the entrance

to the hotel for Marie, an Inuit taxi-driver whom I had booked to take me into the hills outside Fairbanks to see the aurora borealis. She and I met earlier that day when I went for a walk in town.

The empty tourist arcades at midday, the deserted galleries of local artists' work, the clean and vacant streets, all seemed to be waiting for another season, for a short warm summer instead of a long, lingering, northern winter. Walking very slowly through the quiet streets of Fairbanks, Alaska, I found myself thinking of my mother. Testing each step lest the dark patches ahead were treacherous ice, I was remembering how at around my age Mother stopped leaving her little house except to shop or visit her doctors and even then only with an escort. My right foot slid a little on an innocuous-looking scrap; I gasped, righted myself, and on the instant I knew, I felt in my very bones, my mother's terror of slipping on a pavement and shattering her hip or knee, should she dare to leave the controlled safety of her house. That was the reason, the real reason, Mother remained virtually housebound from her seventies. It was not the ennui or the snobbishness that she affected, but fear of falling on ice, real or metaphorical. Fear of falling kept my mother increasingly housebound, as it does countless other old women with our generic tendency to osteoporosis. Marie's taxi had passed at just that moment of revelation in the otherwise empty street; I hailed it on the spot to take me back to the hotel, a short distance away, but perilous. En route I arranged for her to return later and take me a few slippery miles to where the Northern Lights might best be seen.

Marie picked me up promptly at the time requested and drove me in her taxi into the hills beyond Fairbanks where, she said, we would see the aurora borealis undimmed by the town lights. As we travelled, she told me about her family who lived further north. Her three sisters were married with families; she was the only one still single. In the flickering light

Marie appeared not much more than thirty years old; her face was lean, a face that laughs a lot but is not merry: a drinker's face. Her brother, she told me in her breezy conversational tone, had a few months earlier killed himself; he was eighteen. At breakfast in the hotel that morning I had a brief conversation with a woman sitting alone at the next table. She turned out to be a social worker attached to the nearby American army base. She told me that among men stationed there the suicide rate is unconscionably high, almost as high as it is among local Native Americans. Young men especially find the long, long Arctic winters prematurely debilitating. Unable to imagine an end to that primordial darkness, they cannot believe it will ever come.

'This is no country for young men,' I whispered, silently begging the poet's forgiveness.

'My boyfriend says I am the only happy angry person he has ever met,' Marie said.

We parked in a hollow in the middle of nowhere and stepped out into the cold. Next to me Marie was as thin as a sapling. She wanted a cigarette, nicotine stains mottling her bony fingers; however, it was not done to smoke, not even in the open air, not as long as a no-smoking fare was at her side. Stars unfurled over our heads in streams and banners, hoarding their light and casting none on us, assuming an importance they can never match when seen through city smoke and neon signs. And suddenly there it was: a billow of phosphorescence on the horizon, a silken undulation like a green curtain at the far end of a vast banqueting table: the aurora borealis.

'My God, Marie, the earth is flat after all!'

'Yes, yes, maybe. But it is round too,' said Marie. 'That's what they teach at school.'

Again darkness fell around the silver stars and we waited in silence. Then once more the green light arose, this time as a quivering rectangle as if constructed on the surface of the globe itself; stars caught within its frame ceased to sparkle, appearing mysteriously round and green and as still as apples on a tree. I clapped my hands.

'Oh, this is nothing; this is not very great,' said Marie. 'I wish you could see a great one. When the lights are great, they are red and blue and every colour. And sometimes you can hear a crackling in the air. My mother says she can smell the aurora.'

'Marie, believe me, this is wondrous enough for me!'

I could hardly explain to one so young how, on winter walks along the Channel coast where I have my hidey-hole in France, and sometimes early in the morning before the sun rises outside my London window, I find myself moved by beauty more pastel than primary, more understated than the brilliance and flare required by youth. Old taste becomes impressionistic, a yen for glowing opals rather than diamonds.

And it happened again, the great movement in the sky prompting the memory of a forgotten ambition. My dream when I was a girl was to walk the planet, inch by inch, step by step – the wind in my sails over water, trekking from oases to oases in the desert – to see the whole world and meet its entire people. How many steps taken since then, and how many buses, trains, boats, planes? How many people met; how many almost met? How many wonders seen? And, oh, heartbreak! How many to leave unseen and unknown?

'A person should always look forwards, not backwards,' Marie said, reading my mind. Or had I spoken aloud?

We the aged are for ever being ordered by condescending youngsters, and sometimes by each other too, to abjure retrospect, to forgo regret, to surrender reminiscent comparisons, to keep our cloudy eyes fixed on the short and bumpy road ahead.

'Really, Irma, you must stop always looking back,' my younger friend, Janie, chided me when we met for a drink before my trip north.

She had just told me about her recent visit to Venice.

'Cherish the memory,' I had replied. 'Venice is a thrill the first time only.'

To return was to visit a theme park, I warned her; fabulous, yes, but increasingly just film-set and photo-opportunity.

'When I saw Venice fifty years ago it was in daily use by Venetians; it still belonged to the descendants of its founders; it was their ancient home, their garden . . .'

'Irma, you really must stop living in the past,' she said for the umpteenth time.

'But the past,' I told Janie and now Marie, 'lives in me. That is what it means to grow old.'

And why is the past these days considered of little value? Why should the past be any less important than the future that grows out of it? Is it because no financial advisor invests in 'pasts', only in 'futures'? Because advertisers promote tomorrow as if it arrived brand new, as if tomorrow were independent, as if it ever actually arrived and were not simply yesterday *in utero*? But nobody buys a flashy new car or absurdly overpriced boots to travel into the past, do they? Silly fools, the future is ever diminishing for each of us; only the past increases. An old woman's past is a feast, her future barely a snack.

'What did you say?' asked Marie. 'I couldn't hear you.'

The aurora borealis undulated again along the horizon and then rose, this time miraculously cup-shaped and brimming. How beautiful it was! I recognised the wonder I was feeling; I had seen it in my grandson's eyes the first time he felt the stinging cold of ice cream melt into chocolate on his tongue. So wonder does sometimes return with wisdom. My eyes stung with unexpected tears. The cup is now; now is a cup. The aurora shimmered; the cup spilled over. A glorious second childhood: to know once again the enchantments of the present.

'Now is the best, Marie. I was forgetting; I had almost forgotten; I will never again forget. Keep faith with now, Marie; it holds both past and future, problems and solutions, too. Now may not be all we have, but only now has it all. Love now, Marie; I love it again. And I love this big round place where the present is perpetually delivered.'

A mighty green ribbon streamed in the stratosphere.

'Oh, look! See? So full of wonders! Guard it, Marie. Enjoy it. We must hold onto our present tense; it is as close as we come to a perfect tense, even when we misuse it. Now alone holds promise. And now, right now, is worth every moment we have to pay for it.'